ROUTLEDGE LIBRARY EDITIONS:
AGING

I0127707

Volume 21

HOUSING FOR
THE ELDERLY

HOUSING FOR THE ELDERLY

Planning and Policy Formulation in Western Europe and North America

LEONARD HEUMANN
AND
DUNCAN BOLDY

Routledge
Taylor & Francis Group

LONDON AND NEW YORK

First published in 1982 by Croom Helm Ltd

This edition first published in 2024
by Routledge
4 Park Square, Milton Park, Abingdon, Oxon OX14 4RN

and by Routledge
605 Third Avenue, New York, NY 10158

Routledge is an imprint of the Taylor & Francis Group, an informa business

British Library Cataloguing in Publication Data
A catalogue record for this book is available from the British Library

ISBN: 978-1-032-67433-9 (Set)
ISBN: 978-1-032-69692-8 (Volume 21) (hbk)
ISBN: 978-1-032-69771-0 (Volume 21) (pbk)
ISBN: 978-1-032-69770-3 (Volume 21) (ebk)

DOI: 10.4324/9781032697703

Publisher's Note
The publisher has gone to great lengths to ensure the quality of this reprint but points out that some imperfections in the original copies may be apparent.

Disclaimer
The publisher has made every effort to trace copyright holders and would welcome correspondence from those they have been unable to trace.

Housing for the Elderly

PLANNING AND POLICY FORMULATION IN
WESTERN EUROPE AND NORTH AMERICA

LEONARD HEUMANN AND DUNCAN BOLDY

CROOM HELM
London & Canberra

ST. MARTIN'S PRESS
New York

© 1982 Leonard Heumann and Duncan Boldy
Croom Helm Ltd, Provident House, Burrell Row,
Beckenham, Kent BR3 1AT

British Library Cataloguing in Publication Data
Heumann, Leonard
    Housing for the elderly.
    1. Aged – Europe, Western – Dwellings
    2. Aged – North America – Dwellings
    I. Title   II. Boldy, Duncan
    363.5'9   HD7287.E/
ISBN 0-7099-1234-X

First published in the United States of America in 1982
All rights reserved. For information write:
St. Martin's Press Inc., 175 Fifth Avenue, New York, N.Y. 10010

Library of Congress Cataloging in Publication Data
Heumann, Leonard.
    Housing for the elderly.

    1. Aged – Dwellings. 2. Aged – Great Britain – Dwellings.
I. Boldy, Duncan. II. Title.
HD7287.9.H48   1982   363.5'9   82-10684
ISBN 0-312-39349-0

Typeset by Mayhew Typesetting, Bristol
Printed and bound in Great Britain

CONTENTS

To Hildegarde, Alfred, Roberta, Sarena, Aaron and Micah;
Ruth, David and Phillip

NOTES ON AUTHORS

Dr Leonard F. Heumann is Associate Professor of the Departments of Urban and Regional Planning and Housing Research and Development, University of Illinois at Urbana – Champaign. He is the author of numerous articles in books and journals on housing planning, housing needs assessments, and housing policy alternatives in relation to low income and elderly households, and also on issues of racial integration.

Dr Duncan P. Boldy is Senior Operational Research Scientist in the Institute of Biometry and Community Medicine at the University of Exeter. He has a particular interest in research related to the elderly and is joint author of a book on the Home Help Service, as well as author of many other publications. In addition, he is the editor of the book *Operational Research Applied to Health Services* (Croom Helm, London; St Martin's Press, New York, 1981).

PREFACE

Housing and social welfare policy as it affects the elderly is changing throughout Western society. Conventional high rise apartments and institutionalised nursing or residential homes are no longer the sole public responses to housing the elderly. In place of these two extremes on the housing continuum is a variety of intermediate supportive systems that aid independent living. Assisted Independent Living (AIL) programmes are designed to keep the elderly in as independent a living environment as possible despite increasing functioning disabilities and frailties that often accompany advancing age. By the mid-1970s, AIL housing had become recognised in every Western industrialised country as an important long-term housing alternative to institutionalised homes for those elderly with functional disabilities.[1] Assisted independent living is 'the alternative refuge' to long-term care in institutions for the old and infirm. It allows disabled elderly persons to remain in control of their lives, to have the dignity of as much independence as their functional limitations and personal determination allow. AIL housing also keeps the extended family involved in the care of their elderly relatives without the excessive burden of total responsibility; and because of personal and extended family care, AIL housing can be far less costly than total care institutions.

The AIL programmes have different names in different countries. For example, the programme is called 'sheltered housing' in Great Britain, 'congregate living' in the United States, 'Altenwhonheime' in West Germany, and 'Servicehus' in Sweden. British sheltered housing has been recognised as the world leader in the development of AIL accommodations.[2] Where the majority of Western countries have only recently begun to develop AIL programmes, the British have had sheltered housing schemes for over 30 years. They now house more than four times the number of elderly in AIL units than any other Western nation; proportionately, generally much more.

The typical AIL scheme, as found throughout Western Europe and North America, follows the basic British sheltered housing model. The units are independent apartments, which are intended to be 'barrier free'. Each flat or apartment is connected by intercom or alarm system to nearby help in case of emergencies, and visiting support services are provided to help elderly residents maintain their independence as

11

they become increasingly disabled or frail. Where such communal facilities as a lounge and laundry room are provided, these encourage socialising and shared domiciliary care, especially as the residents become more housebound. Usually, bedfast, severely mentally confused and terminally ill residents requiring constant nursing and/or medical attention cannot be accommodated in sheltered housing. Elderly with other less severe levels of functional disability have been able to remain in their independent unit with the help of only visiting support services. As we will show in this book, many functionally disabled elderly are currently able to live out their lives in sheltered housing, with or without extended family support. Our research indicates that there could be a considerable reduction in the number of total care institutional beds now in use in the United States and Great Britain by fully implementing AIL programmes.

The elderly population, particularly the very old and frail, will be increasing in the foreseeable future throughout Western society due to improvements in lifelong medical care and accident prevention, and new life sustaining medicines and medical techniques which are especially effective as regards chronic diseases of the aged. The very old and frail elderly will be surviving with a wide variety of support needs, surviving in a wider range of household types and sizes, and coming from a wide variety of socio-economic and life-style backgrounds. A great deal more must be learned about sheltered housing and who it can serve well under various physical, social and support service designs in order to accommodate this growing array of potential elderly users.

This book defines sheltered housing, traces its development in Western society and analyses its success under several variations in Great Britain. The British analysis focuses on those aspects of the sheltered housing programme that have wider relevance to the development of AIL housing policy in Europe and North America. Great Britain is uniquely suited as the best research site for this type of housing among Western countries: Great Britain is currently the only country with a high enough proportion of such housing sites, a large enough variety of such housing, and old enough resident population to allow careful comparative analysis of sites, staff, management and tenant characteristics over time. In particular, the British have pioneered two critical aspects of sheltered housing for which results are sorely needed by national planners in Great Britain and the other Western countries.

The first pioneering aspect of sheltered housing has been in the variety of accommodation. British housing managers have developed a number of distinct categories of sheltered housing. Each category presents a different level of communal living and resident support services. If adequately provided in local markets, this can allow the elderly a real choice among supportive environments. It also provides the analyst with a 'laboratory' for comparing tenant and support staff characteristics and activities as well as movement and transition patterns among schemes. These sheltered housing varieties are representative of the major AIL programmes currently in use throughout Europe and North America. The analysis presented in Chapter 3 shows that each programme type serves a particular set of needs, but each has disadvantages. Together, these different AIL types begin to form the continuum of entry points required by elderly coming from different backgrounds with different support needs.

The second element that is obviously missing from non-British AIL schemes is the resident *warden*. In North America, the word 'warden' is usually used to describe the director of a prison, but in Britain, the term is used in connection with sheltered housing to describe a person, usually a housewife, who lives in the sheltered housing site with her family; a 'friendly neighbour' on call, often 24 hours a day, in case of emergency. As we shall see, the warden is one of the most critical components of successful long-term independent living for those elderly becoming increasingly frail and disabled. An analysis of the warden's role and activities, by sheltered housing category type and over time, is presented in Chapter 4. We show that wardens provide far more than friendly visits as residents become frail and housebound. Many make critical decisions about when and when not to call in family and support services, provide extensive social counselling and direct domiciliary care, and help organise creative social activities. Depending on their skills and understanding, wardens can generate either an engaging and supportive environment in which to live, one that renders residents isolated without needed support or one which makes residents overly dependent on a warden's services. It is the overcaring or undercaring aspects of the warden role that particularly concerns European and American gerontologists. Other Western AIL schemes have either a resident caretaker with none of the visiting or socialising responsibilities of a warden, or a daytime social worker, caretaker, or home help assigned to a scheme, or no regular staff visitor at all, just a phone or signal connection from a scheme to a central management office. The majority of these non-British schemes are new, and most of the tenants are still young and relatively active. In Chapter

4 we compare the variation in warden activities in relation to tenant characteristics, by category of scheme in Britain. Our conclusions support the continued use of 'lay'-wardens in many settings, but indicate an increasing need for, and advantage in, using professionally trained wardens. In Britain, wardens have proved to be a unique and indispensable service provider for disabled elderly attempting to maintain an independent household.

Chapter 5 discusses the role of management in sheltered housing. British sheltered housing is administered by both voluntary (nonprofit) associations and public administrations. Public sector administrations include both housing authorities and social service agencies. Because of these numerous administrative sources, Great Britain again provides an excellent location for analysing alternative management schemes. Our findings indicate that the national management of a programme can be directed by either housing or social service departments without much variance in the final product, so long as there is a co-ordinated approach to management and service delivery between health, housing and social services at the local level. Local management creates the initial mix of tenants, appoints resident service staff and has a major say in the balance and integration of the resident-population in an AIL site over time. This balance of tenants by age and functional ability and their integration with the wider society can only come about by an enlightened management that fully understands the concept of assisted but independent living.

Chapters 1, 2 and 6 define the need and demand for AIL housing, show its growing importance, place the British research in the context of AIL policy development in other Western countries, and summarise the lessons in programme development that can be learned from the British experience.

The data analysed in Chapters 3, 4 and 5 originate from surveys of eight sheltered housing managers from the urban West Midlands and nine managers from rural Devon, and 35 wardens from randomly selected sheltered housing schemes in the West Midlands and 121 wardens from schemes in Devon. The management and warden opinions and characteristics are analysed against site and tenant characteristics. Over 1,500 tenant records are included in the urban West Midlands sample and approximately 3,500 tenant records in mainly rural Devon. The tenant records include health and demographic characteristics, activity patterns and movement/transition patterns. The urban West Midlands data was collected in the spring of 1978; the rural Devon data was collected in 1973 and again in 1977 with 71 schemes (employing 74 wardens) common to both surveys.

Leonard Heumann, University of Illinois
Duncan Boldy, University of Exeter

Notes

1. Noam, E. and Donahue, W., *Assisted independent living in grouped housing for older people: A report on the situation in European countries*, International Center for Social Gerontology, Washington, DC, 1976.
2. Ibid.

1 THE GROWING NEED AND DEMAND FOR SHELTERED HOUSING

Western industrialised societies are entering a period of dramatic change in population demographics, life sustaining medical treatment, and the financial and social structure of the family that will greatly increase the number and proportion of elderly requiring public assistance with daily living. The means of meeting the varied income, health, housing and social service needs of this ageing population is becoming a central concern to Western governments. There are also growing fears that long-term government assistance to the functionally disabled elderly could develop in areas that do not warrant such assistance. Government programme designs of the past have often failed to recognise the limits of public intervention in the ageing process and have been rigid and inadequate in their ability to adapt to the variety of individual needs. These programmes often fail to give the comprehensive support needed, while at the same time becoming oversupportive in areas where assistance *is* provided. Inflexible and inappropriate support can lead to premature loss of functional independence. As the elderly become more dependent and less capable of resisting the institutionalising nature of public service programmes, they can be denied the legitimately private ageing process that gives meaning and dignity to life. This book analyses one form of long-term assisted, independent living − namely sheltered housing. The evidence to be presented shows that sheltered housing represents one of the most promising long-term housing policy options for assisting the well, but functionally impaired and/or socially deprived and isolated, elderly in retaining their independence, privacy and dignity.

Sheltered housing is one of several titles used throughout Western society for essentially the same concept of long-term assisted, independent living in a sheltered environment. Grouped housing and congregate housing are almost synonymous terms which are used to define special alternatives within the family of sheltered housing types. The typical sheltered housing scheme is made up of independent apartments or bungalows which look like conventional housing. However, each private apartment and its surroundings are intended to be 'barrier free', so as to make the activities of daily life as easy and convenient as possible. The private units are often supplemented with communal spaces that make socialising and shared domiciliary care easier as persons become more frail and housebound. Each unit is connected by an alarm or intercom system to nearby help, usually a resident warden or manager, in case of emergencies. Support services are expected to be made available as needed, usually in the form of peripatetic staff, sometimes in the form of permanent on-site staff, but in all cases the philosophy is that support is only provided at that margin of assistance needed to maintain independent living. The individual's privacy and independence are the unique and essential ingredients of sheltered housing.

The implementation of this basic concept varies throughout Western society so that the many sheltered housing programmes define a continuum of supportive environments that range between conventional housing and institutions. Alternatives along this continuum are created by varying the amount and type of peripatetic versus permanent on-site support services, scheme size and the amount of communally shared spaces and daily activities. To simplify the discussion of these varied sheltered housing types, they will frequently be discussed as two groups – 'minimal service' and 'service-rich' sheltered housing. Service-rich environments (also called in Britain 'very sheltered' housing) include more communal spaces and more on-site service staff. In addition to these design and service variations, managerial policy can also influence the character of sheltered housing. Such policies determine the size of schemes, the screening and transition processes by which the elderly enter and leave schemes and the type, role and training of support staff. Comparing and analysing these variations in sheltered housing design, service and management is the main focus of the research presented in this book. Our goal is to define and order the varied types of sheltered housing in an effort to begin to determine which alternatives might be best suited for various elderly. This chapter describes the growing need and demand for sheltered housing throughout Western society and the position that it occupies on the continuum of publicly and privately assisted independent living alternatives.

The Growing Importance of Assisted Independent Living Alternatives

The family has traditionally provided most of the long-term support to the very old and frail in society. When there is no family, or when family and friends are incapable, unable or unwilling to provide assistance, old age homes and nursing institutions have served as the major long-term housing alternative. This section demonstrates the growing importance of publicly sponsored, assisted independent living as an alternative to institutional care. The argument is presented in four stages. The first two subsections show that the number and proportion of elderly in the population is growing rapidly and the number and proportion of the very old and frail who are most likely to suffer functional impairments is increasing even faster than the overall elderly population. The third subsection shows that the family support base is diminishing — in part due to overall demographic trends toward older populations in Western society and in part due to changes within the family which increasingly has more of its potential support providers working outside the home. Next, we show that more and more well elderly are finding their way into old age institutions which were primarily created to provide skilled care for that small percentage of persons who are totally incapable of caring for themselves. These institutions have expanded their function so that probably 30 per cent or more of the elderly they now house are capable of living semi-independently in the community if the proper assistance were provided. These institutions are costly both to the elderly who must give up some or all functional independence and to society which must staff and maintain them. In a final subsection we show that old age institutions (particularly nursing homes) are generally much more expensive than even service-rich sheltered housing, because they provide total care while eliminating elderly self-care and family input.

The Increasing Number and Proportion of Elderly in the Population

The population aged 65 and over has been increasing throughout Western society for over 75 years. In the United States just over three million (4 per cent of the population) were aged 65 or older in 1900. Today about 11 per cent of the population is 65 or over and by the year 2030 55 million persons (about 20 per cent of the population) will be elderly,[1] assuming there is no new baby boom and there are no new bio-medical breakthroughs which extend life expectancy.

The growth in the elderly population of Western European countries has been about 20 years ahead of the United States. By the mid-1970s persons aged 65 and older constituted between 14 and 15 per cent of the population in England and Wales, the German Federal Republic, France and Sweden.[2] In the United States, the elderly are not expected to constitute 14 per cent of the population until about the year 2000, at which time most Western European elderly populations are likely to be peaking at between 20 and 25 per cent elderly. The expected increase in the 65 and older population will average 39 per cent per year in the United States over the last quarter of the twentieth century. In France the expected increase over the same period will be only 29 per cent,[3] whilst in England and Wales it will be only 23 per cent, and the elderly portion of the population is expected to decline from about 1994.[4] For a more detailed discussion of demographic trends in relation to the elderly, see Abrams.[5]

The Very Rapid Increase in the Number and Proportion of Very Old Elderly

Statistically, 65 is not a particularly significant age marker for the onset of functional dependence. Most people who survive to 65 can be expected to live another 10 years or more before significant levels of functional impairment are evident.[6] Hence the more important trend to watch is the increase in population aged 75 and above; this age cohort is increasing even faster than the overall elderly population. Forecasts for the United States covering the period 1975 to 2000, estimate that the 55-64 age cohort will increase by 16 per cent, the 65-74 age cohort by 23 per cent, and the 75 and over age group by 60 per cent.[7] Between 1970 and 1990 the number of United States elderly over 75 years of age is predicted to double.

In England and Wales the major increase in the cohort aged 75 and over should peak in about 1990 and then level off; however, the 10 year period from 1976–86 is likely to show a 24 per cent increase in this group or about the same growth rate as the United States for this period.[8] France expects a 42 per cent increase in elderly over the age of 80 between 1970 and 2000.[9]

The Decline in the Number of Family Support Providers

Contrary to popular belief, the family is not abandoning in large number its role as primary housing and support provider to the functionally impaired elderly.[10] What is occurring is that fewer family members are available on a 24 hour basis who are capable of providing adequate support for the elderly.

The first line of family support comes from a spouse. Older couples can often maintain their independence by caring for each other. However, of those who survive to old age, an increasing number are widowed or unmarried women. As recently as 1930 there were as many men as women surviving to age 65. Since then there has been a steady decline in the number of men, so that by 1975 there were only

69 men to each 100 women surviving to age 65 in the United States.[11] Two-thirds of all women aged 65 and older now live alone or with someone other than a spouse.[12]

The absence of a spouse places greater responsibility for care on the adult children of surviving widows. Unfortunately, their number have been decreasing as the number of frail and impaired elderly living alone has been increasing. As fertility declines the number of younger family members available to care for the elderly declines. According to the United States Bureau of the Census,[13] there were 13 persons aged 65 and over for every 100 adults between the ages of 20 and 59 in 1900, whereas today there are 29 persons aged 65 and over for every 100 younger adults and by the year 2030 there are likely to be 44 persons 65 and over per 100 younger adults.

Even when there are surviving children they are often entering old age themselves as their parents reach 85 and above. There are an increasing number of cases where elderly children who are themselves facing declining health, energy and finances, are burdened with looking after a widowed parent. It is also not uncommon for the 'young old' to be confronted with dependent elderly relatives on *both* sides of the family.[14]

British studies of the 1950s and 1960s showed that 24 per cent or more of the elderly lived with at least one adult child;[15] recent figures show that only 12 per cent now live with adult children and increasingly more elderly live beyond a one hour drive from children.[16] Living separately, even at some distance, has not, however, prevented female children of disabled elderly from providing support in the past.[17] Women, because of their traditional domestic role at home, have been the primary family members to visit and assist elderly relatives on a daily basis. However, the family structure regarding female children has changed. Treas[18] showed that in 1975, compared with previously, more women in the age group 41–45 had husbands and children whose interests must be balanced out with those of ageing kin. The so-called 'maiden aunt' who cares for elderly relatives is now far less common.

There has also been a dramatic change in the per cent of younger adult women working outside the home. The United States Bureau of the Census[19] found that only 11 per cent of all women were working in 1940. By 1970, 48 per cent were working, and current trends predict that 63 per cent will be working outside the home by 1990.[20] Clearly, working hours cut into the time these women can provide for disabled kin and completely eliminate the security of someone on call 24 hours a day. The economics of family life have also changed. There is evidence that younger families depend on this second income, and that women often cannot quit work to provide daily care for an ailing kin. In 1970, 31 per cent of mothers with preschool children entrusted them to nonfamily services,[21] and all indications are that they would probably do the same in the case of ageing parents. If day care programmes, visiting support services or sheltered housing are not available for the disabled elderly to continue to live in the community, the family will probably increasingly turn to long-term old age institutions to house their disabled and elderly kin.

The Increasing Inappropriateness of Institutional Care for the Elderly

As kin networks offer fewer options and resources to care for the elderly, more elderly enter long-term old age institutions.[22] In the United States, childless or low fertility women have a 15 per cent higher chance of being institutionalised before the age of 75 than women who bore three or more children.[23] The combination of an increasing number of elderly surviving to very old age, and the decrease in family members capable of providing support, means that government programmes will have to augment the family support system in greater numbers and variety. To date societal responses to the needs of noninstitutionalised elderly and their families has been woefully inadequate.[24] The suffering and guilt felt by adult children whose parent's needs exceed their ability to provide are well documented.[25]

Studies beginning in the 1960s[26] document the indiscriminant use of old age institutions to house the isolated low income, and possibly impaired but well elderly. Persons entering these institutions have few housing options and include many who could live in the community if the proper supportive housing was made available. Over 50 per cent of the institutionalised elderly have either no living relatives or no direct contact with them.[27] For many others in institutions their families face economic hardships that prevent them from providing care. Between 60 and 85 per cent of those in institutions are among the poorest of the poor, requiring public assistance with daily living beyond the financial means of their families.[28]

Numerous studies over the past decade have identified institutionalised elderly who could live semi-independently if appropriate long-term housing were provided in the community. Because the analysts undertaking these studies have adopted different criteria, made different assumptions about the availability of support services in the community and surveyed local old age homes of different quality, the estimates of elderly currently in such homes who could live in the community vary dramatically from a low of 12 per cent to a high of 60 per cent with about 30 per cent being the most frequent estimate.[29]

So long as old age institutions provide skilled nursing care for very ill elderly, the use of an institutionalised hospital design is tolerable. However, we are seeing this institutional model being adapted to long-term housing for persons who can still retain some functional independence. Institutional settings are limited in their ability to adjust to independent living. Their living arrangements tend to preclude privacy and the staff dictate daily activity patterns.[30] Adjusting to institutional living is difficult for a reasonably independent person; for persons moving to an old age institution late in life with poor eyesight or poor hearing, poor mobility, or other functional disabilities, the move is often traumatic, adjustment is almost impossible, and the most frequent result is the total surrender of all remaining functional independence.[31]

In Britain the first extended stay nursing institutions for the elderly were long stay geriatric wings of hospitals. As the number of disabled but well elderly increased, the British developed the old persons home which retained to some degree the institutional model of a hospital geriatric wing but eliminated the on-site nursing.

In other Western nations, such as the United States and Sweden, long-term *nursing* care was removed from the hospital and placed in extended stay care facilities for long-term convalescence after hospitalisation, and in skilled care nursing homes for long-term care without previous hospitalisation. As the number of disabled but well elderly in need of housing increased, United States nursing institutions were allowed to expand their scope from skilled nursing care to include 'intermediate care' for persons requiring only simple medical treatment and intermittent nursing care. From 'intermediate care' they were then allowed to expand to cover 'sheltered care' which is entirely non-skilled assistance with daily living. However, like the British, the institutional model borrowed from hospital accommodation was retained for these more independent residents. An extensive study of Illinois nursing homes[32] showed that 'skilled care' residents of nursing homes are properly housed but fully 78 per cent of the 'sheltered care' and 28 per cent of the 'intermediate care' residents entering nursing homes could live in assisted independent housing.

The Rising Cost of Dependent Care Relative to Sheltered Housing

In addition to loss of independence to the elderly resident and the psychological cost to their family, premature and inappropriate institutionalisation of the elderly puts a tremendous drain on family and government financial resources. There are three reasons why the costs of institutional care are higher and rising faster than sheltered housing costs. First, institutions are dependent living environments where *all* daily living services are provided *for* the residents. Therefore, unskilled domiciliary staff are needed for the preparation of all meals, cleaning, laundry, maintenance, etc. Second, this dependent setting often results in the premature loss of many other social and daily self-care functions by the residents. Therefore, the institution is frequently required to organise and supervise social and recreational activities in order to impose some level of physical activity on otherwise inactive residents. In addition, the institution may also have to provide premature support with personal care tasks such as feeding, dressing and bathing. The required presence of 24 hour skilled nursing personnel, whether they are needed or not, is the single most costly service in the United States model. Third, there are the extra capital and other costs associated with the physical building, which must be designed to meet the needs of the most dependent residents.

In contrast, the residents of sheltered housing provide much of their own care, and the visiting skilled care that is needed is provided only at the margin that will help residents maintain their independent unit. There is a conscious effort to avoid creating an over-caring environment that is wasteful of service resources and detrimental to the elderly residents' personal efforts at self-care and social engagement. While the individual resident of a sheltered housing unit requires more personal space than an institutional resident, sheltered housing facilities have none of the medically related communal rooms found in nursing homes (e.g., specialised therapy rooms, nurses stations, staff assigned rooms, etc.). The cost per square foot of constructing and maintaining a sheltered housing unit is comparable to that of a conventional housing unit and far below that of a skilled-or-intermediate care nursing home unit.

Research by the International Center for Social Gerontology and recent testimony at a US Congressional Hearing, found that care in sheltered housing is approximately 40 per cent cheaper to provide per month than intermediate nursing care.[33] In testimony before a United States Senate committee looking into congregate housing for the elderly, the executive secretary of the San Antonio Housing Authority estimated that the Authority could provide an extremely service-rich environment including meals, personal assistance and housekeeping, for about $2 to $5 per person per day compared to local nursing home costs of $25 to $30 per person per day.[34] The major difference appears to be the presence of medical care staff and equipment in the nursing home. Nursing and medical care for the elderly currently exceeds twelve billion dollars a year in the United States. If, for example, only 20 per cent of the present and future nursing home elderly who could benefit from sheltered housing were provided such accommodation, the savings would be enormous. Between 1965 and 1975, medical costs of the elderly in the United States, including nursing home support, increased 29 per cent per year faster than did overall medical costs.[35] Given a rising elderly population, new more economical programmes to assist elderly efforts to retain independence are long overdue.

In Britain the cost of care in sheltered housing is traditionally compared with old age homes and not nursing homes. Old age homes do not provide the expensive nursing services on-site but do provide meals, personal assistance and housekeeping. Even with this comparison, sheltered housing fares relatively well. A study completed in Essex[36] found that sheltered housing had a weekly margin of £3 to £4 per person on average in domiciliary service costs before reaching the equivalent cost of care in an old age home. On the other hand, Plank[37] found that if persons with similar levels of ability to care for themselves were provided with a *similar level of care*, then domiciliary care in sheltered housing was almost equivalent in cost to care in an old age home. However, as we have already argued, it may often be inappropriate to provide a person in sheltered housing with a level of care equivalent to that provided to a similar person in an old age home, since the level of care provided in an old age home may often be excessive in relation to a particular individual's abilities.

Many of the assisted independent living programmes are interdependent. For example, as the population in minimal service sheltered housing ages, more residents will require at-home care from visiting services. Therefore, the parallel development of these visiting service programmes is vital. The development of visiting home services has been frustrated by the myth that they are uneconomical and costly. Morris[38] has shown that home visitation services are economical for 15–25 per cent of the currently institutionalised elderly and 14 per cent of the noninstitutionalised elderly when living in scattered-site conventional housing. Sheltered housing may increase the percentage of elderly for whom visiting services would be economical. The clustered design of sheltered housing can result in economies of scale in travel and visitation time for visiting service providers while shared home care and social support by residents can reduce or even eliminate the need for some visiting services.

Determining the Need for Sheltered Housing

The changes in elderly population demographics and in extended family support patterns projected in the previous section demonstrates a growing need for all types of assisted independent living. This section estimates the specific need for sheltered housing. We have purposely chosen to estimate need rather than measure market demand because sheltered housing is still a largely unknown product to the potential customer, and because much of the potential need is the result of low incomes and functional impairments which prohibit the elderly from participating in the conventional economic market and thereby registering a demand. We have made *very conservative assumptions* concerning need throughout this section so as to define only that subgroup which would most clearly and obviously benefit from sheltered housing.

The characteristics taken as implying the need for sheltered housing are divided into two basic subgroups. As shown in Figs. 1.1 and 1.2, these are respectively 'functionally impaired' and 'socially deprived' elderly. As regards functional impairment, Fig. 1.1, we assume that only those noninstutionalised elderly who suffer frequent or constant problems completing multiple activities of daily living (ADL) tasks are considered impaired enough to warrant sheltered housing. Persons who suffer occasional problems with one or more ADL tasks or frequent or constant problems with only one ADL task are excluded from the analysis and assumed to be best served by some alternate long-term support service. Based on data presented later in this section, these assumptions reduce the number of persons likely to need sheltered housing to between 14-17 per cent. We then further reduce this number to between 3.3-4 per cent of the non-institutionalised elderly by considering only those who live alone and do not receive visits from family or friends at least once a week. We assume that those elderly with frequent or constant support needs with ADL tasks who receive at least weekly visits or who live with others get all the support they need and want from those acquaintances or visiting social services and that they prefer their current housing arrangement over sheltered housing. Finally as we have already indicated, estimates of institutionalised elderly who could live semi-independently if proper

Figure 1.1: A Conservative Estimate of the Per Cent of Functionally Impaired Elderly in Need of Sheltered Housing

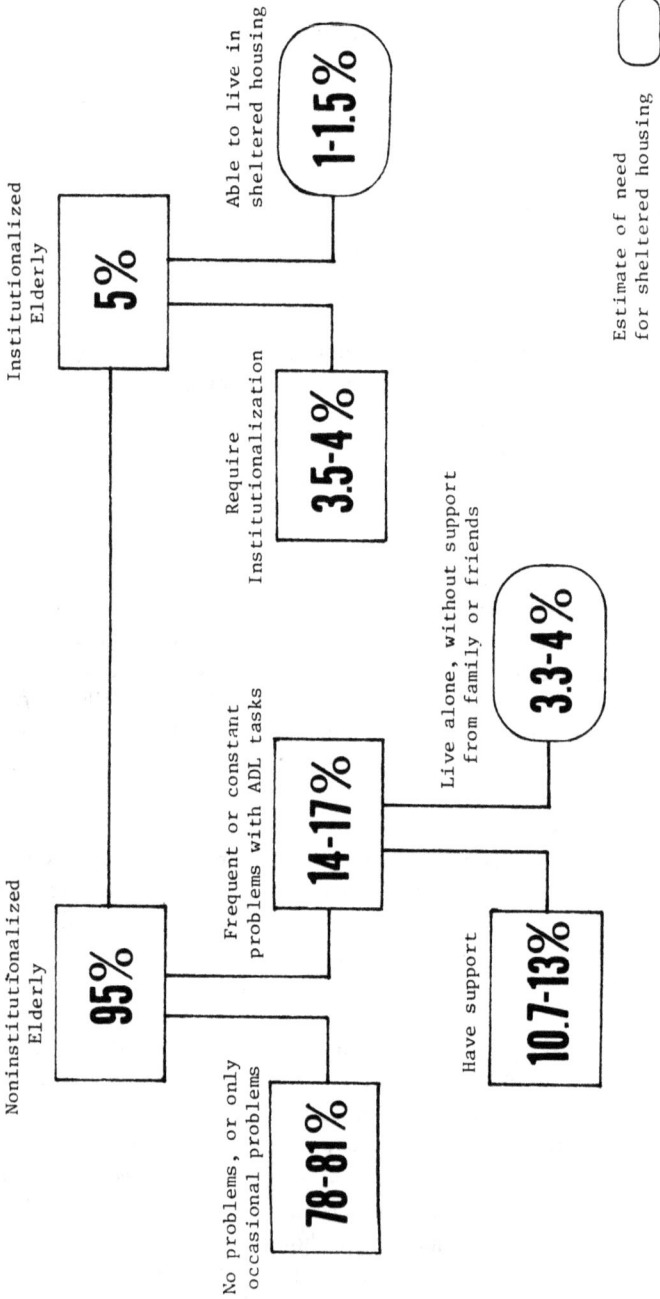

Noninstitutionalized Elderly

95%

Institutionalized Elderly

5%

Able to live in sheltered housing

1-1.5%

Require Institutionalization

3.5-4%

Frequent or constant problems with ADL tasks

14-17%

No problems, or only occasional problems

78-81%

Live alone, without support from family or friends

3.3-4%

Have support

10.7-13%

Estimate of need for sheltered housing

Figure 1.2: A Conservative Estimate of the Per Cent of Socially Deprived Elderly in Need of Sheltered Housing

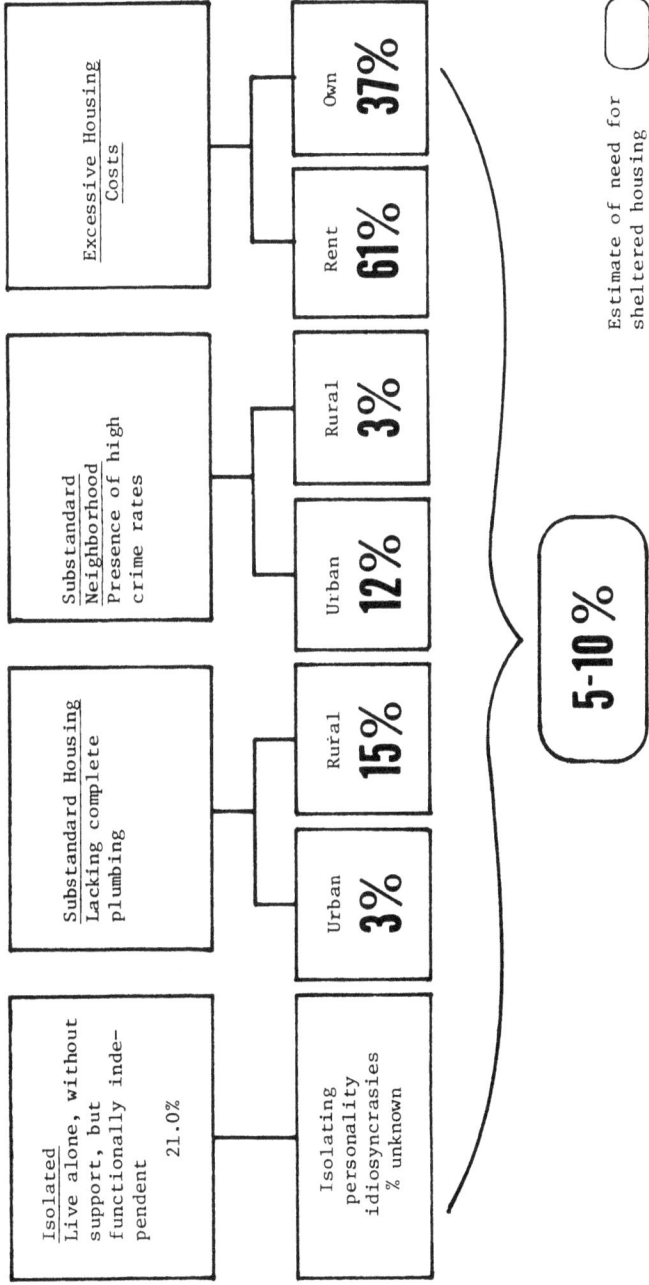

Isolated Live alone, without support, but functionally independent 21.0%	Substandard Housing Lacking complete plumbing		Substandard Neighborhood Presence of high crime rates		Excessive Housing Costs	
Isolating personality idiosyncrasies % unknown	Urban 3%	Rural 15%	Urban 12%	Rural 3%	Rent 61%	Own 37%

5-10%

Estimate of need for sheltered housing

long-term supportive housing were available run as high as 60 per cent. We assume that only 20-30 per cent of the institutionalised elderly would be both able to, and would want to move to sheltered housing. This assumption results in an additional 1-1.5 per cent of the elderly who could benefit from sheltered housing.

The definitions of social deprivation are many and varied. As shown in Figure 1.2, it is not possible to crosstabulate these variables and create a composite definition and estimate of socially deprived elderly using existing data. Our estimate of elderly who are in need of sheltered housing, as a result of social deprivation, independent of the need generated by elderly with functional disabilities, is based on empirical observations of resident populations in British sheltered housing. These observations suggest that another 5-10 per cent of the elderly could benefit from sheltered housing.

Functional Disabilities

One of the primary purposes of sheltered housing is to provide assistance with independent living to those chronically impaired but well noninstitutionalised elderly who have difficulty in functioning in conventional environments. However, even a basic estimate of those most likely to benefit from sheltered housing is not an easy task. National statistics on functional independence have not been collected and analysed in a manner that automatically results in such estimates. Universally monitored medical data does show that in the USA, 86 per cent of those over 65 suffer from one or more chronic conditions such as high blood pressure, arthritis or heart disease.[39] This, however, is a useless statistic for the purpose of estimating the need for sheltered housing. Different people are disabled to different degrees by such chronic diseases; some are totally impaired and could not manage even in a sheltered housing scheme, while most are not impaired to the degree that a move to sheltered housing is warranted. A more useful approach is to measure daily functional ability directly. However, such data are not automatically and uniformly gathered as part of a census. The estimates of daily to weekly needs for assistance found in the few nationwide sample surveys that have been conducted vary from 11-23 per cent of the elderly population, depending on variations in the definition of need, the country sampled or the sampling technique used.[40]

In order to illustrate how these estimates can legitimately vary, we now present an analysis of the 1968 *National Senior Citizens Survey* (NSCS), a random survey of 4,000 noninstitutionalised United States elderly.[41] Two widely recognised measures of activities of daily living (ADL scales), 'mobility' and 'self-care', were used. The questions asked in the NSCS followed typical ADL schedules:

Mobility
1. Do you need help walking up and down stairs?
2. Do you need help in going out of doors?
3. Do you need help in getting around the house?

Self-care
1. Do you need help cutting your toenails?
2. Do you need help washing and bathing?
3. Do you need help dressing and putting on shoes?

For each question the respondent was asked if he/she:

1. Never had problems with the task.
2. Occasionally had problems with the task.
3. Frequently had problems with the task.
4. Always had problems with the task.

This combination of three tasks and four frequency responses can produce 64 possible response combinations for each ADL measure. In order to narrow the levels of disability to a logical yet workable number, the following steps were taken. First, a conservative assumption was made. Respondents who answered that they 'never' or only 'occasionally' had problems with these activities were assumed to have enough functional independence to be excluded from further analysis. Second, to collapse the response types further a Guttman scale was postulated. This requires the analyst to place the tasks in order of difficulty; a person unable to complete the simpler tasks is thus presumed to be unable to complete the more difficult tasks. For the 'mobility' tasks the Guttman scale collapsed the varied answers into the following four levels of continuum of disability:

(0) Totally mobile:	Those who never have problems or only occasionally have problems with all three mobility tasks
(1) Climbing barrier:	Those who frequently or always have problems with stairs but never or only occasionally have problems getting out of doors or around the house

(2) Housebound: Those who frequently or always have
                           problems with stairs and getting out
                           of doors but never or only
                           occasionally have problems getting
                           around the house

(3) Home help dependent: Those who frequently or always have
                           problems with stairs, getting out of
                           doors, and getting around the house

A similar continuum was constructed for self-care tasks:

(0) Totally self-sufficient: Those who never or only occasionally
                               have problems with the three self-care
                               tasks

(1) Minor support needs: Those who frequently or always have
                               problems with cutting toenails but
                               never or only occasionally have
                               problems with washing, bathing or
                               dressing

(2) Weekly support needs: Those who frequently or always have
                               problems cutting toenails and washing
                               and bathing but never or only
                               occasionally have problems dressing

(3) Home help dependent: Those who frequently or always have
                               problems cutting toenails, washing and
                               bathing, dressing and putting on
                               shoes

The actual fit of the NSCS sample to these continua was statistically
excellent. The coefficient of reproducibility for the mobility scale was
0.995, for the self-care scale 0.985. (A coefficient of reproducibility
of 0.9 and above is generally considered to indicate a valid scale.) For
other statistics and display of the Guttman scale tables, see Heumann.[42]
Table 1.1 shows the results of the Guttman scaling.

While we would expect some correlation between the severity of
mobility disabilities and the severity of self-care disabilities, difficulty
in the mobility and self-care tasks need not occur simultaneously. For
example, heart disease may have greatly limited functional mobility on
stairs and long walks out of doors but may not have affected in-home
self-care tasks at all. The effects of a stroke or arthritis may affect
manual dexterity and other self-care functions but not mobility.

Table 1.1: The Percent of Persons in the United States Needing Support with Mobility and Self-Care Tasks

Support continuum:	Activity type	
	Mobility %	Self-care %
0) Totally mobile/self-sufficient	87.9	88.4
1) Climbing barrier/minor support needs	6.6	7.3
2) Housebound/weekly support needs	3.2	2.1
3) Home help dependent	2.3	2.2
	100.0	100.0
Total with some support needs	12.1	11.6

Source: *National Senior Citizens Survey*, 1968.

Therefore, Table 1.2 was created, which crosstabulates the mobility and self-care scales. This crosstabulation produces very different percentages of elderly requiring help with functional disabilities. Cell number 1 now contains the totally independent persons or those having no problems or only occasional problems with both mobility and self-care tasks. Cells 2-16 represent various combinations of frequent or constant problems with ADL tasks. Note that the column totals for those with self-care problems irrespective of mobility problems totals 16.6 per cent and the row totals for those persons with mobility problems irrespective of self-care problems totals 17.8 per cent. The summation of all 15 cells containing various combinations of mobility and self-care problems totals 23 per cent of the elderly sampled in the NSCS. In other words, Tables 1.1 and 1.2 produce a range of from about 12-23 per cent (depending on variations in definition) with frequent or constant disability with one or more ADL tasks. This is basically the same range of disability estimates that have been produced by the various national studies mentioned above, each developing only a single disability coefficient.

In order to narrow the estimated range of those in need of sheltered housing, we recommend that cells 2 and 3 of Table 1.2 be also eliminated from the total of 23 per cent in need of sheltered housing support. Cells 1, 2 and 3 therefore represent persons who are either totally independent, have occasional problems with single or multiple mobility and self-care tasks, or persons who have frequent or constant problems but only with single tasks. These persons do not necessarily require sheltered housing, because they suffer only minor self-care tasks or climbing barrier problems which can both be assisted by visiting support services, building modifications or rehousing in any

Table 1.2: Crosstabulated Self-care and Mobility Scales

Mobility	Self-care				Total
	0 – Self-sufficient	1 – Minor support needs	2 – Weekly support needs	3 – Homehelp dependent	
0 – Totally mobile	1 2839 77.0%	2 154 4.2%	4 36 1.0%	7 6 0.2%	3035 82.3%
1 – Climbing barrier	3 183 5.0%	5 75 2.0%	8 25 0.7%	11 8 0.2%	291 7.9%
2 – House- bound	6 50 1.4%	9 64 1.7%	12 21 0.6%	14 60 1.6%	195 5.3%
3 – Homehelp dependent	10 4 0.1%	13 15 0.4%	15 16 0.4%	16 133 3.6%	168 4.6%
Total	3076 83.4%	308 8.3%	98 2.7%	207 5.6%	3689 100.0%

307 missing cases

Source: Guttman Scale Levels, produced from *National Senior Citizens Survey*, 1968. This table was originally produced in Heumann and Lareau[43] and Heumann.[44]

type of barrier-free environment. The total in cells 4-16, i.e. 14 per cent of the elderly, could serve as the base figure for persons with disabilities needing sheltered housing. However, as some of those in cells 2 or 3 might also benefit from a move to sheltered housing, the row or column totals, approximately 17 per cent, might serve as a high estimate for a range of persons likely to need sheltered housing.

Two additional points about this analysis are noteworthy. First, we have already seen that the number of very old, with a high potential for suffering functional disabilities, has increased rapidly over the decade since the NSCS survey. Therefore, on this basis alone these esimtates should be considered as conservative. Second, these are only national estimates for the United States, they should be higher in European countries that have a higher proportion of elderly over 75, and have lower median incomes than the United States. The same holds for some local planning jurisdictions within the United States. Table 1.3 shows

Table 1.3: Elderly Characteristics Correlated with Mobility and Self-Care Task Ability

INDEPENDENT VARIABLE = MOBILITY			
Dependent variable:	chi squared	degrees of freedom	significance
1. Number of persons in household	3.64	3	ns (30.37)
2. Owner vs. renter tenure	5.65	3	ns (13.02)
3. Age of respondent	52.39	9	s (.001)
4. Total yearly income	70.94	21	s (.001)
5. Sex of respondent	22.88	3	s (.001)
6. Race of respondent[a]	5.45	6	ns (48.74)
INDEPENDENT VARIABLE = SELF CARE			
Dependent variable:			
1. Number of persons in household	2.88	3	ns (40.98)
2. Owner vs. renter tenure	4.94	3	ns (17.63)
3. Age of respondent	46.91	9	s (.001)
4. Total yearly income	41.98	21	s (.42)
5. Sex of respondent	8.35	3	ns (3.93)
6. Race of respondent[a]	3.84	6	ns (69.86)

Notes: a. Race = white, black, and all other.
s = significant   ns = not significant.

Source: *National Senior Citizens Survey*, US, 1968.

that the percentage of disabled elderly tends to vary according to the age, sex of head of household and income of the elderly. Local counties and municipalities with a higher proportion of very old, low income, and female headed households than the national average will therefore tend to have more functionally impaired elderly.[45]

Family and Friends Support

In this section we estimate the proportion of the 14–17 per cent of the elderly population with frequent and multiple functional disabilities who receive no help from family or friends. We assume that this group has the greatest need for sheltered housing in order to receive consistent and reliable long-term assistance with independent living and the monitoring of support needs. Once again we begin with two conservative assumptions. We assume that *all* the disabled elderly who live with someone else, or have relatives nearby who pay regular visits receive all the help they want and need, and they prefer this combination of housing and assistance to moving to sheltered housing.

Research over the last two decades shows that most elderly who need support receive at least some from relatives and friends. British statistics show that 70-75 per cent of the elderly live with someone else,[46] and in the US, 84 per cent of the elderly either live with their children or less than one hour away.[47] A study of British, American and Dutch elderly[48] found that 75-80 per cent of those who live alone have children or siblings nearby, and 69 per cent of these elderly receive some help with daily living from these relatives. There is also strong evidence that as the elderly get older and disabilities increase they tend to move in with, or receive more visits from, relatives.[49]

These findings can be built upon by analysing further the NSCS sample of noninstitutionalised United States elderly. The NSCS asked respondents the following: if they had help nearby, if they had mobility problems, and if they suffered from self-care disabilities. Crosstabulating this data we found that 23.4 per cent of the elderly with mobility problems and self-care disabilities had no help of any kind (family or friends) nearby. If this ratio is applied proportionally to the 14-17 per cent we have estimated have frequent or constant support needs with multiple ADL tasks, then between 3.3-4.0 per cent of the noninstitutionalised elderly constitute the group with the greatest need for sheltered housing. This is clearly a conservative assumption since a greater proportion of such disabled elderly are likely to be older and hence the members of their private support network are more likely to have become disabled or died.

In addition to the conservative assumptions already made, there are other reasons for concluding that this is an underestimate of the need for sheltered housing. Once again, a factor is the age of the NSCS sample. Previously we mentioned the probable increase in the propor- tion of disabled elderly since the survey was conducted; now we are reminded of the earlier findings that that proportion and quality of background support has very likely declined over the past decade. If United States public housing trends are any indication, the need for sheltered housing could be as high as three times that estimated above. Elderly public housing in the United States is almost exclusively limited to elderly who are functionally independent. Any loss of functional independence can be grounds for eviction. A recent US survey of 182 elderly public housing sites developed before 1970 revealed that 12.3 per cent of the elderly public housing residents are threatened with evic- tion because they had disabilities that required basic daily support services in order to maintain their independent housing unit.[50] This 12.3 per cent need for sheltered housing cannot be directly applied to non- institutionalised elderly in general, because public housing tenants tend to be disproportionately poorer. Nevertheless, this is a further indication that the higher end of the 3.3–4.0 per cent estimate of sheltered housing need may be more realistic.

Institutionalised Elderly Who Could Live in the Community

Earlier we identified a wide range of studies which estimate that between 12 and 60 per cent of the elderly in institutions could live outside if appropriate long-term housing and support services were provided. The estimates from these studies varied because the nursing and other elderly homes surveyed varied in quality and because the analysts made different assumptions about the support available in the community. The most common estimate was 30 per cent. For our estimates we will use a range of 20–30 per cent. The lower bound allows for those who may be able to live in the community but desire accommodation other than sheltered housing.

Since most Western societies house about 5 per cent of their elderly population in some form of institutional setting, we will assume that 20–30 per cent of that 5 per cent figure could live in sheltered housing if provided. This would add 1.0 to 1.5 per cent to the percent of elderly who could benefit from sheltered housing (see Figure 1.1), and would raise the total to between 4.3 and 5.5 per cent of the total elderly population.

Sheltered Housing Need Based on Social Deprivation

British researchers, using the same variables discussed so far in this chapter, have arrived at similar estimates (5–6 per cent) of elderly who are likely to need sheltered housing.[51] However, the British researchers have also added an additional variable they call 'social isolation'. When potentially isolated and lonely elderly are included in their estimates, the need for sheltered housing rises to between 10 and 15 per cent of the elderly population. These are primarily empirical observations that vary from one locality to another based on variations in elderly population characteristics, population density and local support service characteristics. However, the original data we have assembled and will present in later chapters on the urban West Midlands and rural Devon areas of England support these estimates. We found that over 40 per cent of the residents of sheltered housing are functionally independent or require only occasional help with disabilities. Most of these functionally independent residents reside in sheltered housing because of the social contacts and economic support provided.

The International Center for Social Gerontology has identified the same two factors, namely functional impairment and social deprivation (a more general term for that set of variables that may cause social isolation), as those that could warrant a move to a sheltered type of housing.[52] Elderly suffering social deprivations include persons who live marginally due to very low incomes, and/or who live in housing that is substandard, inadequate or obstructive to independent living, and/or who live in neighbourhoods that trap or isolate them in their homes. Social deprivation could also include able-bodied elderly with personality idiosyncrasies that make them withdrawn and friendless, or persons with mild neuroses or other mental problems that render them forgetful, careless or irresponsible when living alone. Any or all of these factors would result in social isolation and any or all could eventually lead to, or exacerbate, functional disabilities.

Many of the elderly suffering these social deprivations are unlikely to receive appropriate support with independent living if they continue to reside alone in their present housing. Many of them could benefit from a move to sheltered housing because: 1) such housing is designed to be barrier free, is cheaper to maintain and is easier to care for; 2) the location is usually safer, more convenient to shopping and provides nearby support from neighbours; 3) there is an on-site warden who can make daily visits to check on wellbeing, provide social contacts and call in support help if necessary; and 4) the environment provides more opportunity for spontaneous and inexpensive social contact with peers.

At present data is not generally available regarding such social deprivation variables. Those variables for which data is available cannot be crosstabulated with each other, with functional disability levels or with key demographic characteristics. As a result, it is difficult if not impossible to derive levels of deprivation that suggest sheltered housing solutions as opposed to other support service solutions. The following subsections discuss some of the data that currently exists.

Isolation. Table 1.4 presents a social isolation index using the 1968 NSCS data. The table crosstabulates mobility problems, living alone and weekly contact with friends and relatives. The 4.6 per cent high-risk group is larger than the 3.3-4 per cent disabled and isolated identified above, because it includes elderly who have *occasional* problems with one or more mobility tasks and live alone without weekly support from friends or relatives. The 21 per cent who have no mobility problems, live alone and don't see friends or relatives weekly may or may not consider themselves isolated. They are a segment of the elderly population that has probably grown since the NSCS survey was taken and more detailed analysis about them is needed.

Table 1.4: Social Isolation Index

Level of risk	Percentage of NSCS survey population[a]	Portion of estimated 1979 US elderly population
High 1. Do not see family or friends at least once a week 2. Live alone 3. Have mobility problem	4.6	1,134,300
Medium 1. Do not see family or friends at least once a week 2. Live alone 3. No mobility problem	21.0	5,178,200
Low 1. Married or live with someone 2. Regardless of level of isolation 3. Regardless of level of mobility	58.0	14,301,600
Undetermined	16.4	4,043,900
Total	100.0	24,658,000[b]

Sources: a. *National Senior Citizens Survey*, US, 1968; b. United States Bureau of the Census, *Estimates of the Population of the United States By Age, Race and Sex: 1976-1979*, Current Population Reports, Series p-25, No. 870, United States Department of Commerce, Washington, DC, 1980, p. 3.

Personality Idiosyncrasies. It would be particularly useful to know what proportion of that 21 per cent who live alone without weekly contacts with others suffer chronic but mild psychological problems that either result in or from extended isolation; what proportion have personality idiosyncrasies that leave them friendless and lonely, or have mild neurosis making them forgetful or careless when living alone, etc. Unfortunately these problems are even difficult to discern clinicly, let alone through survey responses to large random samples of the elderly population. Many of the personality idiosyncrasies and cases of withdrawal may be only episodic, as older persons adjust to the loss of friends and relatives. For these cases, visiting social services may suffice. For others, widowhood or other causes of depression and withdrawal may require a move to an environment that provides easier, more spontaneous social engagement, more real and psychological security with living alone, and simplified domestic operations and household maintenance. To the degree that there are persons who fall into these categories independent of functional disabilities and housing and income disabilities, we will be excluding their need for sheltered housing and thus underestimating total need, because there are no reliable estimates at present.

Substandard, Inadequate and Obstructive Housing and Neighbourhoods. Table 1.5 lists selected housing and neighbourhood problems from the 1973 United States Annual Housing Survey that suggest major repairs or relocation to more appropriate surroundings. The table illustrates the different problems faced by elderly living in metropolitan versus rural farm areas. Rural farm elderly are two or three times more likely to occupy deficient housing than the total population, while urban elderly are actually less likely to occupy deficient housing than the total population. On the other hand, urban elderly are two to three times more likely to live in inappropriate neighbourhoods than rural elderly.

The final statistic in Table 1.5 shows the high proportion of elderly living in older housing. Older housing in itself is not a problem. It is presented as an indication of how insensitive current census measures are to elderly needs. Older housing may meet all the census conditions of decency, safety and sanitation as they apply to younger households, but decent older housing can also hide numerous entrapments and costs in time and money for elderly in cleaning and maintenance at a time when their resources and strength are waning. The obstructions to functional and financial independence in older housing are numerous: more, steeper and narrower stairs; double hung, painted shut windows, high ceilings hard to clean and costly to heat, high cupboards and shelves that are hard to reach, poor lighting, and so on. Frequently older obstructive housing is located in older neighbourhoods with high crime rates, high noise and air pollution, poor public services, and so on. No really good estimates combining housing and neighbourhood obstructions to independent living presently exist.

Low Income and Housing. Given the high number of low income elderly, it is surprising that so few live in truly substandard housing. One reason for this seems to be that the elderly are more willing to sacrifice other daily living costs in order to occupy decent housing. A much higher percent of the elderly pay an excessively high proportion of their incomes for decent housing than younger households. Many pay so much that it effectively isolates them in that house because after making house payments, they have little money left for telephone,

Table 1.5: Percent of Elderly Households in the United States Suffering from Selected Housing and Neighbourhood Problems

	Total %	Elderly Urban metro areas %	Rural farm areas %	Elderly and nonelderly %
Housing related problems				
Lacking complete or private plumbing	6	3	15	5
Noncentral heating	33	21	59	26
Leaky roof	7	5	15	8
Neighbourhood related problems[a]				
Heavy street traffic	16	19	8	–
Air pollutants	7	8	3	–
Trash (rubbish)	7	9	4	–
Crime	8	12	3	–
Housing built before 1940	53	51	70	37

Note: a. Problems the respondents felt were harmful or disturbing. Not available for nonelderly.

Source: 1973 US Annual Housing Survey (as selected from Tables 1 and 2 of Struyk).[53]

transportation, entertainment, nice clothes, etc. An analysis of the 1974 United States Annual Housing Survey[54] found that 61 per cent of the elderly headed households that rent, pay excessive percentages of income for housing compared to only 45 per cent for all renters, and 37 per cent of elderly home owners with a mortgage pay an excessive amount for housing compared to only 10 per cent of all home owners.

It would be helpful if we could crosstabulate levels of functional impairment with living alone, with the absence of at least weekly visits from family or friends, with inadequate homes and neighbourhoods, with low income and/or paying too much for housing, and with personality idiosyncrasies. Such a crosstabulation would surely define a group whose multiple social deprivations, independent of functional impairments, would imply a need for sheltered housing. Unfortunately we cannot do this. At present we can only make guestimates based on observation of current elderly residents of sheltered housing. The British estimate mentioned previously of an additional 5 to 10 per cent seems reasonable (see Figure 1.2) and is used in the summary estimate that concludes this section of the chapter.

'Service-rich' vs 'Minimal Service' Sheltered Housing

So far in our estimates of need, all sheltered housing has been assumed to be the same. There are in fact many sheltered housing hybrids; these are introduced in the final section of this chapter. At this point we wish to distinguish between the two basic sheltered housing types 'service-rich' and 'minimal service', which were introduced earlier. While both types provide assisted independent living, they generate quite different social environments. The differences in communal living and the availability of on-site support staff and services are attractive to some people and unattractive to others, at the same time beneficial to some efforts at independent living while injurious to others.

Service-rich facilities, with numerous communal spaces, communal activities (such as communal dining) and on-site support staff are often considered to be a necessity for the more socially and functionally dependent. Some observers feel that a high proportion of those persons returning to semi-independent living from an institutional setting would benefit from a service-rich environment because they have become accustomed to communal living and frequent support staff involvement in their daily activities. Service-rich independent living might require less of an adjustment for persons whose socialising and personal management skills have atrophied because of institutionalisation, isolation or severe functional impairment. While the logic of this argument appears sound, in practice service-rich environments seem to be built for and to attract mostly active and functionally independent persons. These elderly apparently prefer a more communal life-style and the security and convenience of having a wide array of support immediately available. Able bodied residents of service-rich environments welcome the varied support services which they feel provide freedom from the drudgery of domestic chores. Upper middle-class elderly in the United States often retire to service-rich sheltered housing, attracted by the hotel-like life-style of communal dining, organised social events and room services with laundry and heavy-cleaning, etc.

Minimal service facilities, with only a lounge and laundry room (if that) in addition to a resident warden or manager, are often thought of as limited to the younger more able elderly. Again, reality does not bear this out. The British experience shows that the support provided by these facilities addresses the varied needs of the elderly as they become increasingly more disabled. In Chapter 3 we show that so long as family involvement, where available, remains strong and/or visiting community services are well developed and efficient, then many elderly can live out their lives comfortably and securely even in minimal service sheltered housing.

When all the residents of a new minimum service scheme are young and active the unit is likely to be used as any other conventional housing. However, this type of housing can involve far more intimate communal sharing as residents age. Neighbours can provide the domiciliary support and social organising on nights and weekends that staff provide in the more service-rich environments. Events and interactions are more likely to evolve from the shared experience of the residents rather than the skilled intervention of staff. Some analysts feel that minimal service sheltered housing is more beneficial in assisting independent living for the majority since most elderly will never suffer the functional disabilities that justify on-site support staff. In addition, it is felt that the absence of on-site staff keeps the elderly more active and socially engaged once they become housebound,[55] while the presence of on-site staff could result in premature dependence on support services, premature decline in socialising and domiciliary skills, and premature or unnecessary transfer to a totally dependent environment.[56] Furthermore, because minimal service sheltered housing is more like conventional housing in design and far cheaper to staff, more and smaller schemes spread throughout the community can be justified. This in turn should provide greater opportunity for the residents to remain engaged in the larger society they have known all their lives, yet provide the sheltered retreat that can accommodate gradual disengagement if this becomes necessary or is desired.

It is clear that both forms of sheltered housing provide important life-style and support choices, and that both should be built and subsidised by government agencies. However, if we are only considering government subsidised housing, then we believe that minimal service facilities probably should outnumber service-rich facilities, perhaps something like two to one or even greater. The reason for this is that government subsidised sheltered housing will primarily house lower- to middle-class elderly who are less likely than upper-income elderly to choose service-rich facilities. Whilst research in this area is still preliminary, it appears the elderly with higher incomes and a higher education are more likely to choose communal living and to use the communal services provided in sheltered housing. One study controlling for income and functional ability looked at three government-sponsored facilities with communal services.[57] This study found that the majority of all residents used medical services, but middle-income elderly wanted and used sociability-linked services (such as meals and housekeeping) more than did lower-income elderly. Another study of the acceptance of communal living[58] found that it was more acceptable to persons whose pre-retirement life-style and occupation involved human associations, e.g. educators, social workers, club members, civic workers, physicians, etc., as opposed to farmers, labourers, artists and housewives without children.

Based on these findings, elderly who have had low to moderate incomes all their lives are more likely to choose minimum service sheltered housing as their long-term sheltered accommodation because it is most like the housing they have been used to. Elderly who only seek sheltered housing late in life when they are very frail and disabled, or elderly who are returning to semi-independent living after an extended stay in institutional care, may benefit from service-rich facilities. As an elected housing alternative the majority of service-rich schemes would be most attractive to upper-income elderly, and could possibly be left to private-for-profit providers to develop, particularly in the US (this may be less likely to happen in Great Britain).

A Final Estimate of Sheltered Housing Need

Table 1.6 presents a conservative estimate of the need for assisted independent living programmes for the next two decades based on available data. The table shows that the family is expected to continue as the primary and desired long-term support provider of assisted independent living. We estimate that it is appropriate for about 81–86 per cent of the elderly to live out their active lives in conventional housing; in most cases the housing they have known all their lives.

Despite the continued heavy reliance upon the family, public and nonprofit sponsored housing and service programmes should be developed and dramatically expanded to meet the needs of the rapidly growing and ageing population of elderly without adequate family support. Current public housing and institutional care programmes are not designed to meet the needs of semi-independent living. The programmes that should experience the greatest growth are visiting support services, day care and sheltered housing. Of the three, visiting support services should experience the greatest growth as they are required to supplement support needs in both conventional as well as minimal service sheltered housing. Furthermore, if past experience prevails, the majority of elderly requiring public support will seek visiting services first in order to delay any form of move for as long as possible.

Table 1.6: Estimate of Elderly Supported Housing Needs for the Last Quarter of the 20th Century in Western Industrialised Countries

	%
A. Conventional Housing Design[a]	81–86
B. Sheltered housing	10–15
1. Minimal service facilities[b]	6–10
2. Service-rich facilities	4–5
C. Institutional care	4

Notes: a. Up to one-third of these people may require public support with rent payments (including conventional public housing), visiting support services and day care programmes in order to remain in conventional housing; b. Elderly in minimal service sheltered housing could also receive visiting services.

Given our conservative assumptions detailed earlier, we estimate that between 10–15 per cent of the elderly will need and/or want sheltered housing. This estimate represents a major investment in a new and important housing alternative. The 10–15 per cent estimate can be disaggregated as follows (see Figs. 1.1 and 1.2): roughly 4 per cent are persons who have no family support and have functional disabilities too severe to allow them to remain in conventional housing with only day care or visiting support services; another 1 per cent are formerly institutionalised elderly who are only able to return to semi-independent housing if sheltered accommodation is provided; and the remaining 5–10 per cent are socially deprived and isolated but functionally independent elderly, and persons who suffer neither severe social deprivations or functional impairments but desire sheltered accommodation over other housing alternatives. Some observers in Great Britain[59] have argued that we should not develop sheltered housing programmes to a size that includes such large numbers of more active and able bodied elderly. However, we believe that the exclusion of more active elderly would fail to recognise the wishes of some among this group and could undermine the success of sheltered housing generally. If sheltered housing programmes are to work they must retain a balanced community which includes both more active as well as less active residents. If sheltered housing is allowed to become a refuge limited to the frail and housebound it can easily take on all the trappings of institutions, despite the independent design and despite all the best intentions of the management and support staff.[60] In fact, the greatest challenge to sheltered housing programmes is to prove that they can maintain a balance of residents and an engaging, resident dominated (as opposed to staff directed), social environment.

This is such an important question that a significant part of this book is devoted to studying the balance of residents within different types of British sheltered housing.

Over the next two or three decades many more elderly will survive to very old age with increasing levels and variety of support service needs. For many of these elderly, the design of their current homes and their location in the community are going to be critical contributors to their growing functional dependence. For increasing numbers of elderly, only specially designed sheltered housing will ensure the consistent and natural flow of support services to maximise independence, preserve dignity and maintain the options of engagement in, or disengagement from, society. As sheltered housing becomes a proven success in providing a secure, worry free and socially invigorating environment at the hub of elderly life in the community, demand for sheltered housing could easily top the higher estimate of 15 per cent presented in Table 1.6.

The next section discusses the success of sheltered housing to date and the growing demand for it.

The Success of Sheltered Housing Programmes

There is growing evidence that many elderly desire sheltered housing over other housing alternatives, and that the popularity of sheltered housing will increase rapidly as the concept of supported independent living becomes more widely known and programmes are developed and implemented. The previous section of this chapter considered those elderly likely to need sheltered housing; this section considers why elderly who are socially engaged, economically secure and functionally independent choose sheltered housing. For many independent elderly a move to sheltered housing, while they are still active, represents a type of insurance which guarantees that if they live to be very old and frail they will be able to retain maximum control over their independence and privacy. Sheltered housing insures against becoming trapped by, and isolated within, a conventional house late in life when one has neither the energy to care for the house nor the energy to move from it. Sheltered housing also insures that as long as an elderly person remains well and retains some functional independence he/she will not have to move to an institutional environment in which he/she will lose the greatest degree of control over his/her life. Where sheltered housing is already an established and common housing alternative it can frequently become the focus for social life in the elderly community. It can represent age segregation by choice without necessarily leaving the larger community, family and younger friends. As will be illustrated below, research results over the last half decade have shown that there is widespread satisfaction with sheltered housing. Sheltered housing residents *appear* to live longer, remain functionally independent longer, and avoid total care institutions more often than do elderly remaining in conventional housing.

Desire for, and Satisfaction with, Sheltered Housing

Attitude surveys of the elderly are fraught with difficulty. It is a well established fact that when interviewed, the elderly tend to be less critical than younger persons and are more likely to favour the housing environment which they know, over alternatives they have not experienced.[61] For that reason it is not surprising to find that when elderly occupying conventional housing are interviewed, 80 per cent or more prefer their own home or a similar housing type.[62] It is equally not surprising that when elderly who have moved to sheltered housing are interviewed, 80 per cent or more of them also express satisfaction with their housing.[63]

In order to try and distinguish differences in elderly housing preference, researchers have compared responses from those more likely to want or need to move, with responses from the general elderly population. The desire for more congregate and assisted living increases significantly among elderly residing in conventional housing who are older or more functionally impaired, or who live in deficient housing or neighbourhoods.[64] A study conducted in Minnesota[65] also concluded that as functional abilities decrease and dissatisfaction with current neighbourhood and social isolation increase, desire for sheltered housing increases dramatically. United States studies of housing satisfaction that have included an experimental group who moved to more traditional housing for the elderly, have revealed that the sheltered housing residents showed better relative improvement in morale and satisfaction over time.[66] A study in England by the Greater London Council, which surveyed a sample of elderly persons in residential homes, sheltered housing and private households, found sheltered housing residents to be the most satisfied with their situation.[67]

Longer, Active Life

The sheltered housing concept is designed to help the elderly remain

active and engaged at the margin of their functional abilities. Living in
a private sheltered dwelling encourages an elderly person to plan and
carry out domestic operations. This stimulates a level of daily mental
and physical activity which promotes fitness, alertness and engagement
in society; as such it provides a unique advantage over total care
institutions. At the same time, sheltered housing gives the elderly the
security and confidence that they will not become slaves to domestic
obligations when faced with episodic illnesses or worsening chronic
disabilities associated with old age. This is a unique advantage over
conventional housing. Sheltered housing can provide physically, socially
and psychologically secure and supportive environments which
apparently pay off in longer, active lives.

There is a great deal of preliminary data that *suggests* that groups
living in sheltered types of accommodation have lower mortality rates
than do control groups. Harel and Harel[68] show that residents of age
segregated housing have higher survival rates than tenants of age
integrated housing. Decreased mortality rates among those who move
to sheltered housing without heavy medical support were observed
in an eight-year follow-up of elderly residents in a San Antonio
housing project.[69] Sherwood, Green and Morris compared elderly
entering sheltered housing which had a heavy medical support capacity
with a carefully monitored group of elderly who were not admitted.[70]
They also found a significant decrease in mortality among those who
moved to sheltered housing. Brody found that elderly who decided
not to move from their former houses have a higher mortality rate
than elderly who follow through with a move to either sheltered
housing or some other independent but more secure environment.[71]

There is also extensive evidence that fewer sheltered housing
residents than conventional housing residents are admitted to long-term
care facilities. Two of the studies mentioned above[72] show better
health indices and significantly fewer admittances to long-term institutional care facilities among their experimental groups. These findings
are supported by the data collected and presented later in this book.
Both the Devon and West Midlands samples of British sheltered housing
show significantly fewer residents transferred to institutional care from
sheltered housing than from conventional noninstitutionalised housing
found in the community at large. However, it is not clear if this
significance remains even after accounting for those sheltered housing
elderly who sought transfer to institutional care but were denied
entry by crowded institutions which give priority to elderly applicants
from conventional housing. Additional study is required in this area.

Maximising Life-long Independence and Avoidance of Total Care Institutions

A growing body of research has revealed the importance of *choice* and *control* in the life of an individual.[73] Lack of choice and lack of control are apparently primary reasons for the extensive trauma and poor adjustment rate of elderly moving to old age institutions.[74] Old age institutions have become synonymous with loss of choice and control, yet once past the age of 65, a person has a one in four chance of entering such an institution in societies that have no other long-term supportive housing alternative.[75] As the following references illustrate, a move to an old age home usually means the end of personal decision making.

(1) The decision to enter a home for the aged is usually made at a time of crisis when the person being moved is not in control of their lives.[76]

(2) Homes for the aged are among the most restrictive institutions in society, scoring the highest on measures of alienation and on conditional or limited freedom.[77]

(3) Homes for the aged are custodial as opposed to rehabilitative environments. They almost never provide for, or encourage, independent living.[78]

(4) Homes for the aged are countertherapeutic. They encourage 'learned helplessness' and docile dependence on the support staff.[79] Residents usually atrophy both physically and socially, making it increasingly less likely they can return to independent housing the longer they reside in an institution.

(5) Less than a quarter of the persons entering a home for the aged ever return to independent housing in the community.[80]

These quotes are from recent research, but this image of old age institutions has been widely publicised in a number of books as well as newspapers and magazines throughout Western society over the last two decades.[81] It is not surprising, therefore, that many elderly who are able to exercise some control over their housing in old age try hard to avoid the chance of becoming institutionalised. As sheltered housing has become better known and more available it has been recognised as one means by which one can avoid institutionalisation and the trauma of moves late in life. Moving to sheltered housing while still active and able allows a person to shop around and find the scheme most compatible with his/her tastes. The elderly person makes what will probably be his/her last move at a time when he/she is in control of the move and can adapt to the new environment. Sheltered housing maximises the likelihood that independent housing will be retained for the rest of one's active life, and that premature institutionalisation will be avoided if, in fact, some period of institutionalisation becomes necessary at all.

Nowhere have these reasons for choosing sheltered housing been more evident than in the growing demand for a type of service-rich American sheltered housing known as 'total life' or 'continuing care' facilities. Total life care facilities are typically private market, profit motivated schemes that cater for upper middle income, active elderly. This group is the most likely to plan its old age housing to avoid moves late in life when there is a lack of choice and control. Total life and continuing care facilities are designed and advertised to be the last move an elderly household will *ever* have to make. The buyer purchases an independent apartment but the facility into which he is buying contains virtually every possible support service he may need including a nursing wing; thus the terms 'total life' or 'continuing care'. As residents become impaired they can avail themselves of any number of services. There is a meals service, laundry, home help services, and the residents can move in and out of the nursing wing or remain in nursing care for many years, whichever is felt appropriate. Their independent apartment remains theirs until they die, at which time it reverts back to the owners of the facility.

These facilities are costly. There is an initial entry fee that can range from $20,000 to more than $70,000, and the residents can usually recoup only a portion of this fee if they choose to leave in the first year, and none of it thereafter. Therefore, this is a long-term commitment that is usually attractive only to persons who are active and able bodied when they move in. The attraction of the facility is three-fold. First, the elderly buyers have the knowledge that they are moving to an independent apartment where they retain privacy and self determination for as long as they are able or desire. Second, the supportive environment is designed to preserve their functional independence for as long as possible. All domestic chores and responsibilities are simplified. Usually one communal meal and all heavy cleaning and laundry are made part of the service from the start. Finally, while they may forfeit some privacy to the communal environment at first, they acquire the security in later years of knowing that all domiciliary and housing decisions are taken care of. They know where they will live for the rest of their lives. Total life care facilities are very popular

in the US and new developments are being built throughout the
country.

Being in control of your own disengagement from society is
apparently a powerful desire of all elderly, and all types of sheltered
housing, not just the service-rich total life care facilities, promise this
control to some degree. In many ways minimal service sheltered
housing types are superior to total life care. They require the fewest
sacrifices of conventional living while providing support and security
for as long as one remains well and has any functional independence.
Only severe and chronic illnesses and functional deterioration should
require a move to an institution.

Sheltered Housing as a Preferred and Established Life-style

This final reason for preferring sheltered housing is applicable only in
those places where sheltered accommodation is relatively well
established, abundant and is a common form of elderly housing. At
present this is most likely to occur in Great Britain where some
localities have had sheltered housing for well over 20 years and which
house two to four times the current national average of about 5 per
cent of the elderly population (see Table 2.1). The Wyre Forest District
in the English West Midlands is typical of the older more established
programme. Roughly 16 per cent of the elderly in this district reside
in sheltered housing. The accommodation ranges from bungalows or
high rise flats which have been converted to minimal service schemes,
to purpose-built facilities with communal lounges, kitchens and
laundry areas. Many of the purpose-built schemes have luncheon
clubs, social organisations and a wide variety of weekly, monthly and
annual events that attract as many elderly from the surrounding
neighbourhood as residents of the scheme. The district has a
substantial waiting list despite the fact that they house three times the
national average. Waiting time for a flat is 18 months.

The Wyre Forest District may be a forerunner of what sheltered
housing can become once it is established in a community. Individual
schemes become the centre of social life in the elderly community.
Each scheme generates its own market as the scheme and the neighbourhood population evolve and age. A neighbourhood resident may
first come to know the scheme and its events because a parent lives
there. While they may eventually move in themselves for many of the
reasons already mentioned (security, convenience, low rent and
support), they are also likely to be attracted by the sense of community and the close ties among the residents and warden. As will be

shown in Chapter 4, those elderly who live alone without close family ties often gain a family proxy (i.e. the warden) by moving into such sheltered accommodation. The close communal ties and neighbourly relations that develop with other residents and the warden in advance of any illness or disability, often pay off in the best possible support services if the resident becomes sick or frail.

So far this introductory chapter has identified a growing need and a growing desire for sheltered housing. We have also presented preliminary evidence that sheltered housing is a successful support environment that can prevent premature institutionalisation and possibly extend the active lives of residents. Earlier in the chapter we presented evidence that sheltered housing is less costly than institutional care. Most analysts of sheltered housing agree that it is an important long-term housing alternative that deserves more developmental resources than it has received to date. However, there have been criticisms of some aspects of sheltered housing that have slowed its development and thus require further research. Sheltered housing represents a continuum of support environments. Variation in the design, the size, the on-site versus visiting support staffing and the management screening and transfer policies account for the major differences in, and problems with, various sheltered housing programmes.

The Necessity of a Variety of Sheltered Housing Choices

We believe that a continuum of entry points to semi-independent living arrangements is required for optimal acceptance of and adaptation to, assisted independent living for the whole range of elderly. Unless sheltered housing is designed to provide the appropriate level of financial, physical, social and psychological support required by a given individual, it can exacerbate the problems that triggered that individual's need to move. Either oversupportive or undersupportive environments can worsen the situation.

In many countries fledgling sheltered housing programmes define only one or two rigid formats which cannot adapt to varied marginal support needs. Some elderly are cut off from their social networks by a move and are unable to adapt to the alien communal nature of life presented by the type of sheltered housing provided. Others are inadvertently overcared for by untrained or ill-supervised support staff. They can suffer needless disengagement and atrophy of social and domestic skills. These doubts and fears are particularly directed at sheltered housing programmes that provide no alternative choices, that are 'service-rich', and require extensive communal living. Such housing comes closest to institutional care and thus can produce similar social pathologies.

Questions such as how many and what types of housing alternatives are needed, and what type of person is best suited to each alternative, are extremely complex. Such questions have largely gone unasked, therefore unanswered. Throughout this book we attempt to shed new light on these questions, although a full answer must await many more years of extensive research and experience.

Figures 1.3–1.5 represent a taxonomy of the major types of assisted independent living found within Western industrialised countries today. Together these supportive housing facilities make up the range of alternatives necessary to provide all elderly with adequate entry point choices to assisted independent living. While some countries, like Great Britain, already have examples of almost all these alternatives, no country provides more than a few of the public subsidy choices within any single local housing market. The shaded cells in these three figures represent the emerging forms of publicly subsidised, purpose built facilities to aid the semi-independent elderly. The cells numbered five to ten in Fig. 1.4 represent the range of sheltered housing alternatives.

Figs. 1.3–1.5 represent the three broad sub-types of supportive housing: 'long-term private support alternatives' (Fig. 1.3), 'long-term public or nonprofit support alternatives' (Fig. 1.4) and 'short-term or part-time public or nonprofit (voluntary) support alternatives' (Fig. 1.5).

Long-Term Private Support Alternatives

There are three basic alternatives presented for long-term private support: support provided by family or friends visiting or living with the elderly household, support provided by family or friends in a household headed by or shared with the support provider, and privately contracted support. Illustrated from left to right in Fig. 1.3 are those progressively more extensive support services which can be provided. Privately contracted support is seldom used as a long-term alternative by anyone except the very wealthy. However, the two slanted arrows within this group of support alternatives indicate that many middle-class families will employ a combination of private support over the short term in order to allow an elderly parent to remain in a private home in the long term. For example, an elderly person who becomes increasingly disabled due to a terminal illness may receive visiting support in his/her own home from the family so long as it is limited to

Figure 1.3: Long-term Private Supportive Living Alternatives for Elderly in Western Industrial Societies

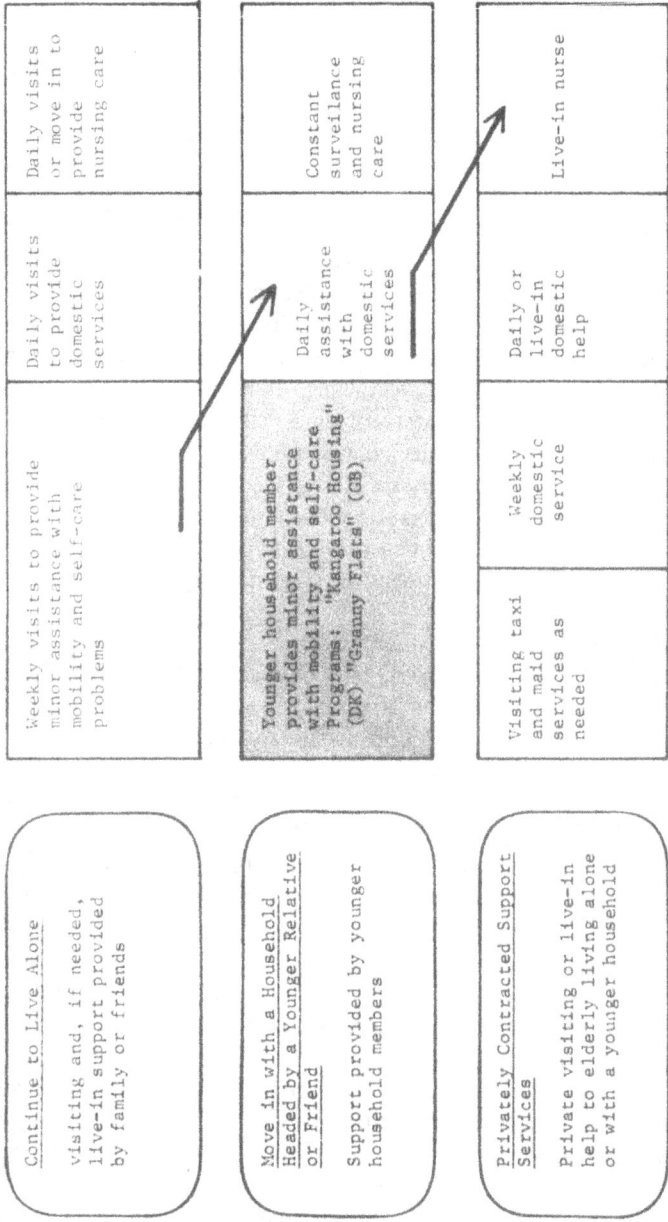

Continue to Live Alone visiting and, if needed, live-in support provided by family or friends	Weekly visits to provide minor assistance with mobility and self-care problems	Daily visits to provide domestic services	Daily visits or move in to provide nursing care
Move in with a Household Headed by a Younger Relative or Friend Support provided by younger household members	Younger household member provides minor assistance with mobility and self-care Programs: "Kangaroo Housing" (DK) "Granny Flats" (GB)	Daily assistance with domestic services	Constant surveilance and nursing care
Privately Contracted Support Services Private visiting or live-in help to elderly living alone or with a younger household	Visiting taxi and maid services as needed	Weekly domestic service	Daily or live-in domestic help	Live-in nurse

Figure 1.4: Long-term Public or Nonprofit Supportive Living Alternatives for Elderly in Western Industrial Societies

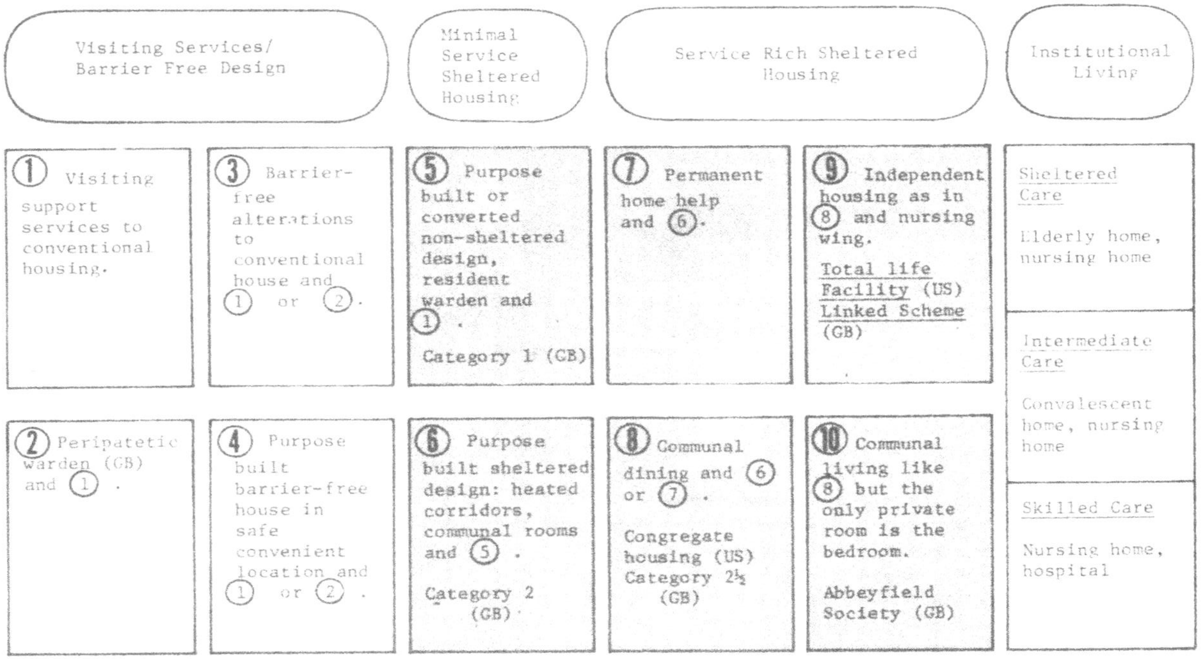

Visiting Services/ Barrier Free Design	Minimal Service Sheltered Housing	Service Rich Sheltered Housing	Institutional Living

① Visiting support services to conventional housing.

③ Barrier-free alterations to conventional house and ① or ② .

⑤ Purpose built or converted non-sheltered design, resident warden and ① . Category 1 (GB)

⑦ Permanent home help and ⑥ .

⑨ Independent housing as in ⑧ and nursing wing.
Total life Facility (US)
Linked Scheme (GB)

Sheltered Care
Elderly home, nursing home

② Peripatetic warden (GB) and ① .

④ Purpose built barrier-free house in safe convenient location and ① or ② .

⑥ Purpose built sheltered design: heated corridors, communal rooms and ⑤ . Category 2 (GB).

⑧ Communal dining and ⑥ or ⑦ .
Congregate housing (US) Category 2½ (GB)

⑩ Communal living like ⑧ but the only private room is the bedroom.
Abbeyfield Society (GB)

Intermediate Care
Convalescent home, nursing home

Skilled Care
Nursing home, hospital

Figure 1.5: Short-term or Part-time Public or Nonprofit Supportive Living Alternatives for Elderly in Western Industrial Societies

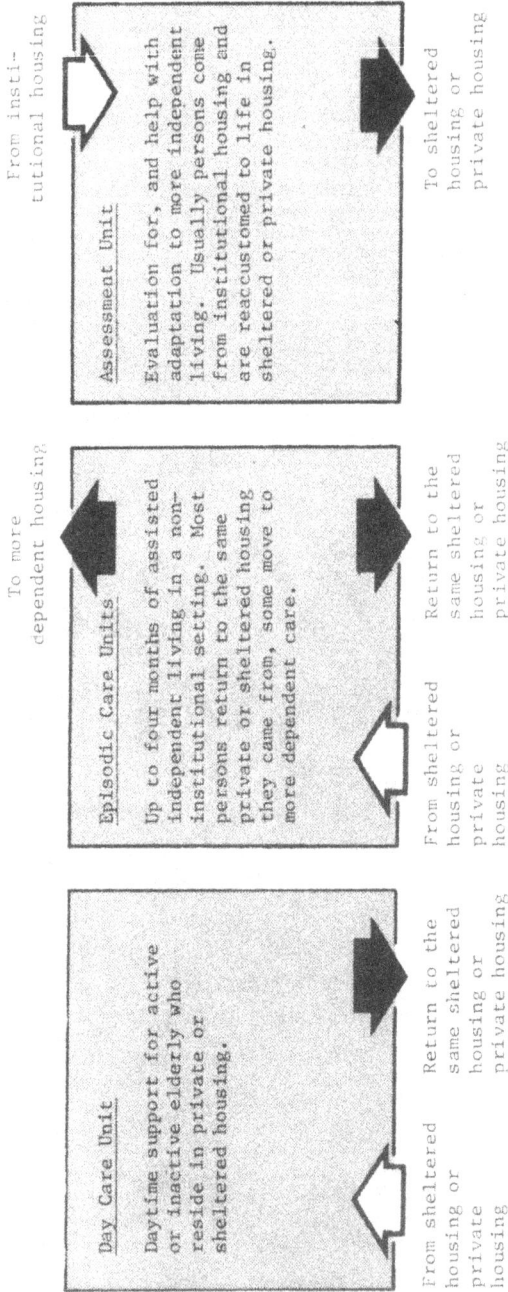

From insti-
tutional housing

Assessment Unit

Evaluation for, and help with adaptation to more independent living. Usually persons come from institutional housing and are reaccustomed to life in sheltered or private housing.

To sheltered
housing or
private housing

To more
dependent housing

Episodic Care Units

Up to four months of assisted independent living in a non-institutional setting. Most persons return to the same private or sheltered housing they came from, some move to more dependent care.

From sheltered
housing or
private
housing

Return to the
same sheltered
housing or
private housing

Day Care Unit

Daytime support for active or inactive elderly who reside in private or sheltered housing.

Return to the
same sheltered
housing or
private housing

From sheltered
housing or
private
housing

weekly support with transportation and domestic chores. The family may move the elderly parent in with them (first arrow) when the parent becomes housebound and daily assistance is needed with feeding, dressing, bathing, etc. Finally, the family may contract with a private nurse (second arrow) over the final weeks of life to provide medical aid which the family is incapable of administering.

Other combinations of private services exist. Perhaps the most common is the one in which an elderly parent lives for many years on his/her own with minor functional disabilities and then moves in with children for another long-term period where he/she remains chronically impaired but not terminally ill. 'Kangaroo housing' as it is called in Denmark, and 'granny flats' as it is called in Great Britain, are purpose-built housing solutions for just such a long-term situation. The housing consists of two linked apartments, each with its own private entry. The elderly unit is usually just an efficiency (using the American term) or bed sitter arrangement (using the British nomenclature). With a granny flat both the elderly and younger households can retain their privacy but still have ease of access, and the elderly have support nearby.

Long-term Public or Nonprofit Support Alternatives. Reading Fig. 1.4 from left to right, long-term public or nonprofit support alternatives present more specialised on-site services, shelter arrangements and communal living. Each separate cell represents a programme alternative. While the array of cells can be seen as individual stopping points on a conveyor belt-like continuum leading to increasingly more dependent care as functional disability increases, this is *not* how we advocate that these programmes function. Each cell should be seen as an alternative *entry point* to assisted independent living. Elderly, choosing an alternative shown toward the right of Fig. 1.4 may be functionally independent when they enter even though they choose a facility with more sheltered design and on-site support staff. In fact, we advise that each programme seeks a balance of residents by age and functional impairment. We would also expect that each individual scheme would be flexible and provide increasing support services as needed. The programmes without on-site services cannot, of course, provide 24 hour support on a long-term basis, and only those toward the far right can provide continuous nursing care.

In the first programme (cell 1), the elderly continue to live in conventional housing as they become impaired while receiving visiting public support services in the community in order to assist them in retaining their independent household. For this to be a viable alternative, the elderly must be aware of the services that are available. In the second programme (cell 2), a peripatetic or visiting warden (a paid visitor, usually a lay person) is assigned to a neighbourhood and pays regular check visits to the elderly and calls in support services for them as needed. In cells numbered 3 and 4, the same support services are provided, but in addition the elderly either have their own house adapted to barrier-free design to ease the onset of functional mobility problems or move to purpose built barrier-free housing which is located in a more appropriate neighbourhood free of crime and pollutants, and within a critical distance of shops and public transportation.

Programme cells 5 and 6 represent minimal service sheltered housing. Here the (usually) purpose-built flats or bungalows are clustered and the independent units have an alarm or intercom connection to a warden (or friendly neighbour). The nonsheltered designs (cell 5) match what the British have titled Category 1 sheltered housing. Each flat or bungalow usually has a private exterior entrance and there are few, if any, communal spaces (although there can be a communal lounge). Sheltered designs (cell 6) fit into the definition of British Category 2 housing. A block of private apartments or flats are attached via heated corridors with a communal entry to the building and at least a communal lounge and laundry. Often a kitchen and meeting rooms are included. At this level of congregate living the role of the resident warden is usually expanded from just a daily visitor to a resident social organiser and advisor.

Programme cells 7 to 10 represent various levels of service-rich sheltered housing. They usually have a sheltered design and include permanent on-site support staff to aid or replace the resident warden. The first level (cell 7) provides permanent home help (to aid residents with domestic chores) and the next level (cell 8) provides a communal kitchen and communal dining. In Britain this and cell 10 have unofficially been entitled category 2½; in the United States this is known as congregate housing. 'Total life' or 'linked' schemes (cell 9) provide a nursing wing (or linked residential home) to which residents can be transferred as needed for episodic or chronic illnesses. Communal living (cell 10) is frequently just one step away from institutional living. All meals are eaten communally and even bathroom and toilet facilities are communal. The only private room the elderly retain is their bedroom.

Short-term or Part-time Public or Nonprofit Support Alternatives. The
three short-term or part-time housing solutions of Fig. 1.5 are seen as
supplements to the various public and private long-term support
housing arrangements. All three may enable elderly persons to remain
in long-term assisted living by providing a temporary refuge in times of
crisis or partial support on a daily basis. Day care facilities can range
from 'drop-in' to 'drop-off' centres. 'Drop-in' centres are usually
for the active and independent elderly who are lonely or destitute and
seek companionship or a warm meal. 'Drop-off' centres can provide
day care for a wide variety of disabled elderly including persons who
are severely impaired to the point of being chairfast and in need of
nursing surveillance. Such centres can be of value to elderly residing
in private households or minimal service sheltered housing facilities.
'Drop-off' centres are also designed to provide free time for a family
member or resident warden who is unable to leave his disabled elderly
charge alone in order to attend to other chores.

In the United States 'drop-in' centres have become quite popular
and serve a variety of functions from neighbourhood nutritional sites
serving hot midday meals, to senior centres providing cultural and
educational activities. In 1973–4 the National Council on Aging
calculated that five million elderly participated in senior centres and
seven million more would do so if centres were accessible to them.
There are two models of 'drop-off' centres in the United States, a
medical model and a social model. The medical model provides nursing
care and is primarily a community outreach function of hospitals and
nursing homes. The social model is provided by numerous public and
nonprofit groups but is limited to functionally and mentally disabled
but well elderly.

The 'episodic care unit' is a form of temporary service-rich sheltered
housing which the elderly can use for up to three or four months. One
type of episodic event is recovery from an accident (e.g., broken arm)
or an illness (e.g., a case of flu that has left the elderly person very
weak). In such cases the resident is temporarily unable to maintain his
own home, or is an excessive burden to his extended family or to the
warden and other residents in his sheltered housing scheme. Therefore,
he may temporarily move to the episodic care unit. The unit is also
available when a family wants to travel on vacation, but an elderly
member is too frail to go along or to stay home alone. Occasionally,
very frail elderly do not recover the level of independence they had
before their episodic illness or injury, even with the special therapy
provided by the episodic care unit. If they cannot return to the private

household they had, they are advised of more appropriate sheltered housing arrangements. Convalescent institutions modelled on a nursing home are quite common, but episodic care units stressing maximum independent living are still a rarity in most Western countries. In the United States episodic care units were first recognised as a useful housing type by nonprofit (voluntary) agencies that provide a full spectrum of housing for the elderly (e.g. conventional housing, sheltered housing, nursing home and hospital). These agencies could clearly see that episodic inability to care for conventional or sheltered housing did not warrant a permanent move to a more dependent housing type. The Council for Jewish Elderly in Chicago provides a good model.

The 'assessment units' are especially designed to take persons from a more dependent care setting (usually an institutional care facility) and reaccustom them to more independent living in sheltered housing. Assessment units are probably the most rare of the three short-term housing alternatives because they require the co-operation of all the public agencies that house and/or provide support to the elderly. The Wyre Forest District in the West Midlands of England, mentioned previously, provides a good example. There a co-operative programme to plan, staff and finance such a unit was accomplished by the district health, social services and housing councils.

Figure 1.3–1.5 illustrate only the physical aspects of housing and social service alternatives. Not shown are the different financial arrangements. For example, any of the sheltered housing settings may or may not be accompanied by a financial subsidy for rent and/or services. In the case of 'kangaroo housing' (granny flats) there might be a tax excemption or subsidy incentive to aid the younger household caring for the elderly member. There are also cases in which elderly individuals have privately banded together and formed a true commune, pooling their financial and domestic resources.[82] Also not shown is the variety of service providers. The 'total life' facility, under service-rich sheltered housing, is a US example where private-for-profit developers build and manage the housing. The 'linked scheme' is a similar British arrangement (sheltered housing adjacent to an old people's home) but is sponsored by public housing authorities, public social service agencies or voluntary (nonprofit) associations.

In Chapter 2 we discuss the extent to which these varied entry points exist in Great Britain and how the British evolved their varied sheltered housing programme almost two decades ahead of other Western societies.

Notes

1. Katz, S.H., 'Anthropological perspectives on aging', *Planning for the elderly* (special editor) Marvin E. Wolfgang. In Richard D. Lambert and Alan W. Heston, (editors), *The Annals of the American Academy of Political and Social Science*, 1978, 438, pp. 1–12.

2. Noam, E., *Homes for the Aged: Supervision and Standards*, National Clearinghouse on Aging, United States Department of Health Education and Welfare, Washington, D.C., 1975, pp. 1–5.

3. Katz, 'Anthropological perspectives on aging'.

4. Department of Health and Social Security, *A Happier Old Age*, HMSO, London, 1978.

5. Abrams, M., 'Demographic Trends', in David Hobman (editor), *The Impact of Aging: Strategies for care*. Croom Helm, London, 1981, pp. 20–32.

6. Katz, 'Anthropological perspectives on aging'.

7. Brotman, H.B., 'Population Projections, Part 1: Tomorrow's older population (to 2000)'. *Gerontologist*, June 1977, 17, pp. 203–9; Uhlenberg, P., 'Changing structure of the older population of the United States of America during the Twentieth Century'. *Gerontologist*, 1977, 17, pp. 197–202.

8. Department of Health and Social Security, *A Happier Old Age*.

9. Katz, 'Anthropological perspectives on aging'.

10. Brody, E.M., 'The aging of the family'. *Planning for the Elderly*, (special editor) Marvin E. Wolfgang. In Richard D. Lambert and Alan W. Heston, (editors), *The Annals of the American Academy of Political and Social Science*, 1978, 438, pp. 13–27.

11. Treas, Judith, 'Family support systems for the aged: Some social and demographic considerations'. *Gerontologist*, 1977, 17, pp. 486–91.

12. Ibid.

13. United States Bureau of the Census. 'Demographic aspects of aging and the older population in the United States'. *Current population report series*, PC-23, No. 59, USGPO, Washington, D.C., 1976.

14. Townsend, P., 'Emergence of the four generation family in industrial society'. In *Middle Age and Aging*, Nevgarten, B.L. (ed.), University of Chicago Press, Chicago, 1968, pp. 255–7.

15. Riley, M.W. and Foner, A., *An Inventory of research findings, aging and society*. Volume 1, Russell Sage, New York, 1968, pp. 541–4; Shanas, E. *et al.*, *Old People in Three Industrial Societies*. Routledge and Kegan Paul, London, 1968.

16. Department of Health and Social Security, *A Happier Old Age*.

17. Shanas *et al.*, *Old People in Three Industrialised Societies*.

18. Treas, 'Family support systems for the aged: Some social and demographic considerations.'

19. United States Bureau of the Census. Census of population: 1970. Subject reports, final report PC (2) – 6A. *Employment status and work experience*. USGPO. Washington, D.C., 1973.

20. Fullerton, H., Jr., and Flaim, P., *New Labor force projections to 1990*. United States Bureau of Labor Statistics bulletin No. 197, USGPO, Washington, D.C., 1977, 13 pp.

21. Treas, 'Family support systems for the aged: Some social and demographic considerations'.

22. Ibid.

23. Soldo, B.J. and Myers, G.C., 'The effects of total fertility on living arrangements among the elderly women: 1970'. Paper presented at the Annual Meeting of the Gerontological Society, New York, 1976.

24. Brody, E.M., *Long-Term care of older people: A Practical Guide*, Human

Sciences Press, New York, 1977.
    25. Brody, E.M. and Spark, G., 'Institutionalization of the aged: A family crisis'. *Family process*, 1966, 5, pp. 76–90; Spark and Brody, E.M., 'The aged are family members'. *Family process*, 1970, 9, pp. 195–210.
    26. Townsend, P., *The Last Refuge*. Routledge and Kegan Paul, London, 1962; Townsend, C., *Old Age: The last segregation*. Grossman, New York, 1971.
    27. Butler, R.N., *Why Survive? Being Old in America*. Harper and Row, New York, 1973.
    28. Ibid.
    29. Booz, Allan and Hamilton, *Long-term care study*. Volume II, State Department on Aging, Springfield, Illinois, 1975; Butler, R.N. *Why Survive? Being Old in America*; Deetz, V.L., 'Congregate housing a growing need'. *HUD Challenge*. United States Department of Housing and Urban Development, Washington, D.C., August 1979, pp. 18–19; Kistin, H. and Morris, R., 'Alternatives to institutional care for the elderly and disabled'. *Gerontologist*, Part 1, 1972, 12, pp. 139–42; Lawton, M.P., 'Institutions and alternatives for older people'. *Health and Social Work*, 1978, 3, pp. 108–34; Thompson, M.M., 'The elderly in our environment: Yesterday and today'. *HUD Challenge*, United States Department of Housing and Urban Development, Washington, D.C., August 1979; Townsend, P., *The Last Refuge*; United States House of Representatives, Select Committee on Aging, Subcommittee on Housing and Long-Term Care. New Perspective on health care for older Americans. USGPO, Washington, D.C., January 1976.
    30. Dudley, C.J. and Hillery, G.A., Jr., 'Freedom and alienation in homes for the aged'. *Gerontologist*, 1977, 17, pp. 140–45.
    31. Ibid.; Kane, R.L. and Kane, R.A., 'Alternatives to institutional care of the elderly: Beyond the dichotomy'. Paper prepared for the American Association for the Advancement of Science, AAAS Intergovernmental R & D Project Workshop on Health and Human Resources: The Elderly, December 1978; Schulz, R. and Brenner, G., 'Relocation of the Aged'. *Journal of Gerontology*, 1977, 32, pp. 323–33.
    32. Booz, Allan and Hamilton. *Long-term care study*.
    33. Nachison, J.S., 'Services for Congregate Housing: A new direction for HUD'. *HUD Challenge*, August 1979; United States House of Representatives, Select Committee on Aging, Subcommittee on Housing and Consumer Interests. Congregate Housing Services, USGPO, Washington, D.C., 1981, p. 47.
    34. Nachison, J.S., 'Services for Congregate Housing: A new direction for HUD'.
    35. Katz, 'Anthropological perspectives on aging'.
    36. Wager, R., *Care of the elderly*, Institute of Municipal Treasurers and Accountants (IMTA), March 1972.
    37. Plank, D., *Caring for the Elderly: Report of a study of various means of caring for dependent elderly people in eight London Boroughs*. Greater London Council, Research Memorandum, No. 512, July 1977.
    38. Morris, R., 'The development of parallel services for the elderly and disabled: some financial dimensions'. *Gerontologist*, 1974, 14, pp. 15–19.
    39. Butler, *Why Survive? Being Old in America*.
    40. Cohn, J., Tell, R.L., and Leveck, T., 'Providing housing/services for the elderly: An allocation model'. Paper presented at the Gerontological Society Meeting, Portland, October 1974. Glassman, J.J., Tell, R.L., Larrivee, J.P. and Itelland, R., 'Toward an estimation of service need: A community planning technique'. DEHS Model Project, monograph, Los Angeles, September 1975; Heumann, L.F., 'Estimating the local needs for elderly congregate housing'. *Gerontologist*, 1976, 16, pp. 397–403; Shanas, E. *et al.*, *Old People in Three Industrial Societies*.
    41. Schooler, K.K., *National Senior Citizens Survey* (NSCS). SRS Training Grant

93-p-7504-915, United States Department of Health Education and Welfare, Administration on Aging, Syracuse University, 1968.

42. Heumann, L.F., 'Planning assisted independent living program for the semi-independent elderly: Development of a descriptive model'. *Gerontologist*, 1978, 18, pp. 145-52.

43. Heumann, L.F. and Lareau, L., 'Local estimates of the functional disabled elderly: Toward a planning tool for housing and support services programs'. *International Journal of Aging and Human Development*, 1979, 10, pp. 77-93.

44. Heumann, 'Estimating the local needs for elderly congregate housing'.

45. Heumann, L.F., *Identifying the Housing and support service needs of the semi-independent elderly: Toward a descriptive planning model for Area Agencies on Aging in Illinois.* Housing Research and Development Program, University of Illinois at Urbana-Champaign, 1977, 135 pp.; Heumann, L.F. and Lareau, L., 'Local estimates of the functional disabled elderly: Toward a planning tool for housing and support services programs'.

46. Department of Health and Social Security, *A Happier Old Age.*

47. Riley and Foner, *An Inventory of research findings, aging and society.*

48. Shanas, E. *et al., Old People in Three Industrial Societies.*

49. United States Department of Health Education and Welfare, Public Health Services, *Home care for persons 55 and over, United States: July 1966-June 1968.* Vital and Health Statistics, Series 10, No. 73, July 1972.

50. Thompson, 'The elderly in our environment: Yesterday and today'.

51. Bettesworth, R.A., 'Present function and future possibility of sheltered housing'. *Sheltered Housing: A Review*, National Federation of Housing Associations, London, 1978; London Borough of Greenwich. *Older People's homes and sheltered housing in Greenwich.* London Borough of Greenwich, November, 1972; Scottish Development Department. *Local housing needs and Strategies: A Case study of the Dundee sub-region.* HMSO, Edinburgh, 1976; Townsend, P., *The Last Refuge.*

52. Nachison, 'Services for Congregate Housing: A new direction for HUD'.

53. Struyk, R.J., 'The housing situation of elderly Americans'. *Gerontologist*, 1977, 17, pp. 130-9 (a).

54. Struyk, R.J., 'The housing expense burden of households headed by the elderly'. *Gerontologist*, 1977, 17, pp. 447-52 (b).

55. Lawton, M.P., 'The relative impact of congregate and traditional housing on elderly tenants'. *Gerontologist*, 1976, 16, pp. 237-42.

56. Lawton, M.P., 'Supportive services in the context of the housing environment'. *Gerontologist*, 1969, 9, pp. 15-19.

57. Lawton, 'Supportive services in the context of the housing environment'.

58. Beckman, R.D., 'The acceptance of congregate life in a retirement village'. *Gerontologist*, 1969, 9, pp. 281-5.

59. Gray, J.J.A., 'Housing for elderly people: heaven, haven and ghetto'. *Housing Monthly: The Journal of the Institute of Housing*, 1976, 12, pp. 12-13; Tinker, A., 'Can a case be made for special housing?' *Municipal Review*, February 1977, pp. 314-5; Tinker, A., 'The way ahead'. *Sheltered Housing: A Review*, Monograph published by the National Association of Housing Associations, 1978.

60. Boldy, Duncan, 'Is sheltered housing a good thing?' In *Some Unresolved aspects of sheltered housing for the elderly and the disabled*, Institute of Social Welfare, 1977; Boldy, Duncan, 'Sheltered Housing for the Elderly: – The Alternative Refuge?' *Community Care* (in press).

61. Griffin, J. and Dean, C., *Housing for the elderly: The size of grouped schemes.* Department of the Environment, HMSO, London, 1975.

62. Gray, 'Housing for elderly people: heaven, haven and ghetto'.

63. Carp, F.M., 'User evaluation of housing for the elderly'. *Gerontologist*, 1976, 16, pp. 102-11; Rose, E.A., *Housing for the Aged.* Saxon House, Teakfield,

Westmead, Farnborough, 1978.
64. Lawton, 'Supportive services in the context of the housing environment'.
65. Findlay, R.A., 'Social determinants of design of housing for the elderly'.
Monograph, Department of Architecture, Iowa State University, Ames, Iowa,
1977.
66. Brody, E.M., Kleban, M.H., and Liebowitz, B. 'Intermediate housing for
the elderly: satisfaction of those who moved and those who did not'. *Gerontologist*, 1975, 15, pp. 350–6; Lawton, 'The relative impact of congregate and
traditional housing on elderly tenants'.
67. Plank, *Caring for the elderly: Report of a study of various means of
caring for dependent elderly people in eight London Boroughs.*
68. Harel, Z. and Harel, B.B., 'On-site coordinated services in age-segregated
and age-integrated public housing'. *Gerontologist*, 1978, 18, pp. 153–8.
69. Carp, F.M., 'Impact of improved living environment on health and life
expectancy'. *Gerontologist*, 1977, 17, pp. 242–9.
70. Sherwood, S., Green, D.S., and Morris, J.N., 'A study of the Highland
Heights Apartments for the physically impaired and elderly in Fall River'. In
Byerts, T. *et al.* (editors), *Gerontological Monographs*, Garland Press, New York,
1979.
71. Brody, E.M., 'Community housing for the elderly: The program, the
people, the decision making process, and the research'. *Gerontologist*, 1978,
18, pp. 121–9.
72. Carp, 'Impact of Improved living environment on health and life
expectancy'; Sherwood *et al.*, 'A study of the Highland Heights Apartments for
the physically impaired and elderly in Fall River'.
73. Seligman, M., *Helplessness*. Freeman Press, San Francisco, 1975.
74. Ferrari, N. *Institutionalization and Attitude Change in an Aged Population*. Unpublished Doctoral dissertation, Case Western Reserve, Ohio, 1962;
Schulz and Brenner, 'Relocation of the Aged'.
75. Kastenbaum, R. and Candy, S.E., 'The 4% Fallacy: A methodological and
empirical critique of extended care facility population statistics'. *Aging and
Human Development*, 1973, 4, pp. 15–21.
76. Kane and Kane, 'Alternatives to institutional care of the elderly: Beyond
the dichotomy'.
77. Dudley and Hillery, 'Freedom and alienation in homes for the aged'.
78. Auston, M. and Kosberg, J., 'Nursing home decision-makers and the social
service needs of residents'. *Social Work in Health Care*, 1976, 1, pp. 447–56.
79. Mercer, S.O. and Kane, R.A., 'Helplessness and hopelessness in the
institutionalized aged: A Field experiment'. *Health and Social Work*, 1979, 4,
pp. 90–116.
80. National Center for Health Statistics. A comparison of nursing home
residents and discharges from the 1977 National Nursing Home Survey for the
United States. *Advance data*, GPO, Washington, D.C., No. 29, May 1978.
81. Butler, *Why Survive? Being Old in America*; Mendelsen, M.A., *Tender
Loving Greed*, Knopf, New York, 1974; Townsend, C., 'Old age: The Last
Segregation'; Townsend, P., 'The Last Refuge'.
82. Hochschild, A.R., *The Unexpected Community*, Prentice Hall, Inc.,
Englewood Cliffs, New Jersey, 1973.

2 THE EVOLUTION OF SHELTERED HOUSING

For the last decade, national policy in the countries of northern Europe and North America has been to reduce the amount of new construction of institutional homes and to increase the investments in supportive systems that assist the elderly with independent living. Despite this growing investment, no Western society had developed specific legislation for the construction of sheltered housing as of 1976.[1] Western countries which have built sheltered housing to date, have had to fund the buildings under existing general housing laws. This has meant that only a portion of the funds appropriated for existing programmes have been assigned to sheltered housing; these laws typically only subsidise the construction of barrier-free units, and do not usually provide assistance with support services and/or communal spaces. As a result the development of sheltered housing has been slow and uneven, with a tendency not to build it in areas where local sponsors lack the wealth, sophistication, staff or will to develop and fund the needed parallel support services on their own. The formulation of specific legislation has begun since 1976. The United States, for example, passed a Congregate Housing Service Program (CHSP) in 1978,[2] and experimental implementation of the programme is now underway.

The Type and Amount of Sheltered Housing Built to Date

Table 2.1 displays the estimated amount of sheltered housing built to date in the German Federal Republic, Great Britain, Sweden and the United States. These four countries have been chosen because they represent the spectrum of sponsor types found in Western societies where sheltered housing is being built. In West Germany, federal programmes are administered by the Social Welfare Agency and local sponsors tend to be large nonprofit organisations that are associated with the major religious and political bodies. In Sweden, federal funding and administration rests with the National Board of Health and Welfare but the local sponsors are municipal social welfare offices. In the United States only about 30 per cent of the sheltered housing is federally subsidised and then not by the health and welfare agency but by the Department of Housing and Urban Development. The local

Table 2.1: The Extent of Sheltered Housing Development in the German Federal Republic, Great Britain, Sweden and the United States

	No. of units	% of residents to total noninstitu- tionalised elderly	Dominant sponsor type
German Federal Republic	25,000	0.36[a]	Large nonprofit welfare association
Great Britain	327,000	5.00[b]	Local housing authority
Sweden	3,500	0.80[c]	Local social welfare office
United States	71,000	0.15[d]	Small private for profit or nonprofit developer

Sources: a. Noam, Ernst and Wilma Donahue, 'Assisted Independent Living in Grouped (Congregate) Housing for Old People', International Center for Social Gerontology, Washington, DC, 1976. The percentage shown for the German Federal Republic is for 1970. The German Federal Republic has built far more *Altenwohnheime* in recent years; however, no consensus on the number of units exists. Interviews with German Federal Republic officials and Research Institutes revealed estimates of from 1.1% to 1.8% of the noninstitutionalised elderly in sheltered housing by 1978. b. 'A Happier Old Age', Department of Health and Social Security, London, 1979. The percentage for Great Britain is a 1979 estimate. An England and Wales survey, carried out by Oxford Polytechnic on behalf of the Department of the Environment, indicated a figure of about 4% as of September 1977.[5] c. Based on statistics presented by the Office of Planning and Organisation, Swedish Planning and Rationalisation Institute of Health and Social Services, Stockholm, 26 June 1978. d. 'Federally-Assisted Congregate Housing Development for the Elderly', Special Concerns Staff, Office of Housing Programs, Housing Management, Department of HUD, Washington, DC, Jan. 1976. The American Association of Homes for the Aging in testimony before the US Senate Subcommittee on Urban Affairs, Congregate Housing Service Act Hearing, 1978. This estimate combines these two sources after eliminating overlaps: 22,559 units are identified by the Department of Housing and Urban Development and 55,366 units are identified by the American Association of Homes for the Aging. This is an estimate, limited to the US definition of congregate housing which means housing connnected to a central dining facility where at least one communal meal is taken each day.

sponsors are small nonprofit developers. The remaining 70 or so per cent of US sheltered housing is sponsored by small private, for-profit developers or small nonprofit religious groups and other philanthropic organisations.[3] In Great Britain, about 85 per cent of the units are built by public housing authorities and about 15 per cent by voluntary (nonprofit) Housing Associations of varying sizes.[4] As with the other European examples, most of the British development receives central government subsidy; but, like the United States, the national funding and administration is handled by the department which is responsible for housing – the Department of the Environment.

Table 2.1 shows that all four countries are well below the 10–15 per cent estimated need for sheltered housing derived in Chapter 1. Great Britain, with about 5 per cent of the elderly in sheltered housing,[6] comes closest to meeting it. This amount of sheltered housing is roughly that estimated as necessary to meet the needs of the most functionally impaired elderly (including those in institutions) who are without family support (see Figures 1.1. and 1.2).

The United States lags far behind other Western societies in the development of sheltered housing, and the projects that do exist are largely private developments that cater for middle- and upper-income consumers. One mitigating factor, however, is that the United States statistics represent only congregate housing, or purpose-built, independent apartments connected to a common dining facility. There is some evidence that nonprofit and public housing for the elderly, which was originally designed to have no support services and to cater only for the totally independent elderly, is being adapted as the elderly population ages (if the sponsor can afford it) to the minimum service definition of sheltered housing. If the new Congregate Housing Service Program is continued past 1982, it should help local public housing sponsors build and convert existing projects to sheltered housing.

British sheltered housing is concentrated at the opposite end of the support continuum to American congregate housing. The typical British scheme fits the minimum service definition with an alarm or intercom system connecting each dwelling to a resident warden with limited communal facilities, e.g. lounge and laundry room, sometimes provided. However, British local authorities and voluntary housing associations have been converting to more service-rich housing as their sheltered housing population has aged.

The German Federal Republic builds sheltered housing under their New Homes Law. This law covers all elderly housing including total care nursing homes. As a result, they attempt to house some elderly with minor functional limitations in *Altenwohnhauser* which parallel British sheltered housing (category 1)[7] or United States public housing for the elderly with no on-site staff or services and no alarm or intercom system. Both *Altenwohnheime* and *Altenwohnstifte* fit the British sheltered housing definition (category 2),[8] except that they also often include a nurse's station with a nurse on duty during the daytime. *Altenwohnstifte* are similar to *Altenwohnheime* except that they are private, nonprofit developments of superior design for higher income elderly.

The Swedish type of sheltered housing, called a *Servicehus*, is very similar to the British model and is a relatively recent phenomenon limited primarily to the Stockholm area. Sweden has a post-World War II history of placing all disabled elderly requiring care in nursing homes. Over 11 per cent of the elderly are in such homes compared with around 5 per cent in institutions in most industrialised countries. It has been estimated by the Swedish Planning and Rationalisation Institute of the Health and Social Services, that 61 per cent of the elderly now in nursing homes are in a too dependent housing environment. Twenty-six per cent of these elderly probably could have stayed where they were before entering the nursing home; the rest would be better off in a *Servicehus*. Sheltered housing is built with municipal taxes by municipal social welfare offices which also administer home visiting services. Since the federal government now subsidises 35 per cent of the salary costs of home visiting services, most social welfare offices choose to provide home visiting services rather than build sheltered housing.

The number of sheltered housing developments has doubled over the last decade in all four countries shown in Table 2.1. Despite this impressive growth, sheltered housing construction still lags behind demand and remains an unknown housing alternative to most elderly. Detailed discussion of the major constraints to sheltered housing development now follows.

The Major Constraints on the Development of Sheltered Housing in Western Society

Vested Interests in National Housing Policy

Almost every Western government has divided its post-World War II elderly housing policy into two subsidy categories:

a. Subsidies for low-income but functionally independent elderly who need assistance securing standard conventional housing they can afford.
b. Subsidies to those functionally dependent elderly with severe and chronic health related disabilities who require total care with daily living.

Two separate housing/service 'industries' have emerged from these policies. While there has been a growing recognition by both industries of the variety of supportive shelter needs that lie between their two housing extremes, it has, nevertheless, been difficult to develop unique sheltered housing legislation. Both industries are reluctant to expand into this intermediate supportive housing market, yet each has been reluctant to give up that territory to the other. The United States illustrates this strong ambivalence toward sheltered housing combined with strong antagonism between the vested interests which provide traditional elderly housing. Subsidised low-income housing for independent elderly is administered by the Department of Housing and Urban Development. Both the national housing programmes and local authorities which sponsor this housing are influenced by powerful banking and real estate lobbies which have traditionally sought to limit such programmes for fear they would compete with and weaken the private housing market. Experiments with subsidised sheltered housing that include support services are particularly alien to these interests as they involve public intervention in providing both housing and social services for elderly who need not be low income. Only in recent years, as public housing managers have become more professional and receptive to elderly needs have they developed their own lobby group in support of sheltered housing.

The nursing home industry represents the other extreme of public shelter provision for the elderly. In the United States this housing is largely privately built and owned. The subsidies primarily go to the individual low-income or needy elderly to help defray the cost of social, health and housing services provided by the nursing home. The Department of Health and Human Services (formerly Health, Education and Welfare) administers these subsidies. An entirely different but equally powerful lobby made up of the medical industry and nursing home owners and directors influences these programmes. These interests are hesitant to let their programmes expand in the direction of more traditional housing without health services.

Nursing homes can be seen as a 'hybrid between hospital and family surrogate'.[9] They provide long-term, skilled care but use the hospital model of short-term institutionalised housing. Nursing homes have tried to accommodate the growing demand for long-term supportive housing from elderly who lack family support but require less than skilled nursing care. However, the 'intermediate care' and 'sheltered care' programmes developed to date have retained the institutional model, because the reimbursement mechanism developed at this end of the housing spectrum favours institutional care over other housing alternatives. Other powerful professional lobbying groups representing individual doctors and hospitals see no reason to give up the present reimbursement mechanism.[10]

This division of interests has slowed the development of unique sheltered housing programmes. The 1974 United States Housing and Community Development Act called for co-operative development of sheltered housing by health, social service and housing agencies, but nothing materialised. The 1978 Congregate Housing Services Act is being totally administered by housing managers in local authorities. In the United States, the nursing home industry has proved unable and unwilling to administer housing programmes for both independent and dependent elderly.

The Lack of Co-operative Management of Long-term Support Care Systems at the Local Level

Sheltered housing for functionally disabled and socially dependent elderly is a complex programme to initiate and maintain. It not only requires housing development and management resources but health and social services resources as well. In countries in which one central agency has been given administrative responsibility to co-ordinate sheltered housing programmes, local problems and gaps in the delivery of support often result. If the central housing authority is the agency which administers the programme, regional and local housing authorities must seek the co-operation of visiting health and social service providers for the programme to work. If the central government's social service agency is the one which administers the programme, local agencies usually require aid from housing authorities in the development and maintenance of the physical buildings.

The most service-rich sheltered housing developments can duplicate all community support programmes on-site. Thus it is the minimal service sheltered housing programmes that are the most threatened by a lack of co-operative management and support. There are cases in which local housing authority sheltered housing programmes do not receive appropriate co-operation from visiting community services. Equally, there are cases in which programmes run by social service agencies have not received promised assistance from the local housing authority in adapting or maintaining barrier-free design or in providing disability supporting equipment. Also, there are cases in which neither housing nor social service authorities receive appropriate co-operation from community medical authorities. Nursing homes or residential homes sometimes refuse to take sheltered housing elderly who can no longer maintain their independence because they falsely assume that sheltered housing can provide more or less total support care. Hospitals have returned elderly residents to their sheltered housing environments so early in the period of convalescence that daily nursing was still required, again falsely assuming that this service is readily available in sheltered housing.

Most of these problems arise because of a lack of knowledge about what support a minimal service, sheltered housing programme can and cannot provide on-site. The agencies not involved in providing sheltered housing have frequently observed that in the early years of a sheltered housing scheme, when most of the residents are active and totally independent, the resident warden or manager can provide the episodic care, assistance or maintenance which the residents require. The non-involved agencies then adjust their own priorities toward serving those elderly who are not in sheltered housing. What they fail to realise is that the resident warden or manager can only provide intensive care for a few residents at a time, and then only on an episodic basis. If such care becomes permanent and/or involves more residents, the entire assistance, surveillance and socialising network which the warden or manager provides to all the residents can become overburdened and collapse, undermining the sheltered housing scheme as a whole. This can become a major problem as the minimum care, sheltered housing programmes age and the amount of dependency among the residents rises.

This problem is addressed from the standpoint of different sheltered housing categories, the warden and management in Chapters 3, 4 and 5. We show that some local authorities in Great Britain with over 20 years of experience in the provision of sheltered housing have developed a new 'super-agency' which pools the planning knowledge and resources of local health, housing and social service agencies working with the elderly. Local co-ordination such as this has resulted not only in comprehensive assistance with traditional housing and services but, also in the development and implementation of important new management innovations in the delivery of sheltered housing; these are discussed in Chapter 5.

Problems with the Legal Status of a Contract Between a Public Authority and Elderly Residents of Sheltered Housing

The lack of assurances that support services will be forthcoming is enough to discourage many local authorities from building sheltered housing. Compounding this uncertainty is the lack of a clear definition of exactly what services should be available to sheltered housing residents. There is still no clear legal definition of what is meant by assisted independent living in any Western society. As a result, the extent of the disabilities that can and should be accommodated in a sheltered housing scheme is not clear. Legal criteria to be used in determining when a person is no longer able to maintain an independent housing unit, or when a person should be transferred to a more dependent support facility, have remained unresolved and are likely to remain so. Most of the countries that have built sheltered housing have begun their programmes by housing the relatively young and least disabled elderly. Most of these programmes are so new that they have yet to experience a large number of very old and frail tenants. As these programmes age, many residents may require extensive support services and communal living. Yet it is not clear when a person is 'better off' and requires less costly support by remaining in sheltered housing and when they are 'better off' in an institutional environment. The problem of defining and then interpreting where assisted independent housing should stop and where assisted *dependent* housing should begin has prevented many countries from either beginning or expanding sheltered housing programmes despite an evident and growing demand.

The determination of a very exacting contract between tenant and management is, of course, a two-edged sword. While a legal contract can guarantee the resident a precise level of support services, it can also require the resident to maintain a precise level of self care and independence. Determining 'level of independence' will often require subjective interpretation. Many intervening factors, such as episodic illnesses, amount of help received from friends, neighbours, relatives and staff, will complicate evaluations. Yet an assessed level of independence could be used to evict tenants who are unpopular or 'too much work' in the opinion of the staff. Any contract design must therefore be humane and flexible with proper checks and balances to prevent misuse and abuse by either the tenants or management. Despite attempts to standardise support service levels, residents and staff of individual sheltered housing schemes will always be willing and able to care for tenants in varying degrees. A highly dependent and chronically ill person in one scheme can cause great stress, and could threaten the health, wellbeing and even safety of other residents. Another scheme could create a hospice environment for the same individual and provide 24 hour support until they die. The effort could be a very positive and unifying experience looked upon with great love, joy and pride by the residents.

Some housing planners feel that the answer to the question of varying service needs can and should be handled through the provision of a continuum from minimal service to service-rich sheltered housing environments along which the elderly can be transferred as their support needs change and surpass the capacity of their current housing. However, the legal dilemma facing housing planners would only be exaggerated when this *conveyor belt* approach to housing the functionally disabled elderly is employed. As was indicated in the previous paragraph, there are very few clear and objective signs that indicate when a person should or *must* be moved. Increasing the number of times this decision has to be made can only complicate matters. On the other hand, a continuum of assisted independent living environments does seem appropriate as providing choice for disabled and deprived elderly moving from conventional housing to different levels of on-site support care and different levels of communal living. This continuum of sheltered housing types serves alternative *entry points* to supported independent living; each point addressing different long-term life-style and housing needs. Given the legal dilemmas, each alternative would have to be designed so as to accommodate as wide a range of functional dependency as economically feasible, with clearly defined functional eligibility limits that all residents understand from the outset.

Great Britain, which has the largest number and variety of sheltered housing, is the obvious and best locality for analysing these and other problems. The differences in sheltered housing types is analysed beginning in Chapter 3. Chapter 4 traces the changes in the resident warden's role over time and between different housing types and scheme designs. We also consider the number and extent of disabilities that wardens can handle in different types of sheltered housing. Chapter 5 explores the role of management in sheltered housing and the different schemes developed for screening applicants and evaluating individual cases at the margin of functional independence.

Elderly Knowledge and Awareness of Sheltered Housing Choices

The lack of knowledge about sheltered housing on the part of the elderly has also severely hindered its rapid development. Where sheltered housing programmes are well established, elderly demand is high. Demand began to build up over two decades ago in Great Britain and is currently catching on in West Germany. In the United States and Sweden most elderly are still unaware of the sheltered housing concept much less the alternative housing choices along a sheltered housing continuum. There are no national governments and only a few local governments that have developed comprehensive information and counselling systems to provide information on all possible assisted independent living choices. This, once again, is the result of the dispersion of the many forms of assisted independent living among the different agencies whose original mandate and perceived role is not that of providing sheltered housing. Housing providers invariably have no outreach programme. They rely on community medical and social work representatives and on word-of-mouth within the community to inform the elderly or their families of sheltered housing opportunities. Isolated elderly are frequently dependent on advice from visiting medical and social service providers who are themselves often woefully ignorant of sheltered housing opportunities. There is of course little incentive to advertise sheltered accommodation where the available number of units is small and demand is high. In the United States, where local authorities are required by law to advertise available units, but already have a long waiting list, they usually comply with the law by placing a small classified ad in local newspapers. As a result the most knowledgeable, and not necessarily the most needy, elderly get sheltered accommodation.

Even where there is widespread public knowledge of available sheltered housing, many needy elderly and their families seem reluctant to investigate the possibilities because of acquired prejudice to public housing programmes. As was pointed out at the beginning of this chapter, the elderly in most countries have been offered only two public programme choices over the past 30 years, housing for the poor or total care institutions. Therefore, it is not surprising that they associate loss of dignity or total loss of independence with all forms of purpose-built housing for the aged provided by, or subsidised through, public auspices. In this case, conventional advertisement is not enough. It must be supplemented with educational programmes and even tours of sheltered housing; such approaches are costly and no country has developed such a programme to date.

If sheltered housing is to be fully and properly developed and used, housing, health and social service providers must expand and co-ordinate community information and education concerning the varied choices of assisted independent living available to the elderly. This requires more than co-ordinated mass advertising or even comprehensive presentation of housing, health and social programmes in printed literature and educational programmes. It means intelligent and co-operative screening and 'gatekeeping' at all support care entry points to assure that individual elderly get the best support service for their needs. The organisation and structure of such a programme is addressed in Chapter 5.

The Origins of Sheltered Housing

We have seen that Great Britain has been a pioneer in the development of sheltered housing. The British have built at least 3 to 5 times more sheltered housing than other Western countries (Table 2.1) and they began to develop national sheltered housing policy some 20 years ahead of most Western countries. This section describes briefly how and why Great Britain was able to pioneer this area, and how Britain's relatively extensive experience with sheltered housing programmes can now serve as an important laboratory for other Western countries which are (or are considering) embarking on a sheltered housing programme.

The next four subsections of this chapter describe the elderly housing environment that led up to the development of sheltered housing in Great Britain. The central argument to be presented is that the development of the 'residential home' instead of the 'nursing home' is the primary reason sheltered housing in Britain predates sheltered housing in most other Western countries by 20 years. The major difference between a residential home and an American or Swedish nursing home is that the residential home houses functionally dependent but well elderly; no nursing staff are present and no long-term medical services are provided. In the British model, general or local hospitals provide geriatric wards which house elderly with long-term chronic illnesses. Hospital models in other Western countries, such as the United States, provide no special geriatric care and only provide short-term treatment. Once a chronically ill patient is stable they are returned to the family or transferred to a nursing home. Over the years the nursing home has become the depository for chronically disabled but not chronically ill elderly coming directly from the community.

The British residential home was among the first long-term housing programmes in post-World War II Western society exclusively for functionally disabled but not chronically ill elderly. Over the same period, the nursing home evolved as the long-term housing alternative for the chronically ill in most other Western countries. This fundamental difference in the service role of residential homes and nursing homes led to variations in the management, design and staffing of the two types of facilities. These variations predisposed the early development of sheltered housing in Great Britain.

The Legacy of the Residential Home for the Aged

Prior to the twentieth century, poor disabled elderly in Great Britain were housed in almshouses or workhouses with all other indigents. By 1909, less than 2 per cent of the elderly in England and Scotland housed in Poor Law institutions were in separate facilities for the elderly.[11] The Local Government Act of 1929 was a reform movement that attempted to create a system of local public assistance institutions, general hospitals and chronic sick hospitals out of the former workhouses. The reform was not entirely successful as is well documented[12] and many age-integrated workhouses survived in kind if not in name until after World War II. Nevertheless, a pattern was established that wherever possible long-term disabled elderly would be divided into two groups and housed separately. The chronically ill would be housed in specialised hospitals or geriatric wards of general hospitals. The chronically disabled but well elderly would be housed in residential homes. The Nuffield Foundation, a private nonprofit social research and charitable foundation concerned with the elderly, appointed a Survey Committee in 1944 which recommended that there be publicly supported small neighbourhood oriented homes (30-35 beds) for 'normal old people who are no longer able to live an independent life'.[13] The survey findings led to the National Assistance Bill of 1947 which gave local welfare authorities the power to establish such 'small' homes with an optimum limit of 25-30 persons. The conclusions of the Survey Committee and the eventual passage of the national bill established this housing model in the public arena. However, this model had already existed for many years in the private market in Great Britain. Charitable organisations had pioneered such exclusive small homes for the well but disabled elderly back in the nineteenth century. By 1944 there were 230 such voluntary homes housing over 9,000 elderly.[14] In the decade from 1950 to 1960 a great many new residential homes were created by the efforts of the government and newly created local welfare and social service authorities. The many new homes and refurbished old workhouses established in this 10 year period were impressive improvements over past accommodation. Nevertheless, these homes were still institutional settings which overcared for many disabled elderly who could have maintained an independent housing unit designed to be barrier free and with proper support services.

The residential home copies the institutional model of medical accommodation but it is not a nursing home. From the start of the programme and still today, residential homes differ from nursing homes in three important ways: they are administered by local social service providers not health providers; the physical design is patterned on a small residential building rather than on a large institutional skilled-care facility; low skilled staff are chosen to give the type of daily support that family members and not professional nurses would provide for the frail elderly. Stated another way, the British have approximately the same proportion of elderly in long-term institutional environments today as the United States, i.e. 5 per cent, however, less than 1 per cent of the British elderly are in nursing care institutions at any one time, while virtually all of the American elderly who are institutionalised are in a nursing home environment.

The Legacy of Social Service Administration

The key difference in the British residential home model when compared to nursing homes in the United States is that the programme is separated from the health service system and is linked instead to social welfare services and sometimes, especially through voluntary (nonprofit) agencies, to housing service providers. The most typical residential home management is a local social service agency which also provides visiting domiciliary and other services to elderly living independently in the larger community. These social service providers are thus in a good position to see where the two sets of housing services do not provide a smooth transition from totally independent to totally dependent living.

Countries that have adopted the nursing home model for long-term housing of disabled elderly are not as likely to recognise the need for assisted independent living because nursing homes are traditionally administered by health service providers. Health service providers have very little contact with the everyday needs of independent elderly even as they become more frail and dependent. The health service focus has traditionally been on the chronically ill elderly and is dominated by a short-term medical treatment model not a long-term care model. No unique geriatric specialists have evolved in America as has been the case in Great Britain. Generally, the learned system of reward in relating to patients by doctors and nurses is treatment, cure and discharge, and not care, maximum independence and comfort with daily living. It is far more difficult, if not impossible, for modern medical systems to evolve a long-term assisted *independent* living programme for the elderly. Nursing home staff trained in a traditional medical model are more likely to favour institutional environments that function to their own optimal concept, rather than the patient/ resident's optimal independence.

The British social service agency administration of homes for the chronically disabled elderly resulted in two important responses to the needs of the elderly which contributed to the very early development of sheltered housing in Great Britain. First, in some localities social service agencies saw the need for sheltered housing and took the initiative in developing and administering it. Because sheltered housing is more like conventional housing than institutional accommodation, local housing departments were the logical developers, and in fact only they could build such housing with central government subsidy. Therefore, where social service agencies took the initiative in developing sheltered housing they developed co-operative management with housing authorities. The housing authority built and maintained the physical plant and the social services authority appointed and administered the warden and peripatetic support services. In the more typical situation, local housing rather than social service authorities took the initiative in developing sheltered housing. However, the actions of social services predisposed the development of sheltered housing. It was the social services who saw that many elderly were having trouble maintaining conventional housing but were still too able bodied to be transferred to a total care residential home. The social services then attempted to postpone the move by providing more reliable and comprehensive visiting support services. The early development of a strong peripatetic support system made it possible for housing authorities to build and manage minimal service sheltered housing programmes. There was also some pragmatism initially, many housing authorities seeing sheltered housing as a means for a more economical use of their total housing stock. By the late 1950s there was a growing proportion of single elderly occupying large public housing units despite an equally large backlog of younger families in need of decent housing. Sheltered housing was used as alternative housing to attract these single elderly into vacating large public housing units. Sheltered housing proved very popular because the elderly were able to retain their independence in a unit that was quieter, safer, easier for them to manage, and over the long term provided the security and temporary support of the resident warden in emergencies and her help in securing appropriate support services.

The Legacy of Small Size

An additional legacy of the British residential home, related to the development of sheltered housing, is the average size of individual schemes. Because residential homes require no nursing care standards in structural design nor expensive nursing staff, they can be built as much smaller facilities and still be economical to run. The British have been able to develop neighbourhood oriented residential homes for the elderly that are financially solvent and retain a humane scale. As a need for more independent supportive housing was identified the British naturally retained the small scheme size of typically 20 to 40 units. They reasoned that if the residential home with more expensive on-site staff was economical at this size both service-rich and minimal service sheltered housing would also be economical at this size. In the 1950s small sheltered housing schemes in the tradition of residential homes began to be built in residential neighbourhoods near the tenants' lifelong friends and relatives without the stigma of an institutional appearance. The modest cost of small sheltered housing schemes encouraged local experimentation with sheltered housing both in the initial years of development and over time as new service, management and housing designs were conceived. Usually the first schemes in a new locality were just adaptations of conventional elderly housing to include an alarm system and warden service, with possibly a communal lounge and/or laundry. In contrast, nursing homes are frequently large facilities (80-250 beds) in order to achieve some economy in building and staff costs. In countries that have adopted a nursing home model and have also experimented with sheltered housing, the sheltered housing schemes typically copy the large size and expensive service-rich environments of nursing homes.

The Legacy of the Lay Warden

In addition to pioneering assisted independent living environments, Great Britain pioneered the role of the warden as the primary daily contact with the elderly residents of sheltered housing. The presence of a lay warden, as we shall see in Chapter 4, helps sheltered housing avoid an institutional atmosphere. It also helps to keep down costs and avoid the large institutional scheme size required for economies of scale when skilled on-site support staff are used. The warden's role in sheltered housing is yet another legacy of the residential home, which demonstrated that highly trained nursing staff were not necessary to provide for even severely disabled elderly so long as they were not ill. Elderly requiring sheltered housing would also require some on-site staff especially in emergencies and to reduce worry, isolation and domiciliary burdens during episodic illnesses. Based on the success of low skilled on-site staff in residential homes, unskilled on-site support was also introduced into sheltered housing schemes. The warden or 'friendly neighbour' role emerged as the logical on-site manager. The warden position is usually filled by a young or middle aged housewife who lives nearby and pays regular visits to the elderly. Her main task has been to spot peripatetic support needs and call them in at the margin of individual need. It was envisioned that this role model would minimise the risk of premature dependency on support staff which had been observed in residential homes, and maximise individual, but secure, independent living.

A Brief History of Sheltered Housing

Recent reviews of sheltered housing policy in Great Britain[15] depict sheltered housing as a grassroots programme evolving from local need inventories and initiatives rather than moulded by national directives. To a large degree this is an accurate picture. National policy statements tend to describe programme modifications a decade (or more) after the modifications are already widely recognised and in use by most progressive local managers. Most central monitoring and new policy directives over the years have been concerned with rationing and controlling capital expenditures and establishing minimum building design standards. Social service 'design', social management 'design', and general performance criteria of sheltered housing have been left to the local sponsor. Local sponsors of government subsidised sheltered housing can be housing authorities, social service authorities, various types of national or local volunteer associations or combinations of these sponsor types. The *ad hoc* evolution of national sheltered housing policy in Great Britain can be divided into three eras.

The Early Pioneers

It is difficult to pinpoint when and where the first grouped housing especially designed for less active elderly with warden services was opened, although this is usually credited to a small west country housing authority, Sturminster Newton RDC, in 1948.[16] This is some nine years before the national government issued any directives describing sheltered housing. (However, the real origins probably lie in some of the pre-World War II almshouses.) Throughout the early 1950s there were other experimental schemes. Most of these isolated experiments seem to have grown out of a perceived local need by housing authorities in that they had increasing numbers of single elderly living in large units who could benefit from smaller more secure units that would require less effort to maintain. The move would, in turn, make available larger council houses for younger families to occupy.

Developments Towards a National Sheltered Housing Movement

In 1957 the Ministry of Housing and Local Government made an inquiry of local authorities to determine what type of accommodation was being provided for the elderly.[17] The 1957 Housing Act, based in part on these findings, identified the need for small group flats and cautiously suggested other elements, such as common sitting rooms, possibly central heating, and the 'additional value' of a warden who might be the tenant of a nearby council house. The Act was the first to give local authorities the power and money to provide what eventually came to be called sheltered housing. In 1958 and again in 1960 the Ministry issued circulars and handbooks[18] describing the purpose, strategy and design standards for sheltered housing, but still in very general terms. The response to this national call for sheltered housing was not carefully monitored in these early years, but by tracing back the oldest existing schemes from the West Midlands and Devon it appears that early adaptation of the idea was very uneven. Some areas enthusiastically shifted elderly housing priorities towards sheltered designs, others (the majority) attempted no sheltered housing schemes at all. This general lack of enthusiasm persisted despite the reporting in the 1960 circular that the first two years of the programme were a great success and emphasising that sheltered accommodation was clearly a different form of elderly housing and not a substitute for larger one bedroom apartments and bungalows for totally independent elderly.

> Most old people living in [sheltered housing] flatlets are very pleased with them. They find them convenient and easy to run, and they greatly appreciate the central heating which is a feature of recommended schemes. They are able to look after themselves without finding this is a burden, and to do things in their own way. If, in an emergency, help is needed, they know that this is close at hand in the warden's service. They can enjoy the privacy of their own lives while sharing in the companionship of other occupants of the block . . . [Local authorities should understand that sheltered housing is] . . . an additional and different form of housing provision designed specially for the benefit of old people who with advancing years become less active and therefore less able to live quite independently of others. The purpose is to provide old people with a comfortable and labour-saving home in which they can be independent

but can also, because they are living in a group, enjoy additional services to meet their special needs.[19]

These publications were followed in 1961 by an important joint circular by the Ministry of Housing and Local Government and the Ministry of Health,[20] urging co-operation between the various services involved with the elderly. The joint circular also set out in some detail (for the first time in a government statement) the sort of role a warden might be expected to play and expressed the opinion that the provision of grouped dwellings for less active old people could help to ease the pressure on accommodation in residential homes. On the role of the warden, the circular stated that:

> Details of arrangements differ, but often a warden undertakes to clean the common-room, bathrooms and W.C.s, landing and stairs, and attend to the central heating: answer the emergency bell system: summon a doctor, relatives etc. in times of emergency: and apply for services needed by the tenants, such as home helps, meals services and supplements to pensions. In addition, many wardens help with household tasks such as putting up curtains and bringing in fuel, and with personal services such as hair washing and bathing. They also draw pensions, shop and cook in bad weather or illness, and organise socials or special parties in the common room.[21]

Such a role clearly exceeds the concept of the warden as a 'good neighbour'.
    The joint circular also advocated a selection policy for sheltered housing which ensured that some of the tenants were fit enough to give help and support the other tenants, i.e. a 'balanced community', thus reducing the pressure on the warden and the demand for support services. The idea of 'linked schemes', i.e. sheltered housing linked to a residential home, was also referred to, although the circular saw little advantage in their provision.
    Throughout the 1960s the sheltered housing programme gained wider support and acceptance at the local level but in most areas remained a small and subsidiary programme to conventional public housing for low income elderly and the residential homes programme. Several factors contributed to this continued reluctance to develop sheltered housing locally. First, many local authorities did not understand its unique service role — just as many local authorities in other countries do not understand it today. Many of these local authority managers felt their public housing elderly could manage in conventional housing

with visiting services until they required (based on the manager's evaluation) accommodation in a residential home. Many of the elderly tenants in conventional local authority housing were still young and active, so these managers saw no gap between the housing service provisions of conventional public housing for the elderly and a residential home. Visits to nearby existing sheltered housing sites may have reinforced this belief. Without precise design guidelines some localities were providing very minimal sheltered housing by just adding an alarm system and part-time warden to existing public housing. Other schemes were very communal with shared bathroom, lounge, even communal dining. Throughout the 1960s research reports by central government and private analysts helped clarify the function and design of sheltered housing, making the objective of the programme clearer and the design and developmental task easier. The widely acclaimed book by Peter Townsend,[22] graphically described the limitations of residential homes as well as the benefits of sheltered housing as a long-term alternative for less active but well elderly. A 1967 government circular[23] established what has come to be known as the 'Parker Morris Standards' for elderly housing. They not only spelled out in greater detail than ever before how to go about designing and building sheltered housing, but divided such accommodation into two types; 'self-contained without communal facilities or warden supervision', and grouped 'flatlets with warden's accommodation and communal facilities'. In 1969 a second circular,[24] with a similar title but focusing entirely on sheltered housing, defined two types that would serve as part of the continuum between conventional and institutional accommodation. As put in the language of the circular the two sheltered housing styles would provide 'a balanced range of different types of accommodation to meet their [elderly] varying needs and preferences'. Category 1, the name given to the first type, would house 'the more active' elderly, and the design would allow for private entrances off the street or nonheated corridors to self-contained private units (typically bungalows, terraced or row housing, maisonettes or garden apartments) with or without community facilities (lounge, laundry, etc.). Category 2 would house 'the less active' elderly and the design would be flats with heated corridors to buildings with a communal entrance, common room, laundry, public telephone, etc. Both categories would receive warden service and have an intercom or alarm bell system.

The Current Phase of Sheltered Housing Development

Between 1957 and 1970 Great Britain built enough sheltered housing to accommodate about 2 per cent of the elderly population. Between 1970 and 1978 an additional 3 per cent of the elderly were accommodated in new or converted structures.[25] As will be shown in Chapter 3, housing authorities, social service agencies and voluntary associations in urban areas began shifting their sheltered housing schemes to increasingly more sheltered designs in the 1970s to accommodate the growing proportion of very old elderly both residing in and seeking sheltered housing. In contrast, rural housing authorities have built and continue to build primarily minimal service (category 1) sheltered housing. They are only now beginning to explore service-rich category 2 alternatives because of their increasing proportion of very old and frail tenants.

Today there is widespread criticism among local housing managers and housing researchers with Circular 82/69,[26] the updating of which is eagerly awaited.[27] During the 1970s sheltered housing experiments developed far beyond this government directive, which describes only category 1 and 2 sheltered housing. The philosophy of sheltered housing has shifted in the 1970s as a result of its very success. Elderly are staying longer in sheltered rather than conventional housing and are reluctant to move. The category 1–2 concept has become insufficient to cope adequately with many of the housebound and frail who require help with meals and domiciliary chores. However, when the only alternative housing is a dependent environment, and this often in short supply, most elderly who can still retain some semblance of independence, either refuse to move or are unable to move because of the lack of available places. As a result, many housing managers now feel they have specific sheltered housing schemes that are in jeopardy because of their very old, housebound, and frail populations which no longer contain a sufficient number of 'fit' tenants to provide social organisation and tenant domiciliary support. The warden in such schemes has become overloaded and the morale among the residents adversely affected. These trends have lead housing managers to invent new scheme types and management policies which have been adopted throughout Great Britain despite the lack of central government directives. One widespread housing type has been colloquially named category 2½. Category 2½ provides the resident with on-site meals, home help and a small flatlet or bedsitter arrangement; all living spaces other than the bedsitter are normally communal. This model obviously increases the likelihood of many frail elderly having the option of remaining in their private household rather than moving to a residential home. A second alternative is the 'linked scheme', which links sheltered housing with a residential home. In this arrangement sheltered housing residents with more episodic needs for skilled or time-consuming support services (bathing, physical therapy, etc.) can make use of such facilities in the residential home. With these (and other) additional sheltered housing types (see Fig. 1.4), managers have a more complete continuum of entry points from conventional housing and hopefully can ease the concentration of very old and frail residents in category 1 and 2 schemes.

In addition to new scheme designs, local sponsors are also developing new management designs. Most managers now recognise that each scheme must either retain a 'balance' of active and inactive residents at all times, to retain an independent tenant dominated environment, or they must adapt services and staff skills over time to accommodate ageing residents. This managerial choice alternative of a 'constant care model' or an 'accommodating care model' is already visible in older American schemes.[28] Very different managerial skills are required, depending on which model is employed. Each requires different screening, 'gatekeeping' and transfer policies, health monitoring, and training of on-site and peripatetic service staff. In addition, these new management models are developing different links with medical and social service agencies, different links with tenants' families, and different counselling techniques for tenants and their families.

Although increasingly discussed, relatively little is known about the *extent* of the sheltered housing programme 'crisis' in Great Britain brought on by an ageing and more dependent resident population. Even less is known about how well local managers, wardens and peripatetic support staff are adapting to or coping with the situation in both urban and rural areas. Until now there has been very little comprehensive research into how much service-rich sheltered housing has been built, and if service-rich schemes are effective in prolonging independent living or accommodating older more frail tenants than minimal service schemes. In the next three chapters these questions are investigated. Data collected from 155 sheltered housing schemes in rural Devon and the urban West Midlands of England are analysed. Throughout the analysis, we discuss the implications of our findings for the United States and other Western countries currently embarking on sheltered housing programmes.

Few countries have developed unique policy standards for sheltered housing outside Great Britain, and no country has had as high a proportion of its elderly population housed in as wide a variety of sheltered housing for as long a time as Great Britain. The governments of Western countries are adapting their existing housing programmes on an *ad hoc* basis, learning as the elderly age to add on or modify support services, physical design standards, management and staff training programes.[29] This trial and error adaptation to elderly housing need is both time consuming and unreliable in a period when Western countries are experiencing a rapid growth in the variety and proportion of elderly surviving to very old age. The British data described in the last section of this chapter and analysed in subsequent chapters were collected in an effort to shed new light on the needs of the functionally impaired elderly and the role of different sheltered housing programmes. It is hoped that other Western countries will be able to learn from, and build on, the British experience.

The Survey Data

In order to analyse the sheltered housing programmes in Great Britain, data were collected from 121 schemes in (mainly) rural Devon (in the southwest of England) in January of 1977, and from 34 schemes in the urban West Midlands (centred on the cities of Birmingham and Coventry) in March and April of 1978. The data in both surveys were compiled from questionnaires administered to the managers and wardens of each scheme. The following data are common to both the urban and rural samples:

    1. *Scheme characteristics:* the year each scheme was built, the type of dwelling units available in the scheme, the number and type of communal facilities provided and the statutory type of sheltered design.
    2. *Tenant characteristics:* age, sex, household composition and the statutory support received by each tenant.
    3. *Warden characteristics:* the individual demographic characteristics of the warden, her household composition, her job qualifications/ training, the length of time she has occupied her post, her work hours, the availability of relief wardens, and the type of alarm/ intercom system available.
    4. *Activities undertaken by the wardens:* both the type of activity and the time spent on each activity were recorded. Types of activity include caretaking and administrative chores within the building and advising, socialising, communal involvement, and long-term, episodic or emergency services provided for the residents.

Such services include: shopping, domiciliary assistance, minor nursing, and liaising with doctors, family, and visiting social services.

The urban/rural differences in the areas covered by the two studies have proved to be a significant factor. As shown in Table 2.2, the Devon schemes are relatively small: 23.4 units per scheme compared to the West Midlands figure of 30.5. This difference becomes more marked when variations in sheltered housing type are discussed in Chapter 3. The size of the schemes along with the variations in support service availability in urban and rural areas affects the warden's role and activities, management policy and programme design; these aspects are analysed in Chapters 4 and 5. The two surveys revealed other differences in addition to the rural/urban setting and these are also discussed in future chapters.

Table 2.2: The Survey Data

	Rural Devon sample (Jan. 1977)		Urban West Midlands sample (Mar./Apr. 1978)		Total	
	No.	%	No.	%	No.	%
Schemes	121	78.1	34	21.9	155	100.0
Persons	3,487	74.4	1,198	25.6	4,685	100.0
Units	2,836	73.2	1,037	26.8	3,873	100.0
Persons/scheme	28.8		35.2		30.2	
Units/scheme	23.4		30.5		25.0	

The Devon Survey

As shown in Table 2.2, the mainly rural Devon survey covered 121 schemes and 3,487 residents. This represents 93 per cent of all sheltered housing residents in 9 out of the 10 district councils in Devon (the District Council of Plymouth being excluded). The survey followed a similar pattern to an earlier survey undertaken in April 1973. A total of 74 out of the 121 schemes were common to both surveys. This allows a longitudinal analysis of resident characteristics and warden activities to be undertaken. The proportion of the elderly population of these nine district councils accommodated in sheltered housing varies from about 0.9 to 4.6 per cent, with an overall average of 2.2 per cent, i.e. quite low, relative to the estimated national figure of about 5 per cent. However, the Devon study includes only local authority schemes. Therefore, the sheltered housing provided by voluntary (nonprofit) housing associations would increase the percentage of elderly in sheltered housing somewhat; there are, however, not as many voluntary associations active in the rural areas as in urban environs.

The West Midlands Survey

The West Midlands survey covered 34 schemes and 1,198 residents. The schemes represent a 25 per cent random sample of selected housing agencies. The large number of voluntary, municipal and district agencies managing sheltered housing in urban areas made it necessary to limit the study to just a representative group of housing managers.

Voluntary Associations Sampled

There are 341 voluntary (nonprofit) associations in Great Britain that manage housing for the elderly.[30] Only four are nationwide associations, these being: the Abbeyfield Society, Anchor Housing Association, Hanover Housing Association and the Royal British Legion. A 25 per cent random sample of the schemes managed by these four voluntary associations within the West Midlands was included in the study, along with two randomly chosen schemes from among those managed by local church, labour or fraternal organisations. (The total voluntary sample equals 16 schemes.)

Public Authorities Sampled

Three public agencies were chosen from among the many in the West Midlands: the Birmingham Housing Authority, the Coventry Social Service Department and the Wyre Forest District Council. The Birmingham Housing Authority is one of the largest local authorities in England and houses a higher proportion of its municipal population than any other large city housing authority in Great Britain. Despite the authority's great size and extensive management programme, it has only relatively recently begun to build and manage sheltered housing (1971). From 1974 to 1979 the Birmingham Housing Authority has built an average of nine new sheltered housing schemes per year and inherited eight other schemes through incorporation into the city of areas with previous sheltered housing programmes. Despite the rapid growth of sheltered accommodation in recent years the authority schemes account for only 0.8 per cent of the elderly population in Birmingham. Coventry, the second largest city in the West Midlands, was chosen because it is an example of where a social service department and not a housing authority is responsible for the management of sheltered housing. While some of the Coventry schemes date back to the 1960s, less than 1 per cent of the elderly in Coventry are housed in sheltered accommodation. The Wyre Forest District represents a smaller city (Kidderminster) and a portion of the suburban metropolitan environment of Birmingham. The Wyre Forest was chosen because it has one of the oldest (1958) and most extensive sheltered housing programmes in the West Midlands with over 16 per cent of its elderly population residing in sheltered accommodation.

The Urban West Midlands study included additional data on the health, activities and movement/transition patterns of the residents, additional characteristics of the physical design and location of the schemes, and a survey of the managers of the sheltered housing programmes within the various voluntary associations and public authorities. Some of these aspects were also covered in the Devon study.

Notes

1. Noam, E. and Donahue, W., *Assisted independent living in grouped housing for older people: A report on the situation in European countries*. International Center for Social Gerontology, Washington, D.C., 1976.

2. United States Congress, Congregate Housing Service Act of 1978. Hearing before the Subcommittee on Housing and Urban Affairs of the Committee on Banking, Housing and Urban Affairs, United States Senate (S2691). USGPO, Washington, D.C., 1978.

3. United States Department of Housing and Urban Development, *Federally-Assisted Congregate Housing Development for the Elderly*. Office of Housing Programs, Housing Management, DHUD, Washington, D.C., 1976.

4. Newman, R., Jenks, M., and Bacon, V., *A National Survey of Local Authority Housing for Elderly People*. Social Services Building Research Team, Oxford Polytechnic, Oxford, September 1977 (a); Newman, R., Jenks, M., and Bacon, V., *Voluntary Organization Housing for Elderly People*. Social Services Building Research Team, Oxford Polytechnic, Oxford, September 1977 (b).

5. Ibid.

6. Department of Health and Social Security, *A Happier Old Age*. HMSO, London, 1979.

7. Ministry of Housing and Local Government. *Housing Standards and Costs: Accommodation specially designed for old people*. Circular 82/69, HMSO, London, 1969.

8. Ibid.

9. Kane, R.L. and Kane, R.A., 'Alternatives to institutional care of the elderly: Beyond the dichotomy'. Paper prepared for the American Association for the Advancement of Science, AAAS Intergovernmental R & D Project Workshop on Health and Human Resources: The Elderly, December 1978, p. 3.

10. Dunlop, B.D., *The Growth of nursing home care*. Lexington Books, D.C. Heath, Lexington, Mass. 1979; Kane and Kane, 'Alternatives to institutional care of the elderly'.

11. Townsend, P., *The last refuge*. Routledge and Kegan Paul, London, 1962.
12. E.g. Ibid, Ch. 2.
13. Ibid.
14. Ibid.
15. E.g. Fox, D., 'Housing the elderly'. In Hobman, D. (ed.), *The Impact of Aging*. Croom Helm, London, 1981, pp. 86–108; Fox, D. and Casemore, J., 'Sheltered Housing: A National policy, locally executed'. *Housing*, December, 1979, pp. 18–20.
16. Townsend, *The last refuge*.
17. Ministry of Housing and Local Government, *Housing of old people*. Circular 18/57, HMSO, London, 1957.
18. Ministry of Housing and Local Government, *Flatlets for old people*. Circular 30/58 , HMSO, London, 1958; Ministry of Housing and Local Government, *More Flatlets for old people*. Circular 47/60, HMSO, London, 1960.
19. Ministry of Housing and Local Government, *More Flatlets for old people*.
20. Ministry of Housing and Local Government and Ministry of Health, *Services for old people*. MHLG Circular 10/61, MOH Circular 12/61, HMSO, London, 1961.
21. Ibid.
22. Townsend, *The last refuge*.
23. Ministry of Housing and Local Government, *Housing Standards, Costs, and Subsidies*. Circular 36/67, HMSO, London, 1967.
24. Ministry of Housing and Local Government, *Housing Standards and Costs: Accommodation specially designed for old people*.
25. Department of Health and Social Security, *A Happier Old Age*.
26. Ministry of Housing and Local Government, *Housing Standards and Costs: Accommodation specially designed for old people*.
27. Boldy, D., 'Sheltered Housing for the Elderly – The Alternative Refuge?' *Community Care* (in press); Fox, 'Housing the Elderly'; Fox and Casemore, 'Sheltered Housing: A national policy, locally executed'; Heumann, L.F., 'The Function of different sheltered housing categories for the semi-independent elderly'. *Social Policy and Administration*, 1981, 15, pp. 164–80; Underwood, J., 'Quality is not enough!' *Housing*, July 1979, 15, pp. 12–13.
28. Lawton, M.P., Greenbaum, M. and Liebowitz, B., 'The Life span of housing environments for the aging'. *Gerontologist*, 1980, 20, pp. 56–64.
29. Noam and Donahue, *Assisted independent living in grouped housing for older people: A report on the situation in European countries*.
30. Housing Corporation, *Directory of Registered Housing Associations*. First Interim Edition, The Housing Corporation, July 1976; National Federation of Housing Associations, *A Guide to Housing Associations*. The NFHA, London 1975.

3 THE FUNCTION OF DIFFERENT SHELTERED HOUSING CATEGORIES

The British sheltered housing programme has a considerably greater proportion of elderly residents, number of older schemes and variety of sheltered housing types than other Western countries, and is, therefore, the focus of analysis in this and the next three chapters. In this chapter we analyse the distribution and use of varied sheltered housing types and show that such different types can provide important support and life style choices for the elderly and help them maintain maximum functional independence. A variety of sheltered housing types also aids local management efforts to retain a balance of more active and less active residents in each scheme. Unfortunately, local British sheltered housing managers do not all provide the wide variety of sheltered housing types available nationally in Great Britain. Many local programmes provide only one type of sheltered housing, i.e. that designed to accommodate the most active and functionally independent elderly. This limited programme is beginning to look inadequate as the proportion and variety of very old and frail elderly seeking sheltered housing increases. The ramifications of a categorical sheltered housing programme and the need for a comprehensive array of different types of sheltered housing entry points are discussed in this chapter. While the British may be experiencing this need for a compre-· hensive array of sheltered housing types several years ahead of countries with younger elderly populations, the process is bound to be repeated. It is not too soon for countries just beginning to develop a single type sheltered housing stock, that will be in service for 40 years or more, to take heed of the British experience.

As was described in the previous chapter, local data on sheltered housing has been assembled for two areas, the mainly rural districts of Devon and the urban West Midlands surrounding and including the cities of Birmingham and Coventry. Five sheltered housing types, all with a resident warden, can be identified between the two areas. The least sheltered design is category 1 without common room(s). This type of scheme is typically just a group of purpose-built and barrier-free bungalows. The second least sheltered type is category 1 with common room(s). This type of scheme could consist of bungalows, maisonettes or terraced housing with at least a communal lounge. Category 1 is followed by the more sheltered category 2 design with flats and common rooms linked by heated interior corridors. Category 2½ repeats the category 2 building design but individual units usually consist of only a small bedroom or bedsitter; all other rooms including dining are communally shared. The most sheltered type is a 'linked scheme' consisting of category 2 or 2½ sheltered housing design linked to a registered home for the aged. All but three of the 155 Devon and West Midlands schemes sampled for this study fit one of these five types. In the three odd cases the sites were mixed category 1 and 2 housing and the warden's records and comments do not distinguish between the residents in each category type. The data for these sites are included in the totals for all sheltered housing statistics presented in the chapter but are omitted from the various disaggregations following Table 3.2. The analysis which follows addresses the following questions:

1. Do the types of sheltered housing provided (and hence choices available) vary among urban and rural localities or public and non-profit sponsors?
2. Do urban, rural, public and nonprofit housing managers perceive of, and use, sheltered housing types in similar or different ways?
3. Does each category type function as housing for distinctly different types of elderly by demographic characteristics and functional activity level, or is there a balance of older/younger and active/inactive elderly in all sites by category type?
4. Is the category 2 type housing as currently designed and located actually better suited for the less active elderly than category 1?
5. Do elderly residents move along a continuum from one sheltered housing type to another? If so, how many? If not, why not? Should they?
6. Does the current mix of sheltered housing types provide an adequate choice of entry points for elderly in urban and rural localities?

The Urban/Rural Differences in Sheltered Housing Development

Our study has revealed considerable differences in the development of urban and rural sheltered housing in Great Britain. One of the most important reasons for providing a variety of sheltered housing categories is to accommodate local variances in elderly housing need

The Function of Different Sheltered Housing Categories

Table 3.1: Number and Size of Sheltered Housing Schemes Surveyed in Devon and in the West Midlands

	Category 1 without common room	Category 1 with common room	Mixed scheme category 1 & 2	Category 2	Category 2½	Linked schemes	Total
			Devon survey				
Persons							
No.	1,777	460	14	1,106	0	130	3,487
%	51.0	13.2	0.4	31.7	0	3.7	100.0
Units							
No.	1,424	355	12	930	0	115	2,836
%	50.2	12.5	0.4	32.8	0	4.1	100.0
Schemes							
No.	72	11	1	32	0	5	121
%	59.5	9.1	0.8	26.5	0	4.1	100.0
Persons/ scheme	24.7	41.8	14.0	34.6	–	26.0	28.8
Units/ scheme	19.8	32.3	12.0	29.1	–	23.0	23.4
			West Midlands survey				
Persons							
No.	189	148	117	607	93	44	1,198
%	15.8	12.4	9.8	50.6	7.8	3.6	100.0
Units							
No.	151	115	96	544	91	40	1,037
%	14.6	11.1	9.3	52.4	8.8	3.8	100.0
Schemes							
No.	4	4	2	16	6	2	34
%	11.8	11.8	5.9	47.0	17.6	5.9	100.0
Persons/ scheme	47.2	37.0	58.5	37.9	15.5	22.0	35.2
Units/ scheme	37.8	28.8	48.0	34.0	15.2	20.0	30.5
Total units within the 7 West Midland agencies surveyed							
No.	1,064		562	2,176	342	80	4,224
%	25.2		13.3	51.5	8.1	1.9	100.0
% sample (units)	25.0		17.1	25.0	26.6	50.0	24.6

and desire. The British sheltered housing policy, as embodied in circular 82/69,[1] does not distinguish between urban and rural development. Nevertheless, flexibility within the standards defined in the circular has allowed sufficient latitude for local adaptation of the programme. Table 3.1 gives details of the number and size of sheltered housing schemes by category type in the rural Devon and the urban West Midlands samples. The first and most striking finding to be drawn from this data, is that neither the urban nor the rural housing managers provide much opportunity for choice among sheltered housing types. Both areas have concentrated construction in one category type, 'bare bones' category 1 bungalows with no common room(s) in rural Devon and grouped category 2 flats in the urban West Midlands. Category 2½ is non-existent in the Devon sample and neither the rural nor urban locations has developed the more sheltered and supportive category 2½ or linked schemes to the point where they could compete as a housing choice with the more traditional sheltered housing categories.

The rural Devon district councils have built twice as many category 1 units as category 2, which is just the reverse of the urban West Midlands sample. Among the category 1 units, 'bare bones' bungalows without common rooms are four times more prevalent in the rural areas. In contrast the more grouped designs of category 1 with attached common room(s) form a greater proportion of category 1 units found in the urban environs. The typical rural scheme also contains a smaller number of units and persons than the typical urban scheme.

At one point in the research we hypothesised that the heavy rural emphasis on category 1 schemes without common rooms was not consciously planned. It was felt these might have been conventional council bungalows built before 1970 (prior to circular 82/69)[2] that were consequently converted to meet sheltered housing standards by adding an alarm system, full-time warden, and undertaking other required changes. However, Table 3.2 shows that this is not the case. With the exception of linked schemes, there were almost as many units of each category type built in rural Devon after 1970 as before, and that not only was the construction of new category 1 schemes without common room the most popular housing type before 1970, but that it also remained the most popular housing type after 1970.

There are good reasons for the popularity of category 1 bungalows and the small scheme sizes found in rural Devon. These schemes blend in well with existing village architecture and life-style. The rural elderly moving into these units are basically retaining a housing environment most like that which they have known all their lives. The relative

Table 3.2: Number of Schemes by Year Built in the Devon and West Midlands Surveys

Year built	Category 1 without common room	Category 1 with common room	Mixed scheme category 1 & 2	Category 2	Category 2½	Linked schemes	Total
Devon survey							
Pre-1970							
No.	37	6	1	16	–	4	64
%	51.4	54.5	100.0	50.0	–	80.0	52.9
1970 and later							
No.	35	5	0	16	–	1	57
%	48.6	45.5	0.0	50.0	–	20.0	47.1
Total							
No.	72	11	1	32	–	5	121
%	100.0	100.0	100.0	100.0	–	100.0	100.0
West Midlands survey							
Pre-1970							
No.	2	1	2	6	1	0	12
%	50.0	25.0	100.0	38.5	16.7	0.0	35.3
1970 and later							
No.	2	3	0	10	5	2	22
%	50.0	75.0	0.0	62.5	83.3	100.0	64.7
Total							
No.	4	4	0	16	6	2	34
%	100.0	100.0	100.0	100.0	100.0	100.0	100.0

flexibility in the sheltered housing standards of circular 82/69[3] has allowed rural district councils to build the type of scheme the relatively young and functionally independent elderly populations entering housing have desired over the years. As we shall see in Chapter 4, it is possible to some extent to adapt the role of the warden to fit this small village and minimal service setting. However, as the rural elderly age and become more frail, the 'bare bones' category 1 schemes, largely untrained wardens, and often limited peripatetic backup support in rural areas, may become a liability requiring changes in the sheltered housing programme as a whole.

Tables 3.1 and 3.2 present quite a different developmental picture of sheltered housing in the urban West Midlands. Many urban districts, like the city of Birmingham, had no sheltered housing programme prior to circular 82/69,[4] so all of their building has been concentrated in the last decade. Most of this sheltered housing development has been in categories 2 and 2½. One reason offered by the urban managers for the greater development of categories 2 and 2½ housing is the recent increase in urban crime. Categories 2 and 2½ offer greater security because they are grouped flats with just one main entrance from the street, where category 1 design typically provides each unit with a street entrance. A second reason offered by urban managers for the greater construction of category 2 and 2½ housing is the high costs of land, construction and housing maintenance in urban areas. The higher density of categories 2 and 2½ can produce economies of scale in land-to-unit construction costs and in heating and maintenance costs when compared to lower density category 1 designs. Because all of these costs are already high and rising rapidly in urban areas, categories 2 and 2½ are more economical than category 1. Notable for its absence among the reasons offered by urban managers for more category 2 and 2½ housing is resident demand. There was no case made by the urban managers for greater user demand for category 2 or 2½ housing over category 1. Nor was there any mention by urban managers of resident complaints with housing category types or wishes to transfer from one type to another.

It may well be that the urban elderly are quite satisfied with the more sheltered category 2 housing design. Many more urban than rural elderly are likely to have lived in grouped apartments on council estates (public housing) prior to entering sheltered accommodation. Like the rural category 1 bungalows, the category 2 grouped flats may reflect what many urban elderly have known most of their lives. Whether as a result of different tastes, needs or financial factors, urban managers are much better prepared to house and care for the growing number of very old and frail elderly as a result of their developmental emphasis on category 2 and to a lesser degree category 2½ sheltered accommodation.

The Managers' View of Sheltered Housing Categories

In addition to the questionnaires administered to the wardens, a structured survey was conducted with the management of each local district council and voluntary association included in both the West Midlands and Devon studies. The resulting comments of the management are interspersed throughout the analysis in this chapter and become a primary focus in Chapter 5. The replies to two particular questions are of interest at this point. Each management agency was asked if they distinguish between category 1 and category 2 housing;

and if they make regular checks on resident functional ability and transfer category 1 residents to category 2 and 'beyond' as needed. If yes, how is this done? If no, why not? The answers obtained were very revealing. They are compared with data about schemes and tenants in later sections of the chapter. Composite and paraphrased responses are presented for selected managers (the emphases are ours).

Do You Distinguish Between Category 1 and Category 2 Housing?

Rural District Councils. None of the nine district councils in Devon distinguished between category 1 and category 2 housing; specific comments included:

(i)   The fact that both categories are warden supervised is considered [the] sufficient [variable not category types].

(ii) The main criteria is the location of a scheme in relation to the tenant's choice of area for rehousing and a tenant's ability to cope with the physical limitations of a particular site (some schemes are located on estates at the top of steep hills).

(iii) All our sheltered housing is category 1 without a common room. Schemes are a fair distance apart and therefore one scheme tends to serve only one particular area.

Urban Public Agencies. The urban managers are far more likely to distinguish between category 1 and 2 and while variance in the activity level of the residents is implied in some responses, most managers identified other factors such as security from crime, variation in the warden's role and activities, and providing choices in communal living, for distinguishing between the sheltered housing types provided.

(i)   We see category 1 and 2 as two different design features of sheltered housing. Category 2 looks more institutional and does provide better security from crime. We have *no building priority* for one category over the other *based on activity levels* of the elderly seeking sheltered housing. In the past we built more category 1 only because it was easy and blended in well on council sites. Now we are building category 2 for the security aspects due to increased crime against the elderly.

(ii) Category 1 housing is always bungalows, category 2 is always a block of flats. The majority of our housing, and all our new purpose-built units, are category 2. We have a growing number of old and frail sheltered housing residents who can still benefit from independent flats. Therefore, we have built new linked schemes joining category 2 and Part III accommodation and, since we are a social service agency, we have also been able to assign permanent home helps to some older category 2 schemes with large proportions of house-bound and chairfast residents.

(iii) We define many different categories based on the description of the warden's job more than housing design. We have a number of private sector wardens each assigned to a town area. We have 'bare bones' category 1 public sector schemes with just a warden and an alarm system. We have both blocks of flats and bungalows with common room and laundry. We have similar schemes with the addition of a luncheon club.

(iv) We see categories 1 and 2 as different choices in *degree of communal living*. Those elderly coming into our schemes have, on the average, the same range of abilities whether they go to category 1 or 2. Men seem to prefer category 1 more, women category 2.

Urban Voluntary Associations. Voluntary associations face an altogether different problem in distinguishing between category types. Most associations build and manage only one category type. Only one association recognised the national policy distinction between 'more active' and 'less active' residents by category type, but they each distinguished their housing type from others and felt they sought a unique resident type.

(i)   The category 1-2 distinction rests on the independence and mobility of the tenants, category 2 accommodating the more dependent and frail.

(ii) We have just one housing type and it is unique from the accepted definition of category 1 and 2. We have a housekeeper, not a warden, who provides 2 meals per day (what has popularly come to be known as category 2½) for about 8 to 12 residents. Loneliness is the chief criterion for acceptance, not functional disability.

(iii) We define just one basic housing type which fits category 2: fully self-contained dwellings each with its own bath and WC, fully centrally heated and hot water supply, lift access to units above ground floor, a three-bedroom warden's dwelling, and alarm/intercom system, lounge/common room, laundry and guest room. Need for sheltered housing is as much a factor of loneliness and isolation as physical impairment. Overall, the majority of our schemes are made up of very young and fit residents.

Do You Make Regular Checks on Elderly Tenants' Functional Ability and Transfer to Other Category Types if Needed?

Rural District Councils. None of the Devon councils made regular checks on tenants' functional ability for purposes of transferring less active tenants to a more secure or supportive category type. Where transfers occur they appear to be tenant initiated and related to housing type 'desires' not support needs. Ironically, where there is a move between category types, tenants are more likely to transfer from category 2 to category 1.

(i) Ground floor category 1 would be regarded as preferable to first floor category 2.

(ii) We do not transfer from category 1 [with a] warden to category 2. From category 1 non-warden to category 2, transfers are arranged as needed and subject to availability, but only when we are notified of need. A regular check of tenants would be totally impracticable with present staff levels.

(iii) No regular checks as such [are made], although a warden would report any obvious cases of difficulty. The main requests for transfer come from tenants seeking the more popular schemes, usually category 1, and not because they are category 1/category 2 schemes.

Urban Public Agencies. As with the rural councils, no regular checks or transfers are made based on activity level. The urban public managers all emphasised their desire to retain a *balance* of relatively active and inactive residents in all category types under their management.

(i) We do *not* screen or relocate residents by category type, we just try to keep a balanced community within a given site, based on disabilities, as vacancies occur.

(ii) We try to create a *balance* of age and ability in each site, but demand for sheltered housing is high and turnover is low, often making it difficult to retain such a balance.

(iii) We screen upon entry, but more to keep a balance of elderly by age and ability in each scheme. We do *not relocate* from category 1 to 2 as a rule, only if the resident wants to move. It is very difficult to transfer persons due to the strong friendship ties they make and lack of vacancies. If the resident must be moved in the opinion of a warden, a team made up of the senior welfare officer and four service personnel assess the situation.

(iv) Since we see category 1 and 2 as choices in communal living and not serving different levels of functionality and activity we do not make checks or transfers based on functional ability.

Urban Voluntary Associations. The voluntary associations are much more likely to comply with the spirit of circular 82/69.[5] They are more likely to institute regular checks on tenant functional ability and attempt to arrange for a move when it is deemed necessary. However, it is far more difficult for voluntary agencies, with only one housing type, to arrange for transfers.

(i)   All tenants are visited at regular intervals and if the area representative or warden feels they should be moved we take steps to arrange this if possible. The problem is our housing association deals exclusively with category 1 schemes, therefore, we have to liaise very closely with local housing authorities and other voluntary associations.

(ii) The local house committee and housekeeper make regular checks on residents and decide when one has to move on to Part III accommodation.

(iii) We take into account the number of frailties in each scheme when assigning vacancies. All new schemes are *balanced* by age/disability and then kept that way over time. A move to a more dependent setting is decided upon by the resident and warden along with the family, local representative, general practitioner and any specialists as needed. In general a move is considered when constant and permanent personal care or constant nursing and medical supervision is needed.[6]

   The responses from both the urban and rural public managers clearly shows that the category types are *not* used in the manner originally conceived in national circular 82/69,[7] namely to distinguish between more active and less active residents. Nor do these managers generally attempt to transfer residents who become less active. Quite the opposite, public housing managers typically see no difference between category types and assign tenants randomly or in a manner that will create a balance of less active and more active elderly in each scheme regardless of category type. The voluntary associations, on the other hand, are more likely to follow the national intent of circular 82/69.[8] They are more likely to build just one housing type, perceived for a certain clientele defined in part by activity level. They are also likely to have a developed procedure for checking on functional ability and transferring tenants.

Tenant Characteristics by Sheltered Housing Category Type

A major policy question when introducing multiple categories of sheltered housing is the purpose of such housing variety. Are category types designed to be staging posts each accommodating increasingly more frail and disabled elderly, or are they designed as different life-style choices each housing a balance of active and frail elderly? Circular 82/69[9] implies that there should be different staging posts for less active and more active tenants, but the local management opinions analysed above clearly favour a balance of less active and more active tenants in each scheme. What in fact has occurred? If the higher numbered category types house increasingly less active elderly we should be able to find significant differences in resident characteristics in each category type by age profile, support service needs and daily activity levels. On the other hand, if the housing managers are integrating the less active and more active elderly in balanced proportions in all category types, we should expect to find no significant differences in resident profiles between categories.

Table 3.3 presents basic demographic characteristics by category type. In the rural area the variance in resident characteristics between category types is very small and no pattern in resident age and household composition emerges. All rural category types tend to house elderly with similar demographic profiles. In the urban area there are also close similarities between the two groups of category 1 sheltered housing. However, there is a patterned change in the demographic profile moving from category 1 to 2 to 2½ in linked schemes. In each more sheltered and supportive environment the average resident is older, there are more very old residents, and more single and generally female households.

Overall, the urban sample shows a greater variance in resident demographic characteristics across category types. This difference probably reflects the greater variance in elderly living in and seeking sheltered accommodation in urban areas. The urban/rural difference in resident characteristics also reflects the variation in the supply of sheltered housing. All of the category types in the rural sample are supplied by district councils, while the urban schemes include voluntary associations addressing the needs of specialised segments of the elderly

Table 3.3: Tenant Characteristics by Category Type

	Category 1 without common room	Category 1 with common room	Category 2	Category 2½	Linked schemes	Total[a]
	Devon survey					
Average age[b]	74.0	73.4	73.4	–	72.3	73.7
% 80+	24.3	24.7	24.9	–	25.0	24.6
% women	72.3	69.5	76.0	–	76.0	73.2
% living alone	59.0	52.8	65.9	–	66.9	60.7
	West Midland survey					
Average age[b]	73.0	72.5	74.6	79.2	80.3	74.6
% 80+	22.8	17.6	24.3	46.2	50.0	24.4
% women	69.8	69.6	75.1	81.7	75.0	74.8
% living alone	59.3	58.8	77.1	81.7	81.8	71.0

Notes: a. Totals include mixed category 1 and 2 schemes. b. Includes all tenants, even those under 65 years of age.

population (e.g. persons from different religious or occupational backgrounds). The very presence of the wide array of voluntary associations in urban areas reflects the concentration of a heterogeneous elderly population made up of many subgroups. In addition, rural councils often provide only one category of sheltered housing in any one locality (village) and the local elderly are often reluctant to live in a different village, irrespective of the type of sheltered housing on offer there. Such an effect is likely to be much less common in urban areas.

Table 3.4 shows the percentage of sheltered housing tenants receiving visiting support services. There is a general increase in the percentage of elderly using these services moving from category 1 to 2 to linked schemes. This is best illustrated in the percentage receiving one or more services in the Devon sample, and for the most highly used individual services in both the urban and rural samples: home help, meals services and chiropody. The pattern is not as clear among the lesser-used health and social visitation services but this may be because of variations in their local availability or because they are supplemented to varying degrees by on-site staff and neighbours.

While Table 3.3 shows that category 2½ schemes house a generally older population than category 2 in the urban areas, Table 3.4 shows that category 2½ schemes house relatively fewer persons receiving off-site or visiting support services (with the exception of chiropody). This tends to support category 2½ management contentions that they seek to house lonely and isolated but well elderly.

Table 3.4: Percentage of Tenants Receiving Visiting Support Services by Category Type

	Category 1 without common room	Category 1 with common room	Category 2	Category 2½	Linked	Total[a]
	Devon survey					
Home help	20.5	23.5	27.3	–	34.6	23.6
Meals-on-wheels or lunch club	10.3	11.7	12.1	–	15.4	11.2
Home nurse	7.8	10.2	7.4	–	14.6	8.3
Day care	2.6	3.0	4.2	–	0.8[b]	3.1
One or more of the above services	28.5	33.5	34.6	–	39.2	31.5
Chiropodist	15.4	12.6	13.9	–	23.1	14.9
Health visitor	6.1	9.3	8.4	–	4.6	7.2
	West Midland survey					
Home help	18.5	16.9	27.5	23.7	77.3	26.2
Meals-on-wheels or lunch club	14.8	13.5	17.1	_b	_b	–
Home nurse	3.7	8.9	8.1	2.2	6.8[c]	6.3
Day care	1.1	2.0	2.8	0.0	_b	1.6
Chiropodist	3.7	12.2	13.1	19.4	25.0	12.8
Health visitor	0.0	7.4	1.1	0.0	0.0	1.8
Social worker	1.6	4.7	2.6	2.2	0.0	2.4

Notes: a. Total includes mixed category 1 and 2 schemes. b. Not applicable, meals or day care are included in the on-site services provided by this housing category in this survey area. c. Some nursing also available on-site.

Table 3.5 compares the abilities of tenants to undertake activities of daily living (ADL) between housing categories for the urban West Midlands sample only. These are a more direct measure of 'dependency' than the demographic characteristics of Table 3.3 or the data on statutory services received of Table 3.4. Hence, they should discriminate more accurately between the residents of different category types. The wardens in each scheme studied were asked to identify the number of residents unable to do 'light house cleaning', 'heavy house cleaning', 'their own cooking', 'their own shopping', to 'bathe themselves', or to 'feed, toilet or dress themselves'. Several distinct differences between category types have resulted. About twice as many category 2 residents are unable to do heavy cleaning (34.1 per cent), cooking (4.3 per cent) and shopping (19.3 per cent) as category 1 residents (17.8 per cent, 1.8 and 11.0 per cent, respectively). The ADL patterns of category 2½ residents are also quite different from

Table 3.5: **Percentage of Residents by Sheltered Housing Category Unable to Complete Various Activities of Daily Living in the West Midlands Sample**

Unable to:	Category 1	Category 2	Category 2½	Linked schemes	Total[b]
Do light housecleaning	4.2	4.6	0.0[a]	2.3	3.8
Do heavy housecleaning	17.8	34.1	51.9	97.1	34.7
Do own cooking	1.8	4.3	–[c]	85.3	5.4
Do own shopping	11.0	19.3	–[c]	63.6	20.6
Bathe self	6.8	8.4	5.4	15.9	7.6
Feed, toilet or dress self	0.3	0.2	0.0	4.6	0.4

Notes: a. Light housekeeping is likely to be much easier in category 2½ than other categories because a private unit can consist of just a single bedroom without a private bathroom or kitchen to clean. b. Totals include mixed category 1 and 2 schemes. c. Not appropriate to this housing category because some or all the cooking and shopping is done by support staff as part of the housing category definition.

category 1 and 2 residents. Most of the light cleaning chores, and all the cooking and shopping activities, are handled communally by support staff in category 2½. The ADL profile of linked schemes is also clearly distinguishable from other sheltered housing schemes, since the vast majority of residents are unable to do heavy cleaning (97.1 per cent), cooking (85.3 per cent) and shopping (63.6 per cent).

Voluntary participation in social activities is yet another way of measuring activity levels. In Table 3.6, social activities for the urban West Midlands sample are divided into two groups: outside activities and inside activities. Categories 1 and 2 are separately identified so we can analyse any shift in activity patterns among category 1 and 2 residents moving from activity involvement outside schemes to activity involvement inside schemes. Category 2 residents have a lower activity rate for most activities conducted away from the housing schemes, but the difference is slight and has no statistical significance. Category 2 residents do make significantly more on-site visits to each other's flats to socialise or provide domiciliary support than category 1 residents. However, when we look at the remaining two voluntary activities conducted within the scheme, we see that category 1 residents are more likely to serve as stand-ins for the warden and are more likely to participate in communal events where common space is provided.

The higher proportion of category 2 participants that pay visits and provide domiciliary care is probably due to the difference in the design of category 1 and 2 schemes. The grouped category 2 units

Table 3.6: Percentage of Residents Participating in Social Activities for Categories 1 and 2 Sheltered Housing in the West Midlands

	Category 1	Category 2
Outside activities		
Go out to visit friends weekly	53.2	49.6
Go to church weekly	10.4	7.6
Go out to pubs and restaurant weekly	13.7	8.7
Attend clubs or other weekly meetings outside the scheme	15.7	15.9
Do voluntary part-time or full-time work	8.6	4.8
Inside activities		
Visit each other within the scheme weekly for tea	13.4	44.0
Provide domiciliary care for each other	12.6	22.4
Serve as assistant warden for an hour or so	15.1	12.5
Attend weekly social activities held in the scheme (omitting category 1 schemes lacking common rooms)	78.4	59.4

connected by heated interior corridors make visiting both safe and convenient. In most category 1 schemes the residents must go outside to visit a neighbour. Since most of the visits for tea and some of the domiciliary aid is probably conducted at night, and given the general inclement weather for half the year in the Midlands, one would expect fewer visits among category 1 residents.

These differences in building design may reflect uniquely different life-style alternatives as one manager and several wardens pointed out. Category 1 provides more personal space and privacy. Usually there is a little yard attached to a self-contained bungalow, terraced house or maisonette. Category 2 units provide much closer contact with elderly neighbours through shared communal entrances, lounges, laundries, heated corridors and even toilet facilities in some schemes.

Summarising the results of Tables 3.3 to 3.6, we find that the various category types *do* house elderly with different support service use patterns and activity levels. However, part of this variance may be the result of screening by management or elderly self screening. In part, the differences are predisposed by the different housing and support service designs in each category type. A certain amount of the variance in social activity can be credited to whether tenants reside in separate bungalows or grouped apartments and a certain amount of the variance in daily living activity to the presence or absence of on-site communal meal services, home help or even nursing staff. The variances are least noticeable between the two types of category 1 and category 2 schemes, which account for 90 per cent of the urban sheltered housing and 96 per cent of the rural sheltered housing (Table 3.1). In this sense there is not that much choice afforded sheltered housing residents. The age, sex and household characteristics in all category types are remarkably similar in the rural area. After accounting for the design and life-style variations of all categories of sheltered housing, the managers have been reasonably successful in retaining a balance of more active and less active tenants in all scheme types. Similar conclusions were also reached by Derek Fox.[10]

Two additional factors that can influence the resident composition of sheltered housing types have yet to be analysed. One is the claim by local managers that the presence of physical barriers to independent living can distort the continuum of increasingly more supportive sheltered housing choice moving from category 1 to category 2. The second factor is whether the five category types serve as transfer points along which the elderly move, or are moved, as they become increasingly less active and more functionally dependent. Stated another way, it is possible that the differences in activity and support service use observed so far reflect management transfer policy along the sheltered housing continuum rather than different entry point choices.

Physical Design Barriers to Independent Living by Category Type

The expressed purpose for distinguishing between categories 1 and 2 in circular 82/69[11] was to make sheltered housing more accommodating to the more active and less active elderly respectively. Yet managers feel the most critical design features enabling the elderly to maintain their functional independence and activity levels are not included in the circular definition of the two category types. As a result, these managers feel category 1 housing is often as accommodating to the less active as category 2 housing and in some instances more so. The two most common problems noted were the failure of the circular to prohibit the necessity to climb stairs in category 2 housing and the failure to require that category 2 schemes be located within critical walking distance of neighbourhood services so that less active households can conveniently shop on their own.

The study data substantiates the claims of management that more

Table 3.7: Location Index[a] Rating Category 1 and 2 Sheltered Housing Sites On Distance to Shopping and Transportation for Sheltered Housing Schemes in the West Midlands

	Category 1 sites	Category 2 sites
Average distance for all trips	1.8	1.6
Location of site to:		
Bus stop	1.4	1.2
Launderette	1.5	0.0
Public telephone	0.6	0.1
Grocery stores	2.0	1.5
Other elderly neighbours	1.0	0.9
Chemist (drug store)	2.6	2.6
Post Office	2.1	1.8
Hairdresser	0.5	0.4
Banks	3.6	4.9
Community centre	1.3	2.4
Churchs	1.9	2.4
Pubs	2.1	1.3

Note: a. 0.0 = on the estate; 1.0 = adjacent to the estate; 2.0 = within ¼ mile; 3.0 = within ½ mile; 4.0 = within 1 mile; 5.0 = greater than 1 mile.

category 2 residents must cope with stairs than category 1 residents. In the West Midlands sample, climbing stairs was required for 30 per cent of the category 2 units, but only 22 per cent of the category 1 units, and 14 per cent of the category 2½ units. All the linked scheme units were barrier free. A similar assessment was not completed in Devon.

For the West Midlands sample, a location index was designed rating different trips away from the scheme by the average distance travelled. Table 3.7 displays the results. The lower the index the shorter the distance. The only activity for which there was a statistically significant travel difference was doing laundry. This occurs because a common laundry room is required in category 2 schemes but not in category 1 schemes. Otherwise there is no significant difference in terms of the location index in the site locations of category 1 and 2 housing. Put another way, when assigning housing for less active persons it is as likely for a category 1 site to be located within the critical distances to shops and transportation as a category 2 site. It is slightly *more* likely for a category 1 unit to be absent of *both* vertical and distance barriers than a category 2 unit. This may help explain why the two category types end up serving elderly with similar activity/mobility levels, and why managers and wardens see little or no advantage to housing a less active person in one type of unit rather than the other.

A third potential barrier to independent living that is more likely to occur in category 2 than category 1 sheltered housing is very large scheme size. Where the scheme is kept small (e.g. 30 units or less), purpose-built sites can be designed to blend into a residential neighbourhood or, an existing street of bungalows can be converted to a sheltered scheme. Small size helps management to occupy a scheme with many elderly neighbours with existing social ties. If size gets too large (e.g. 80 units or more), then the scheme can both stand out and become isolated from the surrounding neighbourhood. Often land costs dictate vertical design of category 2 flats which can isolate residents on different floors from one another even with an elevator present. With large size, fewer schemes are built further apart and the potential resident pool is much larger and more heterogeneous. At some point very large scheme size renders group social activity, group support, group identity and a sense of community inoperable. Also, at some point very large size makes group organisation and communal living so complex that additional on-site management and support staff are required. These are all factors that affect the successful adaptation to sheltered housing, especially as elderly become increasingly more housebound, frail, or confused.

Large scheme size is more common in other European and North American countries than it is in Great Britain. In the development of the residential home British sponsors favoured small neighbourhood-based schemes. With the development of sheltered housing there has been a tendency to increase the scheme size, but national policy (circular 82/69)[12] still recommends 30 as the most units with which the average resident warden can effectively cope. Our study lends support to this view. As shown in Table 3.1, the average size for all category type schemes lies between about 20 and 30 units in mainly rural Devon. In the urban West Midlands, between about 30 and 40 units is the average for category 1 and 2 schemes (excluding mixed category 1-2), and 15-20 units is about average for category 2½ and linked schemes. There were no schemes with more than 44 units per warden in Devon, and only three schemes with 80 or more units in the West Midlands. All three West Midlands schemes with 80 or more units are recent conversions to sheltered housing from existing high-rise council (public housing) schemes. Two of them were not yet ready for occupancy at the time of the 1978 survey. Rising costs have made it difficult for local British authorities to maintain the 30 units limit in recent years. Some have allowed the number of total dwellings in a scheme to rise to 40, with 15 or more additional self-contained elderly dwellings set aside for totally independent households outside the warden's daily care. However, even 55 units is still quite a small scheme compared to the prevailing policy in other European and North American countries where schemes of 100 to 300 units are common.[13]

There has been one small-scale British study that sheds some light on the effect of varying the size of sheltered housing schemes. Jenny Griffin and Cathy Dean in a 1975 Department of the Environment study[14] located four British schemes of just over 100 units and compared tenant interviews from these schemes with tenant interviews from four moderately large schemes (50-99 units) and four within the normal range for British schemes (25-49 units). No truly small schemes were included. There are a number of aspects of the study that make it difficult to translate the results to other European and North American countries where very large schemes are common. First, several of the so-called large schemes were not single tower blocks but several smaller blocks each with their own common room(s). Second, there was no control for category type. Third, the larger schemes tended to be newer with a greater proportion of young and active tenants. Despite these shortcomings, the study found that the advantages of large schemes lie in financial savings and not in resident convenience. Larger schemes were often justified because they produced more staffing flexibility, more efficient use of staff, and because overall tenant satisfaction measures did not vary appreciably among schemes. This latter finding is very likely due to four factors: first, there may not have been enough differences between the scheme sizes, since several of the larger schemes were in fact made up of a cluster of smaller buildings; second, the younger more mobile elderly may have been satisfied with the larger scheme size because they were able to cope with it, while the older more housebound elderly, who tended to live in the smaller schemes, were expressing a very different type of satisfaction; third, elderly traditionally express high general satisfaction with their living environments irrespective of type;[15] and fourth, the interviews were with tenants who had *chosen* these various housing arrangements, not persons who had refused to live in a particular sized scheme.

Nevertheless, the problems with large schemes that were uncovered are worth noting:

1. Larger schemes tended not to have as easy access to shops as smaller schemes.
2. Warden care was considerably less the larger the schemes (average

number of tenants to warden was 87 in the large schemes).

3. Larger schemes did not provide more services than smaller schemes.

4. The larger the scheme the more residents said they had made no friends.

5. Common rooms were used less in larger schemes. A possible short-term explanation for this is that the younger more active residents currently residing in the large schemes are more likely to attend social activities outside the schemes. However, another explantation, offered by the authors of the study, was that common rooms in large schemes were less accessible, larger and more impersonal. In large schemes residents would be less likely to know all their neighbours and more likely to be intimidated or reticent to use common space occupied by 'strangers'.

Recent work in the United States also shows that elderly are having numerous social problems adapting to large high rise schemes, especially if they have no previous experience with this type of living.[16]

Movement Patterns by Category Type

In this section, we analyse two types of movement pattern: movement along the continuum from category 1 to category 2 to Part III accommodation, and all moves from sheltered housing.

The wardens in the West Midlands sample were asked if the residents entering their scheme were screened by activity level to match the housing category type. The responses parallel those given by management. Thirty-five per cent of the wardens felt there had been no screening. There were two common elaborations on this answer. First, some wardens felt that the waiting lists were so large and vacancies so infrequent that the management usually had to assign those at the top of the waiting list the next vacancy regardless of the applicant's activity level or in which housing category the vacancy occurred. Other wardens felt that the management did not have any way to screen for activity level accurately; that the management seldom saw an elderly tenant before he/she moved in because a family member typically filled out the forms and picked up the keys. The second largest response came from voluntary association wardens who said that the question did not apply to their situation because the association managed just one category type; 29 per cent gave this answer. Twenty-four per cent said the management *did* screen. Sometimes an individual within management was responsible for screening, other times elaborate panels made up of agency staff doctors, nurses, social workers and wardens did the screening.[17] Finally, 12 per cent of the wardens said they did not know if the management did or did not screen residents.

When asked if there were regular transfers from category 1 to category 2, every warden said they knew of no such transfer programme. There were three predominant reasons given for the lack of movement: people would have to leave their friends and did not want to; there is no real advantage to making such a move, the same level of support is provided in either setting; and vacancies come up so seldom that regular moves are not possible.

Transfers between units of the same category type do occur, mostly within the same scheme. The typical transfer is an elderly resident on an upper floor in a building without a lift (elevator) being moved to a ground floor flat. Such a move occurs when there has been a severe medical change (e.g., worsening heart condition, arthritis, respiratory condition, eyesight, etc.), or a permanent disability (e.g., resulting from a stroke, fall, etc.), making it impossible for the resident to cope with the stairs. Ironically, the only reported transfers from one category type to another in both the Devon and West Midlands samples were from the upper floors of a category 2 scheme without a lift, to vacancies in a category 1 bungalow.

When asked about moving residents to Part III accommodation, 44 per cent of the wardens said they had had trouble finding vacancies for those of their residents who they felt should move on to residential homes. Of this group, the majority said it was because Part III homes were full and had long waiting lists. They felt the Part III management gave priority to elderly coming from conventional housing and assumed the warden and visiting services could continue to accommodate the sheltered housing applicant. Twenty-one per cent of the wardens interviewed had never had to move a resident to Part III accommodation because their schemes were too new and/or had too young an elderly population. Almost half of these wardens were expecting to have 'trouble' sometime in the future. Finally, 35 per cent of the wardens said that they could move residents on to Part III accommodation with relative ease, although 6 per cent were wardens of linked schemes.

Table 3.8 summarises the movement patterns found in the West Midlands sample. Total moves, as a percentage of total sheltered housing population, are relatively low. The average percentage of yearly moves was only 2.9 per year. The average number of moves per year

Table 3.8: Type and Percentage of Moves From Sheltered Housing by Category Type in the West Midlands

	Category 1	Category 2	Category 2½	Linked schemes	Total[a]
Total moves (including deaths) as a percent of total category population	12.7	22.0	29.6	18.5	21.0
Average yearly moves[b]	2.0	3.2	4.4	9.3	2.9
Type of move as a percentage of total moves					
Deaths	59.2	61.4	30.8	70.0	60.4
Transfer to Part III homes or long stay hospital	20.4	24.0	33.3	10.0	22.3
Move to relatives	10.2	3.5	10.3	–	5.3
Move to a conventional flat or house	4.1	3.5	15.4	10.0	5.1
Move to other sheltered housing	6.1	7.6	7.7	10.0	6.9
Total moves	100.0	100.0	100.0	100.0	100.0

Notes: a. Includes mixed category 1-2 schemes. b. Total moves as a percentage of total sheltered housing population in each category type divided by the average age of the schemes within that category type.

increases for the more sheltered category types with the older residents. This pattern is the opposite to that found among general households aged under 55, where the youngest tend to be the most transient.[18] Category 1 housing, with the fewest persons receiving support services and with the youngest average age, had the fewest moves. The percentage of yearly moves increases moving along the continuum towards linked schemes, as average age and functional dependence increases. The reason for this pattern becomes evident by examining the remaining figures of Table 3.8, which show *types* of moves as a percentage of total moves. First, there is very little movement to other sheltered housing. The sheltered housing transfers shown primarily reflect moves from one location to another, changing sheltered accommodation but remaining in the same category type. The concept of a 'conveyor belt' approach to housing the elderly is simply not evident. As we have seen, this is in part the result of local management policy not to transfer elderly unless absolutely necessary, partly because it is not physically feasible given the low vacancy rates in all sheltered housing categories and, the most important reason, because the elderly themselves refuse to give up the friendship and support ties they have established. The vast majority of elderly persons make just one move to sheltered housing and remain there until they are 'forced' to move by a very pronounced shift in their ability to maintain an independent unit or until they die.

Table 3.2 shows that the majority (65 per cent) of schemes in all category types were built in 1970 or later, so the average tenant has not resided in their unit very long. Category 1 tenants on average have the youngest and most functional independent elderly of all five housing types. Therefore, category 1 elderly have the longest time before a likely change in health or functional ability would precipitate a move. This explains their lower rate of moves. Category 2 residents are slightly older and have slightly higher functional dependencies. Linked scheme residents are considerably older (average age over 80 – Table 3.3) and far more dependent. Once again, the exception to the pattern seems to be category 2½ schemes where, as shown in Table 3.4, generally fewer residents receive visiting support services than category 2 residents. The reader will recall from earlier statements that category 2½ is claimed by managers to serve more lonely and isolated but well elderly, who are attracted to the communal atmosphere of a shared living environment. It would appear from Table 3.8 that more of these elderly also choose to return to conventional housing while still active and functionally independent, whilst as many as a third transfer to Part III or long stay hospital; proportionately far fewer remain until they die, compared with other category types.

Only 8.4 per cent of the entire West Midlands sheltered housing population studied had moved since entering a sheltered housing scheme; while 12.7 per cent had died in their sheltered housing unit. In other words, 60 per cent of all the moves (including deaths) in the West Midlands sample were as a result of deaths. This figure is comparable with other findings. A study of Anchor Housing Association schemes found that 56 per cent of all moves were the result of death,[19] and an earlier study covering 24 schemes in rural Devon found that between 1963 and 1971, 53 per cent of all moves were the result of deaths.[20]

It is interesting that, for these three studies, the earlier the study the lower the percentage of moves resulting in deaths. Table 3.9 controls for the date of initial occupancy of schemes in the West Midlands sample, and shows that the newest schemes have the lowest percentage of total moves and the lowest number of deaths in proportion to total moves. However, on a yearly average the newly occupied

Table 3.9: Percent of Moves from Sheltered Housing by the Age of the Scheme in the West Midlands

| | Age of the schemes | | | |
	First occupied 1976–8	First occupied 1968–75	First occupied prior to 1968	Total schemes
Total moves as a percent of total population	10.2	23.8	27.9	21.0
Average yearly moves[a]	6.4	3.8	2.2	2.9
Type of move as a percent of total moves				
Deaths	54.9	60.4	62.0	60.4
Transfer to Part III homes or long stay hospital	21.6	21.9	22.8	22.3
Move to relatives	7.8	4.2	5.3	5.3
Move to conventional flat or house	7.8	4.2	4.7	5.1
Move to other sheltered housing	7.8	9.4	5.3	6.9
Total moves	100.0	100.0	100.0	100.0

Note: a. Total moves as a percentage of sheltered housing population in each 'age of scheme' category divided by the average age of the schemes in that category.

schemes have the most mobile residents, with the highest proportion returning to conventional housing on their own or with relatives.

Variations in Tenant Characteristics Over Time

Housing managers are of the general opinion that sheltered housing tenants are becoming a lot older and hence more frail. There is the fear that the situation will 'get worse', due to the general demographic trends toward a higher proportion of elderly surviving to very old age and the expected difficulties of transferring particularly dependent tenants to residential homes and geriatric hospitals. The Devon and West Midlands survey results reveal some evidence to support this view.

As we have seen, Table 3.9 indicates that the average yearly turnover of residents declines as schemes get older, making it difficult for managers to maintain a balance of younger more active tenants and older less active tenants. This trend has implications for the workload of the warden and the growing need for more support services as both the elderly in general, and sheltered housing tenants in particular, continue to survive to very old age. This aspect is discussed further in

Table 3.10: Variation in Tenant Characteristics Between 1973 and 1977 for the Devon Sheltered Housing Sample

	Tenants	
	April 1973	Jan. 1977
Under 65 (%)	12	10
65–74 (%)	42	41
75+ (%)	45	49
Median age[a]	75.4	75.8
% women	72	73
% living alone	57	60
% Receiving:		
Home help	21	24
Meals (luncheon club)	9	12
District nurse	4	8
Day care	3	2
Chiropodist	10	13
Health visitor	1	6
% receiving one or more support services[b]	28	31

Notes: a. Those age 65+ only. b. Excluding those receiving chiropody and/or health visiting only.

Source: Data provided by wardens from 74 schemes surveyed in 1973 and 1977.

Chapter 4. The other statistic of importance is the rate of transfer to Part III accommodation or long stay hospital. Table 3.9 shows that it hardly changes, irrespective of the age of a scheme. This tends to support what wardens and managers have said, namely that it is difficult to find vacancies for sheltered housing tenants in long-term dependent care facilities. If this is true, and continues to be true in the future, it will also have strong policy implications for sheltered housing staffing and staff skills, as the schemes become older.

Table 3.10 shows that the median age of elderly tenants in the Devon study was 76 years. This is roughly mid-way between that of the equivalent general elderly population (69 years) and that of the residents of Devon old people's homes (83 years). However, some ageing of the tenant population is evident between 1973 and 1977, together with an increase in the proportion of women, the proportion living alone and the proportion receiving statutory support (particularly the 'medical support' services of district nurse and health visitor). This shift has occurred in the comparatively short time of less than four years, despite the fact that the data applies to schemes many of which are still quite new with relatively young residents. As individual schemes and districts evolve very old and dependent sheltered housing populations they will require major management and staffing policy changes.

One particular district council in Devon provides an example of how rapidly the age distribution of a local sheltered housing population can shift. In March 1979 this district council recollected data equivalent to that provided for Table 3.10. Just over the two year two month period from January 1977, the median age of sheltered housing tenants rose from 74.8 to 78.0 years. In addition, the proportion of women went up from 77 to 78 per cent, and the proportion living alone rose from 61 to 65 per cent. Prompted by these figures, the district council, in conjunction with the local social service agency, set about exploring the possibility of providing some category 2½ type schemes in order to 'bridge the gap' between conventional sheltered housing and Part III accommodation. This local policy change may be typical of adaptations to ageing populations throughout Great Britain. The main reason the Devon district council housing providers gave for considering the provision of category 2½ sheltered housing was to provide housing appropriate for the very old and frail elderly in the general population seeking sheltered housing *for the first time*. It was not seen as a new staging post to which current category 1 tenants would be transferred. The new category 2½ units are planned as a means of relieving the pressure of assigning *all* the old and frail elderly on the waiting list to vacancies in existing category 1 schemes. Some vacancies in category 1 units can thus be filled by younger more active elderly in order to maintain the balance between fit and frail tenants in these schemes.

Conclusions

There are significant variations in sheltered housing design that can affect the type of elderly who will be attracted to, and be comfortable with, a given scheme, and in the character of living arrangements and type of support provided. Three key variables can substantially alter the character of sheltered housing; they are the way in which services are provided, the extent of private or communal living arrangements and the overall size of the scheme or sheltered housing community. These three variables are displayed as a continuum in Fig. 3.1.

The 'support service' continuum varies from peripatetic to permanent on-site support staff. The more on-site services provided for residents (e.g. housekeeping, congregate or communal meals, organised social activities, physical therapy, nursing), the more service-rich the

Figure 3.1: Variations in Sheltered Housing Types

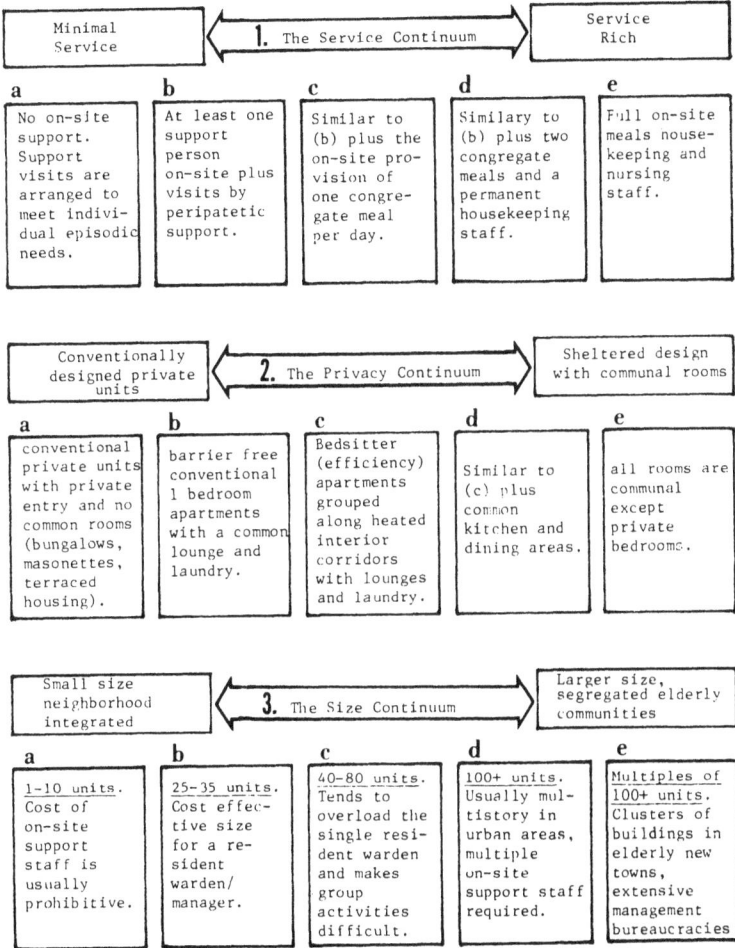

Minimal Service	1. The Service Continuum			Service Rich
a	**b**	**c**	**d**	**e**
No on-site support. Support visits are arranged to meet individual episodic needs.	At least one support person on-site plus visits by peripatetic support.	Similar to (b) plus the on-site provision of one congregate meal per day.	Similary to (b) plus two congregate meals and a permanent housekeeping staff.	Full on-site meals nousekeeping and nursing staff.

Conventionally designed private units	2. The Privacy Continuum			Sheltered design with communal rooms
a	**b**	**c**	**d**	**e**
conventional private units with private entry and no common rooms (bungalows, masonettes, terraced housing).	barrier free conventional 1 bedroom apartments with a common lounge and laundry.	Bedsitter (efficiency) apartments grouped along heated interior corridors with lounges and laundry.	Similar to (c) plus common kitchen and dining areas.	all rooms are communal except private bedrooms.

Small size neighborhood integrated	3. The Size Continuum			Larger size, segregated elderly communities
a	**b**	**c**	**d**	**e**
1-10 units. Cost of on-site support staff is usually prohibitive.	25-35 units. Cost effective size for a resident warden/manager.	40-80 units. Tends to overload the single resident warden and makes group activities difficult.	100+ units. Usually multistory in urban areas, multiple on-site support staff required.	Multiples of 100+ units. Clusters of buildings in elderly new towns, extensive management bureaucracies

scheme. For some elderly, the presence of on-site staff is very rewarding and a key to successful independent living. These elderly may have frequent and multiple support needs, or just value the security, convenience and friendship such permanent staff provide. For other elderly the presence of on-site support staff can be interpreted as stifling independence and presenting an unwanted, overprotective, and even institutional atmosphere. In some cases on-site staff could result in actual premature surrender of many independent functions.

The 'privacy' continuum of Fig. 3.1 represents variations in scheme design from very private to very communal living, the most private sheltered housing design being conventional single-family bungalows with no common rooms and only minimal modifications to eliminate physical barriers and provide personal security. The most communal designs provide just private bed/sitting rooms grouped along heated interior corridors connected to common rooms for lounging, dining, recreation and toiletting. For some elderly, particularly rural elderly, private, low density living is all they have ever known. Communally shared intimate spaces and the constant close proximity of others would produce depression, confusion, stress or anxiety for these elderly. For others, communal environments mean an escape from boredom and isolation, renewed involvement with others, and a feeling of belonging, worth and security.

The 'size' continuum describes variations in the number of units in a scheme and/or the number of schemes clustered in an old age community. The variation in size of a sheltered housing scheme or community not only determines the degree of segregation from, or integration with, the general community, but also the degree of separation from familiar neighbourhood surroundings and established family and friendship ties. Large schemes also increase the complexity of tenant organisation and communal living, independent of variations in the service or privacy continua. Large scheme size can produce feelings of stress or confusion in some elderly; and can produce feelings of security and identity in others.

The Need for a Variety of Sheltered Housing Types at the Local Level

By combining points from each continuum in Fig. 3.1, one can describe the various sheltered housing programmes available in Western countries. For example, in rural Devon in England, sheltered housing consists principally of minimal service, conventional design, and relatively small scheme size (1a or b, 2a or b, 3a or b). In northern parts of the United States the pattern is frequently minimal service, semi-communal/sheltered design, and relatively large scheme size (1a, 2c, 3d). In the area surrounding Copenhagen, Denmark, the elderly are housed in service-rich 'old folks towns' (1c or d, 2d, 3e). Great Britain is the only country with a full array of combinations from which to choose. However, we have seen that at the local level there is often only one sheltered housing type available. The situation appears to be most limiting in rural areas. In Devon, there is very little voluntary (nonprofit) sponsored sheltered housing and the average district council only provides enough sheltered housing for about 2 per cent of the elderly population compared with a 5 per cent national average. Sixty-three per cent of the sheltered housing in Devon is category 1, and 80 per cent of that is 'bare bones' bungalows without common rooms. In the urban West Midlands less than 1 per cent of the elderly lived in sheltered housing before 1970. Since then there has been extensive new construction by both voluntary and public sponsors, and in many areas the elderly do have at least a choice of category 1 or 2 schemes and public or voluntary sponsorship. However, the sheltered housing opportunities are very uneven from one urban district to another. Some districts in the West Midlands still house less than 3 per cent of their elderly in sheltered accommodation. The highest percentage in the West Midlands is a district with over 16 per cent of the elderly residing in publicly provided sheltered housing alone. Even in that district, there is a waiting time of up to 18 months if a person requests both a certain sheltered housing type and neighbourhood location.

The Need for a Variety of 'Entry Points' to Sheltered Housing

Many of the possible combinations of sheltered housing support service, privacy in unit design, and scheme size suggested by Fig. 3.1, could provide viable housing alternatives in particular circumstances. However, if only one combination is available to local elderly it would probably be inappropriate for a sizeable proportion. On the other hand, no locality could or should provide all the combinations possible, as many would be clearly inappropriate given the size, distribution, lifestyle and support needs of the local elderly population. As an obvious example, very large high rise/high density schemes are not warranted or appropriate for sparsely populated rural areas. Local sponsors need to define the continuum of sheltered housing between conventional housing and residential or nursing homes that fit the needs of their locality. This could mean as few as two alternatives so long as local elderly consider that they are provided with viable and meaningful choices.

There are several important reasons for providing elderly with such choices in sheltered accommodation. A viable choice means that an important element of personal control is kept in making a move to a potentially less independent environment. A viable choice means choosing the environment that is most 'normal' and comfortable to the individual. This can help ease the trauma of the move and the adaptation to a more supportive environment. Any move that involves a change in life-style is traumatic, even when such a move is made by young and mobile persons with many options open to them. The trauma of a move is compounded when it is *necessitated* by advancing age and functional disabilities. It is natural to want to postpone such a move for as long as possible. It also seems logical that different persons will make this move, if they make it at all, at different times in their adult lives, under different social circumstances, and with different support needs. Therefore, a number of points of entry into different support environments are required. Once they make this move, most residents will sink deep emotional roots into their new sheltered housing environment. We have seen in Table 3.8 that elderly seldom move from their initial sheltered housing choice, and from Table 3.9 we can see that such moves become less likely with time. If the initial sheltered housing choices in our study areas had been more appropriate we would presumably have recorded even fewer moves than we did. The trauma of an additional move for all parties concerned (the resident, his/her family, neighbours and support staff), can only increase as a person becomes older and more dependent. This is probably the biggest incentive to keep an elderly resident in his/her initial sheltered housing choice, and in making that choice the best possible choice for each person. As early as 1965, a United Nations colloquium on Housing for the Elderly concluded that 'the ideal would be for old people to be rehoused at the end of their active life, or when they become incapable of looking after themselves, in a dwelling from which they would not be required to move again – unless their health at some future date required their hospitalization'.[21] Such an aim can best be achieved if the elderly are provided truly viable sheltered housing 'entry points'.

The Inappropriateness of Current Categorical Sheltered Housing Programmes

Countries currently defining sheltered housing policy and promoting just one sheltered housing type should take note of the British programme where an effort to define two separate sheltered housing types has proved insufficient. This chapter has shown that local housing managers today take little if any notice of the 1969 national policy directive to develop two sheltered housing category types separating the 'more active' and 'less active' elderly in Great Britain. There are two apparent reasons. First, the differences in category 1 and 2 sheltered housing as nationally defined failed to produce enough of a variation to serve as viable choices for elderly with different support needs and tastes in living arrangements. Referring to Fig. 3.1, we can see that both categories 1 and 2, as defined in government circular 82/69,[22] are identical on two of the three key sheltered housing type variables. The circular recommends the same service type (1b), and the same scheme size (3b) for both categories. Only on individual unit privacy do the categories vary and then only slightly; category 1 represents points 2a or b, category 2 point 2c. Second, the national circular design criteria were not as tightly defined as they should have been if category 2 was to house effectively the 'less active' elderly. Category 1, as we have seen, is more likely to be built without stairs, and both categories are equally likely to be built outside the critical walking distance necessary to shops and transportation for the 'less active' elderly to remain functionally independent. Since functional mobility is a major problem for less active elderly, category 2 could become more appropriate housing for this group if stairs were not allowed in the design criteria and critical site location criteria were made part of the design standards.

Even if the physical design distinctions between category 1 and 2 were sharpened, these two categories should not remain the only sheltered housing choices. The presentation in this chapter has clearly shown that local housing managers require on-site service provisions and greater communal sharing as design options if they are to provide viable choices for many of the very old and frail elderly currently seeking sheltered housing for the first time. A national sheltered housing policy in all Western nations should be developed that incorporates a range of combinations of the 'service', 'privacy' and 'size' variations suggested by Fig. 3.1. Programmes are required that give local developers the appropriate scope to design a discrete set of category types appropriate to local elderly needs and desires.

Urban and Rural Differences in Developing a Variety of Sheltered Housing Entry Points

Urban areas should have the fewest problems developing a viable array of sheltered housing choices for the elderly for two reasons. First, urban areas tend to have relatively larger elderly populations concentrated in relatively small service areas. In fact many of the elderly most in need of sheltered housing are concentrated in discrete urban neighbourhoods. This concentrated demand makes it feasible to build and fully occupy several sheltered housing schemes in or near areas with which the elderly are familiar and comfortable. Second, there is also a concentration of the various resources needed in order to develop and sponsor a variety of long term supportive environments for the elderly in urban areas. There are both housing and social service organisations, often present in the public, voluntary (nonprofit) and private sectors, which can sponsor housing in urban areas. In rural areas the elderly are frequently dispersed and there is usually neither the demand nor the financial resources to provide a variety of sheltered housing choices within a given town or village. For example, district councils in rural Devon are typically housing only half as many elderly as the national average, limiting themselves to primarily one housing type and building in just a few of the larger villages or towns in their district. This may mean that a more flexible 'all purpose' scheme design may have to be developed for rural areas, a scheme type in which the warden, statutory and voluntary support as well as some spatial features can vary over time, not only to suit the changing dependencies of the existing residents, but also the changing needs and tastes of elderly entering sheltered housing for the first time.

Sheltered Housing Types Serving as Staging Posts on a 'Conveyor Belt' to the Grave

Earlier in this chapter and in Chapter 1, we discussed how stressful and debilitating it can be to move a person at the point in their life when they are faced with a potentially permanent loss of functional independence. Yet, once a country develops a continuum of sheltered housing types, some local managers may be tempted to move the elderly along to increasingly more sheltered and supportive environments every time they become a bit more frail and disabled. The fear of multiple housing types being used as such staging posts may have actually deterred some countries from developing multiple category types. It should therefore be a relief to them to learn that, based on the data presented in this chapter at least, a 'conveyor belt' approach to multiple housing types has not developed in Great Britain. In fact, there seems to be a number of built-in stops that prevent such transfers from occurring. Unfortunately, the reasons that prevent transfers along the continuum also seem to prevent initial *entry* at the point on the continuum best suited to persons seeking sheltered accommodation. The primary deterent is low vacancy rates. The overall vacancy rate in the West Midlands sheltered housing sample was less than 2 per cent in 1978 and almost half of this already low figure was made up of temporary vacancies that could not be used for transfers or new entries (i.e., units belonging to persons temporarily in hospital or new units still awaiting, but already committed to, the first tenant). In Devon, the equivalent figure in 1977 (omitting the temporary vacancies) was under 1 per cent. Demand almost constantly exceeds supply in government funded programmes which subsidise both housing and service costs. The low vacancy rate prevents transfers but also prevents ease of entry and also tends to limit available options when entry is desired.

Another factor preventing transfers is that different sheltered housing types are frequently found in different 'markets' under different managers. This makes transfers difficult, if not impossible, to co-ordinate when compounded by low vacancy rates. In a given area of Birmingham, for example, category 1 housing may be provided by a voluntary association, category 2 by the public authority, and category 2½ by another voluntary association. The separation of managers and markets also makes it difficult for the elderly person trying to find the most appropriate point of entry into sheltered housing. The management in any one market is not necessarily knowledgeable about other opportunities or vacancies. Since most elderly begin their search at or near a point of housing crisis, they cannot patiently shop around. Frequently, they must accept the choices, if any, available from the first management they find with vacancies.

While the movement of elderly people is to be avoided wherever possible, there are times when a transfer is best for the individual and the other residents in a sheltered housing scheme. The providers of more supportive environments often assume that persons entering from conventional housing should have higher priority for the few available vacancies because they are more likely to have no support where they currently reside. The more supportive the housing sought, the stronger this logic becomes. Thus, if there is an excess of demand for beds in residential homes, the applicant coming from conventional housing will often be chosen over someone who has the services of a warden nearby, regardless of whether the warden can cope with that person or not. This policy further explains why transfers, even needed transfers, are so infrequent along the entire sheltered housing continuum. It also points out the need for a co-ordinated transfer policy among all the housing providers for the elderly. This management function is discussed further in Chapter 5.

Finally, and most important, wardens and managers recognise the strong friendship ties and the actual and moral support a resident receives from friends and neighbours in his scheme. This support can often outweigh the advantages gained by transferring the resident to a more sheltered environment. The managers interviewed in this study felt that all sheltered housing types should be flexibly designed to adapt and provide a range of support. While the level of support might remain not too dissimilar for all sheltered housing, the style of support provision, the level of communal living and the level of segregation from the larger society could continue to vary among category types. This similarity in level of support would be the single best protection against unnecessary and forced transfers of sheltered housing residents. The managers also warned that because so much of the existing sheltered housing is relatively new, most of the residents still have the same functional abilities they had when they entered; therefore, fewer transfers are currently required than are likely in the future. This suggests that an increasing proportion of the total sheltered housing units will be required at the more supportive end of the continuum to accommodate both new entrants and transfers as the elderly population both inside and outside of the sheltered housing ages. This is precisely where most of the local development of new category types and the construction of new units has been concentrated in Britain. Overall, the use of existing category types as entry points and transfer points, along with the development of new category types, has been quite sound in the two British areas analysed. Local managers in other areas of Great Britain and other Western countries will, no doubt, respond as thoughtfully and creatively to similar or even more complex multiple sheltered housing type programmes and strategies that may be developed at the national level.

The Need for a 'Balance' of Active and Inactive Residents Regardless of Category Type

What has evolved over the concluding pages of this chapter is a strategy of multiple entry points into sheltered housing, each point representing a different sheltered housing sub-type. The sub-types would vary by amount of on-site or visiting services, private or communal living and scheme size. However, all these sheltered housing sub-types would share the goal of assisted independent living, all would be designed to provide a similar range of support, and all would define the termination of sheltered housing at a similar level of resident functional independence. In this model there would be a continuum of sheltered housing support service and communal living designs, but *not* a continuum of level of care and support to the individual. The level of support and care may vary from scheme to scheme over time depending on the needs of the residents but all sheltered housing schemes could attain a similar level of support if and when residents required it. In some designs, for example, when support with meals becomes necessary it would take the form of individual help to a household with shopping, then preparation of meals and finally the delivery of a prepared hot meal as dependencies increased. In another scheme design, meals would be communally prepared and eaten by all elderly from the time they first enter the scheme. In both cases a similar level of nutritional support could be attained. The elderly resident would have the choice of scheme type that would deliver this nutritional support in a manner compatible with his life-style needs or tastes.

This model is different from the national British policy suggested in circular 82/69,[23] but is similar to the strategy evolving at the local level in Great Britain. The circular calls for the separation of 'more active' elderly into category 1 and 'less active' elderly into category 2. This implies that these category types become staging posts along which the elderly are moved as their functional limitations increase. However, almost every manager interviewed in this study voluntarily pointed out the need to keep all sheltered housing schemes, regardless of category type, 'balanced' between more active and less active tenants. The local management reasoning seems to us the most sound. If a homogeneous group of young and independent elderly are allowed to occupy a scheme and they jointly become less active over time without any new young and active replacements, the scheme can loose its sheltered housing role and become a residential home by default. With uniformly less active residents, tenant initiated and directed social activity would die out. With uniformly less active residents, voluntary domiciliary support provided by neighbours would cease. With more frail than fit tenants the wardens of minimal on-site service schemes would become overburdened. The management would be faced with assigning more and more staff to take over services previously provided by tenants and wardens, risking ultimate staff domination of daily activities in the scheme. The only way to prevent this scenario is to start with, and keep, a balance of more active and less active elderly in each scheme regardless of category type.

The key ingredient in the success of minimal service sheltered housing (category 1 and 2) in Great Britain has been the resident warden. In minimal service schemes the warden is the primary link between residents and support services and provides much of the short-term episodic and emergency care. The balance of fit and frail residents becomes most crucial in these situations. If the warden becomes over-burdened by too many inactive and dependent tenants, her services to all other tenants will be compromised. The effective warden is the key to the continued success of sheltered housing schemes in Great Britain. The next chapter analyses the changing and pivotal role of the warden in different scheme types, in different scheme locations, and in schemes with different levels of resident dependency.

Notes

1. Ministry of Housing and Local Government, *Housing Standards and Costs: Accommodation specially for old people*. Circular 82/69, HMSO, London 1969.
   2. Ibid.
   3. Ibid.
   4. Ibid.
   5. Ibid.
   6. Cowley, R.J., *Caring for the elderly in sheltered housing: A Report of the Anchor Extra Care Study Group*. Anchor Housing Association, Oxford, 1977.
   7. Ministry of Housing and Local Government, *Housing Standards and Costs: Accommodation specially for old people*.
   8. Ibid.
   9. Ibid.
   10. Fox, D., 'Housing the elderly'. In, Hobman, D. (ed.), *The Impact of Aging*. Croom Helm, London, 1981, pp. 86–108.
   11. Ministry of Housing and Local Goverment, *Housing Standards and Costs: Accommodation specially for old people*.
   12. Ibid.
   13. United Nations, *Housing for the elderly*. Proceedings of the Colloquium organised by the committee on Housing, Building and Planning of the United Nations Economic Commission for Europe, Belgium and the Netherlands, October 1965, New York, 1968; Beyer, Glenn, H. and Nierstrasz, F.H.J., *Housing the aged in Western Countries*. Published for the Bouwcentrum, Rotterdam, and the Center for Environmental Studies, Cornell University, Ithaca, New York, by Elsevier, Amsterdam, London and New York, 1967; Noam, E. and Donahue, W., *Assisted independent living in grouped housing for older people: A report on the situation in European countries*. International Center for Social Gerontology, Washington, D.C., 1976.
   14. Griffin, J. and Dean, C., *Housing for the elderly: The size of grouped schemes*. Department of the Environment, HMSO, London, 1975.
   15. Abrams, M., *Beyond three-score and ten: A first report on a survey of the elderly*. Age Concern, London, 1978.
   16. Lareau, L.S., 'Reactions of rural elderly to high rise environments'. *Housing and Society*, 1981, 8, pp. 37–44.
   17. The current function and future roles of these sheltered housing advisory panels in both screening entrants and assessing resident ability to remain in sheltered housing is becoming more common as sheltered accommodation becomes more specialised and as the resident populations age. Further discussion of these panels can be found in Chapter 5.
   18. United States Bureau of the Census, *Geographic Mobility: March 1975– March 1978*. Current Population Reports, Population Characteristics Series P-20, No. 331, United States Department of Commerce, Washington, D.C., November 1978, Table 4, p. 12.
   19. Cowley, *Caring for the elderly in Sheltered housing: A Report of the*

Anchor Extra Care Study Group.

20. Boldy, D., Abel, P. and Carter, K., *The Elderly in grouped dwellings; A profile.* Institute of Biometry and Community Medicine, University of Exeter, Exeter, Devon, 1973.

21. United Nations, *Housing for the elderly.*

22. Ministry of Housing and Local Government, *Housing Standards and Costs: Accommodation specially for old people.*

23. Ibid.

4 THE SHELTERED HOUSING WARDEN

Perhaps the single most important element in the day-to-day success of elderly assisted independent living environments is the support staff. This is particularly true of minimal service sheltered housing where there is usually just a single staff person who serves as the tenants' arbitrator, social organiser, link to housing management and link to emergency and long-term health and social support services. Throughout North America and most of Western Europe, minimal service sheltered accommodation provides no live-in support staff. Where 24-hour security to a site is provided, it often consists of an assigned or visiting social worker, nurse or site manager during the day, and a combination of designated tenants, security personnel and/or a live-in property caretaker for the remaining 16 hours. In some cases the daytime manager is rotated from site-to-site and specific tasks such as arbitrating tenant disputes or liaising with visiting support services is carried out by different management personnel. The more service-rich sheltered housing programmes in North America and Western Europe tend to use an on-site administrator/manager who oversees the numerous personnel who have direct support contact with the elderly tenants.

The British sheltered housing programme centres support on one person — the resident warden. All the various category types of British sheltered housing have a resident warden, and in the minimal service housing types the warden is the only on-site support. The warden is typically a young to middle aged housewife who lives with her family in a private apartment or house attached or adjacent to the sheltered housing scheme. Usually no special skills or training are required to be eligible for a warden position beyond a loving/caring nature, self-confidence, and common sense.

The British word 'warden' is defined in simplist terms as a 'friendly neighbour'. The American use of the word connotes a director of a penal institution; hardly appropriate to oversee long-term assisted independent housing for the elderly. In Great Britain prison directors are called warders. A warden is a very common term and job type; it implies a resident counsellor, organiser and family proxy for such facilities as youth hostels, college dormatories, day care programmes, summer camps or elderly sheltered housing.

126

The warden concept covers all the counselling and organiser roles typically covered by several people assigned to sheltered accommodation in other Western countries. The role of the warden is designed to produce a close friend and neighbour of the elderly tenants while the tenants are still active and independent; and an advocate and family proxy, in place of a professional health or social service bureaucrat, if and when the tenants become inactive and require varying support services to remain in their independent living environment. In fact, there is very little expected of the warden in the way of social organisation or service provision so long as elderly sheltered housing residents remain active and independent. The residents and warden are expected to live in a *reciprocal* good neighbour relationship in advance of any functional dependencies on the part of the tenants. Then, should the elderly tenants require help with retaining social activity and functional independence, the warden begins to serve as a dedicated advocate and family proxy.

The typical management description of a warden's duties centre on the provision of temporary domiciliary help to the tenants such as cooking and shopping during episodic illness or following an accident. Temporary help is defined as filling in until appropriate peripatetic community services or family support can be summoned. Because the tenant and warden dwellings are connected via an alarm or intercom system, the job description also includes answering calls from tenants and taking appropriate action, such as summoning emergency services or family. Beyond these duties management expectations vary from one location to another. A majority of managers expect a warden to visit tenants daily unless tenants expressly disapprove. Most managers also expect wardens to oversee the property and bring needed repairs to their attention. In some cases the husband of the warden is retained by management to complete routine maintenance and upkeep. In some cases the warden is expected to clean common areas within the scheme. Finally, most managers *encourage* the warden to co-operate in social organisation of communal activities. A growing number of managers *expect* the warden to at least start up, if not retain, permanent involvement in a tenants' organisation and weekly social activities. Time off and remuneration for this work is not standardised. Most managers see the job as part-time, although the warden can be on-call 24 hours a day. Remuneration usually consists of free rent and a relatively small stipend.

The resident warden represents a pivotal and dynamic role in the long-term support of frail but independent elderly. The warden can have a profound positive effect on the elderly residents, but the wrong warden or wrong tenant/warden 'chemistry' can have a profound negative effect. The wrong person in the warden role can result in neglect, misuse or abuse of all support functions to the residents. A weak warden can also *be* abused and overworked by management and tenants. The job itself can also change dramatically over time. Even a minor inbalance toward more inactive tenants, and a lay warden can find herself terribly overworked providing domiciliary, social and nursing services to the frail and dependent elderly in the 'off hours' when support services are not available.

This chapter analyses the pivotal role of the warden in British sheltered housing. We begin by presenting the debate over what the role and duties of the warden should be. In the following sections we explore the actual working conditions of the warden today. First, we analyse the warden's weekly workload and activities within different sheltered housing types to determine if there is in fact more than one warden type. Second, we determine the degree to which warden activities include the direct provision of services as opposed to only their organisation. Third, we analyse how the activity patterns of the wardens are changing over time. Fourth, we analyse whether increasing warden skills and responsibilities are being rewarded by management. Finally, we summarise the types of wardens in active service today, and discuss the policy implications for the future both in Great Britain and in the United States, where public programmes of assisted independent living for the elderly are only now being formulated.

The Debate Over What the Role and Duties of the Warden Should Be

After more than 20 years of experience with sheltered housing in Great Britain, the debate over what specific duties a warden *should* perform and what skills a warden *should* possess remains unresolved. In addition, these 20 years plus have seen few studies about what skills practising wardens actually possess and what roles they actually perform. The importance of filling this gap in knowledge is becoming more vital, as the number and variety of wardens increases with the increasing varieties of sheltered housing types.

Our evaluation of what a warden does will be enhanced if we first identify how management perceives the warden role and the types of persons actually being recruited as wardens. Fig. 4.1 presents in simple terms the three warden role types that have precipitated the debate

Figure 4.1: Warden Role Types

Housing managers	Health and social service managers	Possible long-term need
Non-professional support ORGANISER	Non-professional support PROVIDER	Professional ORGANISER/ PROVIDER

over what role a warden should play. For the most part housing authority managers see the warden as an *organiser* of support services and social activities and as an advocate and friend of the tenants.[1] Social services and health agency managers are more likely to interpret the warden role as that of a *provider*; someone who is part of the overall care provision system in a community.[2]

Whether wardens should be professionally trained or not enters the debate when sheltered housing tenants and their needs for on-site services are viewed longitudinally. As was discussed in Chapter 3, the turnover in sheltered housing in very small and some housing managers claim they are unable to maintain a balance of active and inactive tenants over time. Proponents of the professional warden organiser/ provider alternative argue that so long as the warden has a young and active tenant population she can function primarily as an organiser. However, as some of her tenants become less active and require visiting support services the warden role will change to both organiser and provider. As dependence on visiting services increases, it becomes important to remember that even the most efficient peripatetic service system has gaps in service delivery and service quality. These gaps must be recognised and accommodated for in the warden role. Already, most wardens are expected to provide short-term domiciliary and nursing services in an emergency and until long-term visiting services are established. What is not often recognised is that *long-term* gaps in peripatetic services also exist.

As more elderly tenants require services more of the warden's time will be taken up as a provider. Nights and weekends are typically times when no visiting services are available. Long-term provision of services by the warden can also spill over into week days if some services are unreliable or nonexistent. The role of both organiser and provider can also become more complex over time. As some tenants require multiple services the warden may be the only one in a position to co-ordinate and monitor these disjoined support efforts. Even organising social activities and paying visits becomes more complex as the number and variety of tenant functional and mental disabilities increase. As one of us has pointed out elsewhere,[3] wardens in this situation are 'likely to find themselves fulfilling a role more and more akin to that of home-help and home-nurse rolled into one'. One has to ask if wardens in this situation wouldn't be better equipped to handle their job if they possessed specific professional skills as organisers and providers.

In the counter argument to the skilled professional warden it is feared that 'overdefining and confining the work [of a warden] . . . may undermine the main reason for success of the [sheltered housing] concept'.[4] Proponents of the lay warden feel that the success of sheltered housing is in providing independent living rather than in providing social or medical support. They also fear that a live-in professional provider will not only *react* to dependencies, she will *create* dependencies, thus undermining the goal of prolonging independent living.[5] While there is merit in this warning there is no empirical evidence that 'professionals' are more likely to create dependencies than non-professionals. However, it may well be that the lay warden is more prone to create functional and emotional dependencies among less active tenants.

Current Management Views and Guidelines for Hiring Wardens

Most British sheltered housing is managed by housing authorities, and we found a great deal of similarity in the types of persons actually being appointed as wardens in the Devon and West Midlands samples and the publicly professed criteria used for hiring them. There was also a great deal of similarity in the role model most managers sought; it was most closely aligned with the *nonprofessional organiser role*.

Not one of the management agencies interviewed officially required any professional skills in order to be eligible for a warden position. In fact some managers specifically stated that they avoid candidates with professional provider credentials because they feared that such a person could 'over care' and create dependencies, or be very frustrated suppressing their provider skills in an environment that stresses maximum functional and social independence. The managers in the West Midlands sample were asked how they interviewed and screened candidates for the warden position. In all cases they relied most heavily on a subjective interview where they attempted to identify persons with characteristics such as 'self confidence', 'assertiveness' and 'sensitivity to elderly needs and problems'. This latter factor was not meant to imply professional insights or training but 'common sense', 'patience', 'empathy', and a 'loving and tolerant nature'.

It appears from many of the management comments that what they seek in hiring a warden is someone who can and will make strong emotional bonds with the tenants. In a previous account of Devon wardens it was concluded that the warden is hired to function as a paid proxy for relatives and friends and becomes emotionally involved with her 'family'.[6] Managers apparently see the emotional bond between elderly tenant and warden as a unique and important element in the success of sheltered housing. They see this bond as something that does not occur as often between elderly and peripatetic support service staff or between elderly and staff in hospitals, residential accommodation or nursing homes. Most managers feel that by living together in the same scheme as independent households the lay warden and tenant will make close 'family' ties, and the warden will be committed to the tenant's desire to remain independent as he/she grows more frail and develops support service needs.

While this role scenario makes a great deal of sense, and was generally observed in the sheltered housing sites studied, four questions still remain: Is a lay warden more likely to make these ties with tenants then a professionally trained warden? As tenants come to require advanced organiser/provider skills to remain independent, would not a professional nurse or social worker have greater success in helping a tenant retain independent living? Furthermore, if sheltered housing schemes were truly balanced between active and inactive tenants from the start, wouldn't a warden with professional skills be warranted? Is the history of the lay warden in part a product of past sheltered housing schemes beginning with primarily active and independent elderly who required little more than a social organiser?

The Type of Wardens Actually Being Hired

Further to reinforce the emotional bond and commitment of warden to tenants, we found a strong socio-economic and life-style compatibility between them. Of the 34 wardens in the West Midlands sample, 32 were found to have raised families and 14 (41 per cent) still had children living at home. The average age of the wardens was 52, 23 years younger than the average age of the residents. Only three wardens were so young that they were not within the normal age range of a daughter to the average tenant. Of the 119 Devon wardens for which similar information was obtained in 1977, 68 (57 per cent) still had children living at home although only 8 (7 per cent) had any children under 5. The average age of the Devon wardens was 50, with 6 (5 per cent) being under 30 and as many as 18 (15 per cent) being over the official retiring age for women of 60.

In many local authority schemes, the warden and elderly tenants come from the same neighbourhood or same working- to middle-class life-style. The warden's husband tends to hold a blue collar or lower level white collar job (sales, clerical, foreman, etc.). Husbands and older children frequently get involved in assisting the warden. It is not un-common for managers to have a policy that the husbands should help out around the scheme with tasks such as putting out dustbins (trash cans) for tenants when they are too heavy, helping with minor electrical and plumbing repairs and communal gardening work.[7] Thirteen per cent of the wardens in the Devon sample said that members of their family provided important and needed assistance. In the West Midlands sample, 9 per cent of the wardens said their husbands were expected to tend gardens and complete minor repairs, while another 29 per cent said their husbands voluntarily tended to minor repairs and other tenant needs. In 12 per cent of the West Midland cases wardens voluntarily added that their children also provided regular assistance such as taking dogs for a walk or running errands for tenants. As one Devon warden put it: 'This is a job that involves all the family; you then get a family atmosphere among the tenants.'

While sheltered housing managers have been screening warden candidates for those who will hopefully be dedicated family proxies, they have also been hiring more wardens with organiser/provider skills, even if their official job descriptions state that no special skills or training are required. Some managers are developing community college courses and training programmes to provide wardens with skills ranging from first aid to group dynamics. Of the wardens hired over the last eight years by managers in the West Midlands survey, 24 per cent had worked with the elderly before in some nursing capacity, an additional 9 per cent had held white collar administrative positions before becoming a warden, and an additional 32 per cent had taken an orien-tation course developed by the housing authority management.

There has been a marked increase in the number of wardens with professional nursing credentials. In the Devon survey of 1973 only 12 per cent of the wardens had nursing qualifications. Just four years later, 27 per cent of the Devon wardens had nursing qualifications. Fully 50 per cent of the wardens surveyed in the West Midlands sample and hired in 1977 and 1978 (n = 14) had some nursing training, while only 5 per cent of the wardens surveyed who were hired prior to 1977 (n = 20) had some nursing training. Thus while all of the managers continue to advertise their warden positions as requiring no previous skills or training, and some managers still avoid candidates with professional care giving skills, the hiring trend is toward wardens with nursing skills who apparently also possess strong desires for making close 'family' ties with their elderly tenants.

The Actual Workload of the Warden in Different Sheltered Housing Types

Two separate lists of warden activities were constructed from previous research studies[8] and management interviews in Devon and the West Midlands. Forty-two separate activities were isolated, 15 being common to both studies. These 42 activities were then subdivided into four groups: general support, 'emergency' support, communal activities, and housekeeping and administration. Each activity was further identified as either an 'organiser', 'provider' or 'support' activity. The Appendix presents the details of this taxonomy of warden activities. The wardens studied in Devon and the West Midlands were presented with their respective list of activities and asked to record the amount of time spent in a particular week on each activity. The following tables summarise the different workload and activity patterns of the wardens in the two surveys.

Table 4.1 highlights the differences in workload for Devon and West Midlands wardens in each of the five sheltered housing category types introduced in Chapter 3. Chapter 3 showed that the various category types represent uniquely different sheltered housing environments with different on-site service staff. As we shall see in later tables in this chapter, the category differences are reflected in different warden activities, and it may be that several very different warden types are evolving. Table 4.1 shows that the workload of the warden varies by category type and tends to increase, with one noted exception to be discussed below, as the on-site communal activities and support activities increase.

Chapter 3 also revealed that government policy considers the category types as exclusive staging posts ranging from housing for the most active tenants (category 1), to housing for the least active tenants (linked schemes). As a result, the workload of a warden can be dramatically increased in the categories designated for less active tenants. This is also reflected in the workload figures presented in

Table 4.1: The Warden's Weekly Workload by Category Type in Devon and the West Midlands

	Average hours worked per week[a]	Average hours of domiciliary care per week	Average number of persons per scheme	Average hours worked per tenant per week
Devon sample				
Category 1 without common room(s)				
n = 72	24.2	7.8	24.7	0.98
Category 1 with common room(s)				
n = 11	29.8	5.5	41.8	0.71
Category 2				
n = 32	33.8	7.8	34.6	0.98
Category 2½				
n = 0	–	–	–	–
Linked schemes				
n = 5	27.9[b]	6.3	26.0	1.07[b]
Total n = 121	27.4	7.6	28.8	0.95
West Midlands sample				
Category 1 without common room(s)				
n = 4	22.0	4.8	47.3	0.47
Category 1 with common room(s)				
n = 4	29.0	4.8	37.0	0.78
Category 2				
n = 16	34.8	8.1	37.9	0.92
Category 2½				
n = 6	57.0[c]	4.0	15.5	3.68[c]
Linked schemes				
n = 2	69.0[d]	–[e]	22.0	3.14[d]
Total n = 34	38.5	6.8	35.2	1.09

Notes: a. Does *not* include being on call in case of emergency, any time spent cleaning common areas, rent collections, etc. Only direct and routine contact with the tenants is included. b. Excludes work hours in connection with residents of the residential home component of the linked schemes facility. c. Includes meal planning, shopping for food and in some cases cooking. d. Includes work hours for both the sheltered housing and residential home components of the linked scheme facility. e. The warden does not provide domiciliary care because there is an on-site home help and cleaning service.

Table 4.1. One might have expected a more dramatic variance in workload given the government staging policy. However, as was pointed out in Chapter 3, many local sheltered housing managers attempt to achieve a balance of active and inactive tenants in *all schemes* regardless of category type.

As noted above, there is an exception to the patterns just described which was also first noted in Chapter 3. In some localities, especially rural areas, only one category type is provided which must accommodate all eligible elderly regardless of activity level. Such a phenomenon occurs in rural Devon, where category 1 housing with no common room(s) is the most popular, and frequently the only, sheltered housing choice. Table 4.1 shows that when compared to the urban West Midlands, the wardens of a category 1 scheme without common room(s) in Devon put in more than twice as much work per tenant per week. Table 3.4 of the previous chapter, illustrated how many more Devon tenants of category 1 schemes without common room(s) received peripatetic domiciliary support services. The warden must provide most of this domiciliary care at nights and weekends when peripatetic support is not available.

Completing the urban/rural comparison from Table 4.1, there is a remarkable similarity between category 1 with common room(s) and category 2, in the two samples. Linked schemes cannot easily be compared because the Devon survey excluded work hours in connection with residents of the residential home component, these being included in the West Midlands survey.

The Relationship between Resident Needs and Warden Activities

Table 3.5 of the previous chapter showed that in the West Midlands sample the more sheltered the housing category design the more residents require help with activities of daily living (ADL tasks). For example, the percentage of tenants unable to complete heavy house cleaning was nearly 18 per cent in category 1 schemes, this increased to 34 per cent in category 2, to 52 per cent in category 2½, and reached 97 per cent among the sheltered housing tenants of linked schemes. If the prevailing concept of the warden is principally an *organiser* of support services holds in each of these category types, then the increasing proportion of tenants requiring help with ADL tasks should be handled by other on-site staff or visiting services and the warden's activities should remain relatively constant. To test this hypothesis we asked the wardens in the West Midlands sample how many of their residents they can leave alone without any daily check-ups, how many require at least one daily visit, how many require extra checks throughout the day, and how many require daily support from the warden as well as visiting services. Table 4.2 shows the results. Clearly, the number of totally independent residents decreases as the sheltered housing category type increases. This in turn implies different workloads and activities for the wardens of the different category types. Category 2 wardens have about twice as many tenants who require extra checks or support services as category 1 wardens. Spread out over an entire week, this has to mean that category 2 wardens have either less time to spend providing social activities for the more independent residents or their total work hours must increase. Category 2½ wardens have about twice as many tenants who require extra checks and support services as the category 2 wardens. The fact that category 2½ wardens are also involved in planning meals, food purchasing and sometimes cooking communal meals, suggests a totally different set of weekly activities. Linked schemes introduce additional on-site support staff removing the warden from direct support service activities but requiring, by the wardens' own admission, administrator/co-ordinator skills not required in the minimal service schemes.

To discern more clearly whether wardens of different sheltered housing types perform different activites, the wardens in the West Midlands sample were presented with the list of activities set out in the Appendix and asked if these were: (1) activities they must complete as prescribed by management, (2) specific activities management expressly told them not to complete, or (3) activities that were not specifically identified by management but were tasks they or their spouse completed anyway. Table 4.3 presents a comparison of responses by wardens from four sheltered housing types. To simplify the table, only a sample of the most important activities are displayed under four subcategories and only warden responses to management prescribed or voluntarily completed activities are included.

Neighbourly services appear to be central to the concept of a warden as service 'organiser' and 'friendly neighbour'. Almost all wardens regardless of sheltered housing type completed these neighbourly services. In most cases these activities are prescribed by the management, but when they are not the wardens are likely to voluntarily complete them. For all other service categories there is no uniformity in warden activities between sheltered housing types.

Caretaker services are more likely to be required of category 1 and 2 wardens; category 2½ and linked scheme wardens are more likely to have permanent support staff to complete these chores. Social organisation activities illustrate another marked difference in warden roles. The managers of category 1 and 2 housing are more likely than

Table 4.2: Percentage of Persons the Warden Sees Daily by Category Type in the West Midlands Sample

Which of the following statements best fits each resident:	Category 1	Category 2	Category 2½	Linked schemes	Total
Totally independent and can be left alone	57.9	44.8	36.9	22.7	42.8
Must be checked on daily	34.7	39.1	30.8[a]	63.7	39.7
Require extra checks throughout the day	5.9	13.0	26.2[a]	13.6[b]	14.9
Require daily support from warden and visiting services	1.5	2.6	6.1	0.0[b]	2.4
Unable to stay in sheltered housing	0.0	0.5	0.0	0.0	0.3
Total	100.0	100.0	100.0	100.0	100.0

Notes: a. Category 2½ wardens stated that communal meals served as a time when they could check on residents without making special visits to each unit. b. The presence of on-site support staff helps eliminate some of the extra checks and all of the support from the warden or visiting services.

category 2½ and linked scheme managers to require such duties, and category 1 and 2 wardens are more likely voluntarily to complete such activities when they are not specified. There are also variations in required and voluntary activities among wardens in the four housing types for each of the extended service activities. Almost all wardens must secure adequate meals for tenants. However, category 1 and 2 wardens call in meals-on-wheels based on observed individual need, category 2½ and linked scheme wardens administer on-site congregate dining for all sheltered housing residents. Running errands for sick and housebound residents is more likely to be required of category 1 and 2 wardens, and where not required, these wardens are more likely voluntarily to provide this service. However, domiciliary chores are more likely to be required of category 2½ and, in particular, linked scheme wardens. Voluntary provision of domiciliary chores is provided roughly equally by all warden types except linked scheme wardens.

Overall, the results of Table 4.3 reinforce the findings of Table 4.2. There is very little consistency in warden duties among the four different housing categories. Other than neighbourly services, no services are consistently required by management or voluntarily provided by wardens. The differences in minimal service or service-rich design help create distinct differences in warden duties. More category 1 and 2 wardens are expected to complete maintenance and social

Table 4.3: Percent of Wardens from the West Midlands Sample Who Stated They Must Complete or Voluntarily Completed Selected Activities, by Housing Category Type

Activities	Must complete				Completed voluntarily			
	Category 1 (n = 10)	Category 2 (n = 16)	Category 2½ (n = 6)	Linked (n = 2)	Category 1 (n = 10)	Category 2 (n = 16)	Category 2½ (n = 6)	Linked (n = 2)
Neighbourly services								
Pay regular calls on tenants	80	81	67	100	0	13	0	—
Contact relatives when necessary	100	94	50	100	—	6	50	—
Arrange doctor's visits	90	94	67	50	10	6	33	50
Caretaker services								
Clean common rooms	60	25	17	0	0	6	0	0
Arrange for repairs	80	88	50	50	0	13	50	50
Social organisation								
Organise social events and outings	50	44	17	50	30	50	17	0
Start tenants organisation	40	19	0	0	10	31	0	0
Continue to head tenants organisation	30	0	0	0	30	25	0	0
Extended services								
Arrange for meals-on-wheels/ provide meals	90[a]	88[a]	100[b]	100[b]	0[a]	13[a]	—[b]	—[b]
Do errands for sick tenants	30	19	17	0	60	56	17	50
Do domiciliary chores for sick tenants	0	6	17	50	10	25	17	0

Notes: a. Visiting meals arranged. b. Meals provided on-site.

Table 4.4: Average Hours Worked per week by Devon Wardens according to Activity Group and Housing Category Type

Activity groups[a]	Category 1 without common room(s)	Category 1 with common room(s)	Category 2	Linked schemes[b]	Total
General support	21.0	20.5	23.3	23.6	21.6
'Emergency' activities	3.0	4.7	5.3	3.4	3.8
Communal acitivities	0.2	4.6	5.2	0.9	2.0
Housekeeping and administrative activities	2.3	5.0	9.3	3.1	4.4
Total	26.5	34.8	43.1	31.0	31.8
Average hours worked per tenant per week	1.07	0.83	1.25	1.19	1.10

Notes: a. For the type of activities included under each group see Appendix 1. b. Linked scheme wardens were asked to record only the time spent working with sheltered housing tenants and not any time (if any) spent with residential home tenants.

organising duties than category 2½ and linked scheme wardens. Category 2½ and linked scheme wardens are expected to complete or oversee more on-site cooking and domiciliary services.

Table 4.4 breaks down the average hours worked per week by Devon wardens into the four activity groups introduced earlier in this chapter. Not only are there marked differences in the amount of time associated with different activity groups by wardens in different housing categories, but the overall average work load per tenant and per scheme type varies dramatically. The average category 1 warden in schemes without common room(s) works close to a half-time job, while the average category 2 warden puts in more than a 40 hour week. In particular, virtually no communal activities are undertaken by wardens of category 1 without common room(s) and the amount of time spent on housekeeping and administrative duties increases steadily from category 1 without common room(s) to category 2.

Summarising the findings of the first four tables of this chapter, we find that all wardens provide similar general 'friendly neighbour' types of support. Category 1 and 2 wardens are involved in the same types of activities and probably at the same skill level but category 2 wardens must spend more time with emergency, communal, housekeeping and administrative activities on a per-tenant and a per-scheme basis each week. Category 2½ wardens spend more time completing home help (homemaker) chores and require more dietary and meal planning skills. Linked scheme wardens spend more time checking on tenants and thus require skills of a surveillance nature. Since the overall average age of the residents in both samples is less than 75 years of age, the wardens role may yet require more of a direct caring role and additional skills and training as the resident population of these schemes ages and grows more dependent.

Changes in Warden Activity Over Time

In order to test whether wardens' workloads (and particularly 'provider' activities) increase as their residents age, warden activities in the Devon study were analysed over time. Wardens recorded their time spent against a list of 33 activities (see the Appendix) on two occasions, a month in 1973 (April) and a week in 1977 (January). Seventy-four schemes were common to both survey dates. Table 4.5 presents the average number of hours recorded per week by the wardens of these schemes on the two dates. (Similar results were also obtained when only those 47 wardens who had been in post both in 1973 and 1977 were considered. Hence, recorded changes in warden activities are not due to changes in wardens, but rather to shifts in activities among the wardens.) The table analyses the time spent by activity area (General, 'Emergency', Communal and Housekeeping/Administrative), outside normal working hours, and responding to alarm calls. In addition, the warden's time spent on 'provider' service activities was also identified. For the purpose of this study, 'provider' service activities are defined as emergency nursing and long-term nursing and support services provided by the warden. The specific activities considered to be 'provider' activities are identified in the Appendix.

Table 4.5 shows a considerable overall increase in workload over time, as well as in potential stress-creating activities like alarm calls, and in tenant reliance on the warden at times that are disruptive of privacy and normal living patterns. In less than four years there was roughly a 50 per cent increase in the average warden's working week. The increase in both overall workload and provider services occurs in 'general support' and 'emergency' activities, and these are the activities that relate most to tenant dependency. There is actually a *reduction* in the average time spent by wardens on housekeeping and administrative activities over this time period. It is entirely possible that this reduction represents a conscious cut-back on housekeeping and administrative chores in an effort to counterbalance the increase in support service dependencies and keep the overall workload per week within the

Table 4.5: Changes in Support Activities of Devon Wardens[a] Over Time

	April 1973		January 1977	
	Total hours/week	Provider[b] hours/week	Total hours/week	Provider[b] hours/week
General support activities	12.75	5.00	20.25	7.50
'Emergency' activities	2.00	1.00	4.00	1.75
Communal activities	1.00	_[c]	1.00	_[c]
Housekeeping and administration	3.75	_[c]	2.75	_[c]
Total time	19.5	6.0	28.0	9.25
% total time outside of normal working hours	16		34	
Average alarm calls/ warden/week	0.7		3.5	
% 'genuine emergency' alarm calls	61		43	

Notes: a. Refers to 74 schemes common to both the 1973 and 1977 Devon surveys. Times were generally recorded to the nearest ¼ hour and hence the results are only presented to the same degree of accuracy. b. Provider activities are identified in Appendix 1. c. None of the communal, housekeeping or administrative activities used in the Devon survey were considered to be 'provider' activities (see Appendix 1).

bounds of the warden's original job commitment and current financial remuneration. While some wardens may be partially successful in keeping their total work time close to their original commitment by cutting back on housekeeping/administration or organiser chores, the average warden was increasingly putting in time *outside* of normal work hours (i.e. before breakfast, after evening meals or on Saturday or Sunday). Between 1973 and 1977 the average workload outside normal work hours *doubled* in percentage terms, rising to *one-third* of the total work time. This reflects a rapid growth in tenant dependency, especially during times when visiting community support services are usually unavailable.

Average alarm calls per warden per week rose *5 fold* between 1973 and 1977. This statistic also reflects the tenants growing support dependency on the warden for, as shown in Table 4.5, this increase is not mainly in emergency calls. The *percentage* of alarm calls classified as 'genuine emergencies' by the warden declined over the study period from 61 to 43.

The increased warden workload indicated by the figures of Table 4.5 is probably due *in part* to the increased dependency of the tenants. However, this increase appears greater than one might expect, given the change in tenant demographic characteristics and visiting support service use between 1973 and 1977 (see Table 3.10). While part of the increase in warden workload may be due to real decreases in tenant health and functional independence, some may also be due to an untrained but caring warden who is in part creating support demand and not responding to it. It takes a very skilled observer to identify the margin of a tenant's real need, and encourage the tenant to otherwise retain his or her functional independence. An untrained warden could be contributing to her own work overload by being unable to distinguish between 'real need' and 'false dependency'. Even if she can make this distinction she may not have the skill to reverse the group dynamics toward greater dependency which can occur among ageing and frail elderly living together.

In one sense it doesn't matter whether there is a growth in *real* dependency or *created* dependency. In either case the wardens are finding themselves in more of a provider role with greater workloads and working at hours of the day that interfere with tolerable working conditions and a 'normal' private life. Unless adequate on-site support is given to the warden we may see a growing disenchantment with the job of a warden. In fact, the increasing workload may already be contributing to increased warden turnover in Devon. The average annual turnover between 1963 and 1971 was less than 1 per cent;[9] the average annual turnover between 1973 and 1977 had risen to almost 10 per cent.

We feel that the findings of this section strongly support the arguments of Chapter 3 concerning the expansion in provision of sheltered housing. Sheltered housing must provide enough variety of entry points so that each housing type can attract both active and inactive elderly, and provide elderly with different life-styles a choice in living arrangements. If there is but one type of sheltered housing and the supply of that housing is far below elderly demand, managers will be forced to accommodate the most needy all at approximately the same functional dependency level, and will be unable to create or maintain schemes with a balance of active and inactive tenants. The original concept of sheltered housing will not survive under these conditions; it will over time, be inexorably pushed into a dependent housing environment. The interim victim will be the overworked warden, the final victim will be the underserved and prematurely dependent elderly.

Working Conditions

Various British panels and commissions have been assembled over the years to analyse the working conditions of wardens and to set standards for warden service.[10] As the warden concept evolved, British housing and social service analysts realised that the warden works under unique conditions and can easily be misused and abused. As early as 1962[11] studies were recognising that because the warden lives and works at the same place, and because her 'clients' frequently become like family, she can be pressed into 24-hours-a-day service. As we have already seen in this chapter, the needs of ageing tenants can easily create workloads and support tasks that far exceed the role of 'friendly neighbour'. This section considers the special working conditions of the warden. We look first at the allowed 'time off' from the job and whether this expands as the job grows more psychologically demanding. Second, we look at the financial remunerations received by wardens under different managements and different workloads.

Time Off

In the early days of sheltered housing, management naively assumed that the warden's job description involved only four to six hours of duties per day (making rounds, some cleaning, some socialising and calling in support services), and that the rest of her time was her own. They failed to see: (1) how even benign chores could fill far more time as tenants become more dependent; (2) how the list of chores would expand in time and skill demands as tenants aged; and (3) that the introduction of an alarm system meant that so long as the warden was home she was 'on call' 24 hours a day.

The pressures of being 'on call' in particular, require some institu-tionalised form of relief to guarantee time off whether the warden stays at home or goes out. She should be allowed time off without worrying about the safety and well being of her tenants. Without structured time off there can be literally no free time for many wardens. If they stay at home they are subject to disrupting calls, and without qualified relief many feel compelled to stay at home. A number of wardens interviewed in both the Devon and West Midlands samples had no adequate relief and said they were 'afraid' to leave the scheme or were anxious about their tenants while away, particularly when the tenants are left unattended or attended by a person who is not adequately trained or reliable.

If time off is left to be arranged by the warden and not provided by the management, it becomes an added chore. Too often it can become a low priority, constantly postponed by increasing tenant demands and needs. As schemes get older and acquire more frail tenants the anxiety about leaving a scheme unattended can grow. A situation can arise where a warden is taking less time off as her on-duty tasks become more demanding in time and energy. Such a situation could ultimately lead to a total breakdown of warden services.

It would seem logical that the emotional strain of being 'on-call' 24 hours a day should be formally recognised by management, and that clearly defined, ample off-duty periods with pay and assigned relief wardens should become standard policy. However, such policy is still often lacking. The 1972 Age Concern report[12] is used as a bench-mark for comparing current standards. This report proposed that between 1¼ and 2 days off per week should be the norm, recognising that in cases where 'outside hour' calls are common and the wardens daily workload is already high, even 2 days per week totally free of alarm calls or away from the scheme was not seen as unreasonabe. Table 4.6 displays official management policy on weekly time off for 135 West Midland wardens (8 management agencies) in 1978, 83 Devon wardens in 1973, and 119 Devon wardens in 1977 (9 management agencies).

The West Midlands data comes the closest to the 1972 standard for weekly time off. The majority of wardens got 1 day off per week plus 1 weekend per month. However, only 19 per cent of the West Midlands wardens got 2 official days off per week. The situation in Devon is far worse. In 1973, 84 per cent of the wardens had no official time off prescribed. While there is a marked improvement by 1977, over half are still below the recommended minimum time off set by the Age Concern report.[13]

The second and third parts of Table 4.6 show that while official policy may exist in some places it does not mean that management actually provides paid and reliable relief wardens. In the urban West Midlands almost 8 per cent of the wardens receive no help in securing weekday relief assistance according to the management; an additional 28 per cent must make the first effort to find a relief person and only if none can be found will management assist, *if asked*. When the 34 wardens who were directly surveyed were asked about this policy, 29 per cent said they received no help securing a relief warden no matter what management policy claimed, and almost 9 per cent said that only after exhausting their own sources for a relief person would management assist them. In the mainly rural setting of Devon in 1973

Table 4.6: Time Off and Relief Warden Arrangements in Devon and the West Midlands

	West Midlands March/April 1978		Devon April 1973		Devon January 1977	
	No.	%	No.	%	No.	%
Official weekly time off						
No official time off prescribed	0	—	70	84	36	30
Officially allowed 1 day/week or less	88[a]	65	3	4	31	26
Officially allowed more than 1 day/week but less than 2 days/week	22	16	10	12	24	20
Officially allowed 2 days/week or more	25	19			28	24
Total	135	100	83	100	119	100
Relief warden arrangements						
Management does not provide	2	2	80	96	40	34
Management provides only for annual holiday	10	6	0	0	54	45
Warden must make first attempt to find replacement (usually an able tenant)	37	27	0	0	0	0
Management provides paid relief warden	86	64	3	4	25	21
Total	135	100	83	100	119	100
Warden's opinion of responsibility for providing relief warden						
Management does not provide, warden must	10	29	Not asked		25	22
Management provides only for annual holiday	0	—			28	24
Management provides only for weekly days off	2	6			0	0
Warden must make first attempt to provide	3	9			0	0
Management provides	19	56			63	54
Total	34	100			116	100

Note: a. In 86 cases wardens receive 1 day/week off, plus 1 weekend off per month.

almost no managers provided relief warden arrangements. Although there is again a marked improvement by 1977, fully 79 per cent of the wardens received no help securing adequate relief on a weekly basis according to management. Oddly enough, warden opinion is not as critical of management, with less than half claiming that it was the management's responsibility to arrange for weekly relief wardens.

The poor working conditions of the warden are compounded by low pay, few, if any, increases in pay for increased services, and inadequate support as workload increases over time. These conditions are described in the next sub-section along with the policy implications of the overall working conditions of wardens.

Pay Scales

We have seen that wardens have increasingly higher entry level skills, experience longer work hours over time, and acquire increasing responsibilities as their tenants become less self-reliant. Nevertheless, the average British sheltered housing programme in the study areas tends to underpay wardens and has no formula or review mechanism to increase pay for variations in workload, changes in duties or increasing skills through on-the-job training. Neither the local sheltered housing managers or the national subsidy programmes have adequately addressed the question of a fair base salary or equitable increases in salary as workload and responsibilities change.

Table 4.7 shows salaries and housing benefits for 135 wardens in eight management programmes in the West Midlands. Most programmes are similar in that they offer a small weekly salary and free rent and utilities (i.e. public services) in the warden dwelling attached to the sheltered housing scheme. Beyond these basic similarities there are wide disparities in salary and benefits for similar job descriptions. When the variation in actual workload is considered the disparities in pay can become staggering. Comparing programmes 1 and 7 in Table 4.7 illustrates such a disparity. Wardens in programme 1 receive £8.00 per week plus rent, with no utilities. Several of these wardens administer schemes with 40 or more residents, put in more than 40 hours work a week, and have 10 to 15 years of service experience as a warden. In contrast, a warden in programme 7 receices more than three times this weekly salary plus rent *and* utilities. The typical scheme in programme 7 provides the warden with a new and roomy flat and is limited to only 30 resident units; the average warden in programme 7 works only 20 hours per week and has only five years of experience.

The management for programme 1 admitted that whenever possible

Table 4.7: Salary and Benefits for Wardens in Eight Housing Programmes in the West Midlands (as of 1978 except as noted)

Programme type	Number of wardens	Weekly salary in £	Housing utilities[e] and benefits	Variability for time on the job and service load
Public	42	8.00	Free rent, no utilities	None
Voluntary[a]	2	10.60[b]	Free rent and utilities	£200 per year plus £10 per unit in the scheme
Voluntary	6	14.50	Free rent and utilities	None
Voluntary	8	16.00	Free rent and utilities	Warden receives meals if she also cooks communal meals for tenants. Her family receives free meals if her husband does caretaking chores
Public	44	20.00	Free rent and utilities	None
Public	10	23.00	Free rent and utilities	None
Voluntary[a]	9	24.12[c]	Free rent and utilities	Salary tables vary by length of appointment and number of units in the scheme
Public	14	24.50[d]	No rent or utilities, instead a flat fee of £68/week	None
Total	135			
Weighted average weekly salary £16.61				

Notes: a. Based on 1977 figures. b. Based on 35 units per scheme. c. Assumes a median time period in length of employment and 31–35 units per scheme. d. Estimate after paying rent and utilities assuming a 3-bedroom house renting at £140/month and utilities at £35/month in 1978. e. I.e., public services such as electricity, gas, water.

they try to encourage the warden to clean common areas in the scheme
so they can pay her for that service at the rate they pay all cleaning
staff, because that rate is so much *higher* than what a warden receives!
In fact, the yearly salary for cleaning staff in this programme is higher
than a warden's equivalent pay in *all* the programmes included in Table
4.7. Thus the *average* warden assigned a permanent cleaning staff to
assist her with cleaning both common areas and tenant flats would be
paid far less than that domestic assistant. The rationale for the difference is that the domestic employee is a full 8 hour a day job while the
warden position is *not intended* to be full time. However, as we saw
in Table 4.1, the *average* category 2 warden works only 5 to 6 hours
less than a 40 hour week and in addition is on-call 24 hours a day and
must juggle time off around tenant needs that increasingly occur
outside normal working hours. Being a warden is truly a labour of love.

Not surprisingly there are signs that wardens are not happy with
aspects of their jobs. Earlier in this chapter we pointed out the growing
turnover rate among wardens in the Devon sample. As the sheltered
housing programme continues to age, and the workload in older
schemes continues to increase, we can expect higher rates of warden
turnover which could threaten the continuity of warden services to
elderly residents. This continuity of service is an important contribution the warden concept introduces to long-term independent living
for the elderly. A warden's success is built on a foundation of long-term
friendship and trust. It pays greatest dividends as elderly tenants
become more support service dependent. Unlike other support service
providers, wardens do not perform a specific task at a constant daily
rate. Warden services grow over time both with the increased disability
of ageing tenants and the increased trust and friendship the tenants
form with the warden. This trust and friendship cannot easily be
replaced if that warden leaves when the workload becomes intolerable.
The low scale of rewards and growing frustration can also become
public knowledge, deterring the best warden candidates from ever
seeking a career in long-term care for the elderly.

The variability in the wardens' workload and responsibilities is
beginning to be reflected in variable pay scales. As shown in Table
4.7, two of the eight housing managers interviewed in the West
Midlands increased warden salaries as the number of units the warden
must look after increases. One of these programmes also increases
salaries based on the length of the warden's appointment. This latter
increase reflects the investment in friendship and trust that develop
between warden and tenant as well as the real likelihood that the

warden's workload will increase as residents age. It also reflects the additional skills and expertise gained on the job and through special courses taken outside of working hours. However, even these more progressive pay systems contain no direct incentives for wardens to improve their skills over time.

There are two ways adequately to support and compensate increasing warden workloads and responsibilities. One is through salary and benefit increases, the second is by providing additional staff and resources to help with such additional workload. These are not trade-offs, as both types of support and reward are equally important. Higher pay alone is not the solution when the increased workload is too great or the type of additional work is inappropriate for a single warden. Increased support service resources alone do not compensate for the increased responsibilities of the warden as on-site service co-ordinator or the increase in the workload after hours, when support personnel are not available.

Adequate support resources and increasing pay and benefits may not be enough to prevent increases in warden turnover as schemes age and the type of workload and responsibilities change. Some wardens may feel that the job has changed so much from what they were originally appointed for that they must either find a new warden position with responsibilities and workload akin to what they originally sought or, if this is no longer possible, cease being a warden altogether. For such wardens neither additional support staff nor higher salary and benefits would make a difference. To what degree this is occurring is not clear. The Devon and West Midlands samples consisted of active wardens, not former wardens who have quit for one reason or another. What does come through, loud and clear, from the wardens interviewed in our study is that management must provide adequate and timely support services and assistance as the workload within a scheme increases, if the original warden concept is to remain viable. This support service role of sheltered housing management is quite complex. It involves monitoring the warden workload regularly. It involves the education and training of wardens to adapt to their changing role. It means careful co-ordination and liaising with social and medical support services in the community to assure that they are present when needed, understood and fit into a programme of assisted independent living. It possibly means developing an in-house peripatetic service staff and semi-permanent assistant warden staff which can be dispatched to assist schemes with an episodic or median term site-management overload. Finally, it means education and liaising with hospitals, residential homes, nursing homes and day care programmes to co-ordinate the episodic and permanent transfer of very sick and disabled sheltered housing tenants. This all important role of programme management is discussed in Chapter 5.

Effective and Ineffective Warden Types[14]

The West Midlands managers were asked to evaluate the performance of their wardens and differentiate between their 'star' wardens and poorest wardens. Four warden types were identified from among the 135 wardens assessed by seven managers; they can be summarised as composite profiles.

The first type is the *model warden*. Ninety-five per cent (n = 128) of the wardens fit this definition and 30 per cent (n = 40) were considered 'star' wardens who are exceptionally gifted at their work. There was total agreement among the managers on what constituted a model warden; it is *someone who keeps the residents independent and actively engaged in society*. Some of the key nuances to this theme were: (a) someone who does not overcare for the residents; (b) someone who provides just enough extra care to keep the residents in an independent unit from becoming unnecessarily dependent on any support service, be it from the warden, a relative, a friend, a neighbour, or visiting domiciliary and professional staff; and (c) someone who makes full use of communal space and activities, especially to attract elderly from outside to social functions held within the scheme in order to help keep the residents socially engaged; and (d) someone who takes residents out on trips or finds group trips for residents to join, and someone who is constantly encouraging the residents to get out on their own.

Three different concepts of an ineffective or negative warden emerged from the management responses. Only 5 per cent (n = 7) of the wardens fit into this group. The first type within this group is *the warden who undercares*. For whatever reason, these wardens are lazy and do not care for their job or the elderly residents. As a result, they do not make the required daily rounds, do not provide the necessary setting and activities to keep the residents socially engaged and do not provide an atmosphere of trust and confidence. The elderly residents do not confide in these wardens and the wardens are usually incapable of identifying any changes in the support needs of the residents.

The next type of ineffective warden is *the elderly dominated warden*. Such wardens lack self confidence and assertiveness. They can easily be intimidated and manipulated by the residents. They often feel sorry for the elderly because of their advanced age and frailty. These wardens may fear, or have trouble understanding and accepting, their own ageing. They cannot say 'no' to resident demand; they are like a permissive parent with a young child. They are truly overworked, and don't like it, but don't understand why. They are constantly looking to place the blame for their lack of control on certain residents or the management for lack of support. They provide many social events and activities for the residents, but the residents provide very little input and there is no strong sense of community within the facility. Residents quickly learn that they can demand extra care from such wardens even when they don't need it. They can easily become dependent on these warden services.

The last type in the ineffective group are *wardens who overcare by choice*. These wardens are typical of the 'old school' of wardens who see themselves more as matrons of their own personal old folks home. They can often work 80-hour weeks and love their job. They provide a great number of social activities but retain tight control over all organisation and planning. They interfere in the privacy of the tenants, as they do not accept the concept of independent living. They provide too much care, often making the residents dependent on their presence. They see a tenant's leaving to go to a more dependent care setting as a personal defeat. Thus they often do not call in outside support when residents need help and fail to evaluate objectively when it is best for a given resident to leave, both for the good of that resident and the scheme as a whole. They often play favourites among residents. While not always creating an institutional feeling within the scheme, they constantly seek to be the central and dominant figure in the environment.

The Emerging Warden Service Roles

Controlled longitudinal studies of equivalent sheltered housing designs and elderly populations with and without a resident warden are required in order to arrive at an accurate picture of the warden's contribution to assisted independent living. However, based on what is already known about the support needs of the semi-independent elderly, the resident warden can provide several unique and critical services.

The Warden as Facilitator of Social Activities

Not all wardens provide their residents with opportunities for social engagement, although 73 per cent in the West Midlands study did. When comparing the truly gifted ('star') wardens with the rest of the wardens, as identified by the managers in the interview sample, the greater talent and energy of the gifted wardens becomes evident. Not only do they make sure some level of social engagement is found for their residents, but in a majority of cases the warden involves the residents in planning and administering communal social activities. This involvement includes weekly social events, bringing entertainment to the site, and taking trips away from the site. Just as there is a progression in the quality of social organisation from schemes run by gifted wardens to schemes run by other wardens, it seems logical that there would be a significant drop in social activity moving from a sheltered housing scheme with resident wardens to schemes without resident wardens. As difficult as it is for the average warden to organise and sustain social activities for residents, it would be even more difficult if the residents were dependent on an occasional visiting social worker or their own organisational talents. The difficulty of organising and sustaining social involvement can only increase where a majority of the elderly residents are disabled by advancing age and frailty. Yet it is the housebound elderly who rely most heavily on communal activities to remain socially engaged and to prevent social isolation.

The Warden as Support Service Advocate

Despite the fact that requesting support when needed is a universal task for all wardens, not all wardens complete the task with equal success. In most large urban areas there are a wide variety of disjointed and overlapping support services, and the demand for those services almost always exceeds the supply. To be able to identify and secure the right services quickly is a skill most wardens acquire, some better than others.

The West Midlands wardens were asked if they were able to obtain support services for their elderly residents within 24 hours of when the services are first needed; 80 per cent of the management identified 'star' wardens said they could, compared with only 53 per cent for other wardens. Among the reasons some wardens get services to respond faster is because they understand the service delivery system better — they know who to call and what to say. A request by some wardens is also respected more than a request by other wardens. In the first case, a service manager may dispatch the service personnel based solely on the telephone request of the warden. In the latter case an inspection to verify the support service need may be made before the service is granted. In an effort to differentiate among the many requests for service, some service agencies require a formal request from the resident's doctor or social worker. As with the support service managers, doctors or social workers may respect the service requests of some wardens without a special visit to the resident, whilst not doing so as regards requests from other wardens. Finally, some support services are so poorly managed that services are not forthcoming even after a doctor or social worker's request. In this case, the management of the housing authority or association must intervene on behalf of the resident, but managers are not likely to intervene unless a strong and effective case is made by the warden.

Overall, the more knowledgeable, forceful and respected the warden, the more effective an advocate she will be in securing support services for her residents. As a support service advocate one would expect the average warden to have a *far better* success rate than could be realised from the private efforts of a disabled elderly resident or the resident's friends or family.

The Warden as Paid Family Proxy

As one author has pointed out, being a warden is not a job, 'it's a way of life'.[15] The warden's home is her place of work, and the residents are her extended family. As one of us has pointed out elsewhere,[16] the vast majority of wardens are actively and enthusiastically involved in maintaining the independence of their elderly residents and would have it no other way.

In sheltered housing, the elderly and the warden can interrelate as fellow residents, friends and neighbours. This is a uniquely different relationship from that likely to evolve between the elderly and the support service personnel they encounter living in a sheltered housing scheme without a warden or living in a nursing or residential home. What are the chances of forming an equal status relationship with a visiting social worker or public nurse with a monthly case load of perhaps 50 to 100 persons? What kind of shared experiences can evolve in a nursing home when the environment is designed for staff convenience and efficiency and not for resident independence?

The close daily proximity of warden and elderly residents is bound to result in numerous shared experiences that have little, if anything, to do with the elderly resident's dependence (if any) on the warden. They may shop together or meet while shopping, chat together over tea in the common rooms, or fold laundry together. It is this reciprocal good neighbour relationship, in advance of an episodic illness or crippling disability, that emotionally bonds a warden and elderly resident. In more cases than not, this relationship pays off as the elderly become more dependent. They gain a family proxy who will look out for their interests better than any other support service personnel.

Policy Conclusion

The present nonprofessional British warden will require increasingly improved financial compensation, back-up assistance, peer and professional consultation, and on-the-job training as she faces an older, more frail and disabled resident population. Despite the evolution toward more skilled support and increasing complexity in the warden's tasks, the evidence from our Devon and West Midlands studies indicates that the majority of current lay wardens *are* capable of handling the expanding responsibilities and need *not* be replaced by a more profes- sionally-schooled warden model, *if* an adequate supply and variety of sheltered housing entry points are available to prevent an imbalance of inactive and frail elderly in any given scheme. If a balance of active and inactive elderly cannot be maintained, and schemes evolve to become care environments, it is questionable if a totally unskilled 'friendly neighbour' is the best co-ordinator of the housing environment.

The evidence to date, and we emphasise *to date*, suggests that the lay warden remains an effective day-to-day contact for the elderly residents so long as there is a balance of active and inactive elderly and the inactive elderly are able to maintain an independent household with outside aid. The needs of the residents usually grow slowly over many months or years, and the lay warden is usually able to grow and learn with the changing demands of the job. Many acquire new skills as they are needed, without losing the most important attributes of neighbour/ familial compatibility with, and affection for, the residents.

Many lay wardens of schemes originally made up of totally active elderly gain the new skills they need to handle inactive tenants through personal initiative and dedication to their job; those who do not, need to be identified quickly. Some unskilled wardens could gain the required new skills if housing managers would provide opportunities through relief time to take appropriate courses. Other wardens cannot acquire such new skills and must be relocated to jobs overseeing totally active elderly, probably not in sheltered housing if all schemes are eventually going to involve a mix of active and inactive tenants. Management must continue to improve screening techniques and criteria in order to identify the best applicants among the candidates for positions as warden. This includes bearing in mind the long-term need for job flexibility and adaptability on the part of the warden. Screening mechanisms are needed that accurately discriminate between candidates on innate intelligence, common sense and a secure and stable personality.

As the warden's job becomes more complex, housing managers will also have to create new professional staff advisers to the wardens on various social, administrative and paramedical problems. Where these special advisers already exist they have initiated monthly forums where wardens can meet and share problems and their possible solutions. The advisers also arrange site visits so wardens can observe first hand the innovative programmes their peers have developed, and design types of special short courses for wardens.

While we feel the lay warden can adapt to the growing needs of her tenants with proper back-up support and a full range of sheltered housing entry points, we should not overlook the benefits of a more professionally skilled candidate. We tend to agree with the widely held belief of many maangers that professional training and skills might be a liability and source of frustration for the warden.[17] We feel that the professional warden might be encumbered by professional jargon and might not be as likely to share important socio-economic ties with the residents, or could become frustrated by day-to-day duties that do not allow them to practise their particular skills. We believe that the more skilled the warden becomes, the more prone she is to create an overly supportive environment encouraging dependence on her skills and training, and that this would be the antithesis of the assisted independent living concept. However, we have found no empirical evidence that any of these assumed 'professional liabilities' exist. In fact there is no reason why a person trained to identify health changes and social welfare needs wouldn't be better suited for the job so long as they possess the warmth and common sense required of any warden. A good deal of our hesitancy in recommending a professionally skilled warden has been the result of observing new schemes where the tenants have been relatively active and independent. Such settings may indeed be inappropriate for a professional nurse and/or community organiser. However, given the obvious need for all schemes to be balanced between active and inactive elderly from the outset, and the likelihood that all schemes are going to experience at least episodic periods of dependency and stress overloads, the professinally trained warden makes good sense. In fact there is an inherent contradiction in the current British warden system. It calls for lay wardens who receive low salaries, who share socio-economic background and interests with their residents, and who are able to develop close personal ties with them. At the same time, it is desirable for the wardens not to become overprotective of their most frail and disabled residents at the cost of normal duties to the more able residents. This level of objectivity to job priorities would be difficult for even the most highly trained and much higher paid nurse or social worker.

The Viability of the British Warden System in the United States

The British system of minimal service sheltered housing with resident wardens could be an important model for long-term assisted independent living programmes throughout the rest of Western Europe and North America, especially in countries such as the United States, just beginning to embark on assisted independent living programmes. There are, however, a number of historical differences between British and American housing programmes, and numerous demographic differences between the elderly populations of the two societies, that raise questions about the viability of transferring the British programme to the United States without modifications. As we have just discussed, the British system *may* benefit by shifting from lay wardens to professionally trained wardens while retaining the basic 'friendly neighbour' character of the job. Hiring *only* professionally trained wardens may be a short-range imperative in the United States. As suggested by the statistics we presented in Chapter 1, the United States may have waited too long to begin its sheltered housing programme. There is already a substantial backlog of public housing and institutionalised elderly with advanced levels of frailty and functional impairments who have no viable alternative except sheltered housing if they are to retain or regain some functional independence. These elderly will have to be given priority for sheltered housing. Even if they are integrated with younger more independent elderly, the presence of these more dependent elderly may prohibit the hiring of untrained wardens who could be trained on the job. Warden duties in most American schemes might require more specialised and professionally trained wardens from the start.

New Commonwealth immigrants to Great Britain seldom move to sheltered housing upon reaching old age. They apparently prefer to live with extended family or return to their native country. As a result, British sheltered housing schemes draw elderly residents from a far more homogeneous population than would the United States.

Some of the places where American housing programmes already provide long-term support similar to sheltered housing, without identifying it as such, are: better small town nursing homes, small county housing authorities and religiously sponsored housing and support service councils. In these cases the elderly and the support staff make up a very homogeneous group. However, in the majority of American sheltered housing schemes the residents will be drawn from a far more heterogeneous pool according to race, religion, income and life-style. Thus the task of socially integrating residents may be far more difficult. Here again, American sheltered housing might require a warden with professional training from the outset.

The British are willing to build small schemes of 30 to 40 units in existing residential neighbourhoods. In contrast, Americans have been unwilling to build such small schemes, arguing that developmental and overhead costs only warrant schemes of at least 100 units. The sheer number of residents in such large schemes prohibits the single resident warden concept. The physical size of American schemes often requires vertical development that tends to destroy ties between residents and often requires sponsors to seek elderly residents from a larger potential pool. This can further prevent residents from sharing neighbourhood ties and ethnic or socio-economic homogeneity. America also has relatively fewer viable neighbourhoods that warrant small sheltered housing projects. Many of the older American inner-city areas have been depleted of community infrastructure by continuous low-density suburban housing development. The elderly have been 'left behind' in neighbourhoods without adequate shopping or transportation nearby, but with high crime rates and air and noise pollution, all of which obstruct independent living and imply more support services.

In order for minimal service sheltered housing to work, the warden must have access to well developed visiting social service system in the community. This would require more and better visiting services than are currently available in many urban and most rural areas of America. It would also require better co-ordination and planning between local housing and social service agencies. The only alternative would be to fund a separate peripatetic service system just for sheltered housing within each local housing management system, or to develop in-dependent service-rich sheltered housing sites. The latter seems to be the option of least resistance in the United States. Given the current trends in sheltered housing development in the United States, management would have to provide the resident warden with many more

rewards and reinforcements than the British counterpart in order to
attract the quality of personnel commensurate with the great complexity and importance of the job.

Developing larger service-rich sheltered housing schemes to meet
some immediate *short-term* demands in the United States seems
both prudent and logical; however, this approach should not be the
sole basis of a *long-term* sheltered housing programme. Even with all
the aforementioned differences between British and American elderly
populations and housing and support services systems, the long-term
needs of the elderly in the two countries are similar. There is a need
for a continuum of entry points into sheltered housing in order to
provide choices and to retain a balance of active and inactive elderly.
There is also a greater long-term need for minimum service as opposed
to service-rich sheltered housing, because, as was shown in Chapter 1,
more elderly seek housing similar to the conventional housing they
have known all their lives, and because most elderly will not suffer
support needs severe enough to warrant service-rich environments.
The British resident warden model is, in our opinion, the most
effective for minimal service sheltered housing. Even if it requires
new management programmes and sponsors and far better peripatetic
support services, these are long-term component programme investments worth making. The following chapter discusses several possible
management programme alternatives.

Notes

1. Butler, A., Oldman, C. and Wright, R., *Sheltered Housing for the elderly:
A Critical Review*, Research monograph, Department of Social Policy and
Administration, The University of Leeds, 1979, 175 pp; Cowley, R.J., *Caring
for the elderly in sheltered housing: a Report of the Anchor Extra Care
Study Group*. Anchor Housing Association, Oxford, 1977; Ministry of
Housing and Local Government. *Housing standards and costs: Accommodation
specially designed for old people*. Circular 82/69, HMSO, London, 1969.
2. Butler, A., Oldman, C. and Wright, R., *Sheltered Housing for the
elderly: A Critical Review*; Age Concern, *Role of the Warden in grouped
housing*. Report of a Working Party, Chairman: A. Wilcocks, London, 1972.
3. Boldy, D., 'Is sheltered housing a good thing?' In *Some Unresolved aspects
of sheltered housing for the elderly and disabled*. Institute of Social Welfare,
1977, p. 7.
4. Institute of Housing Managers, 'Role of the Warden in sheltered housing
schemes: Observations of the Institute of Housing Managers'. *Housing Monthly*,
1975, 11, pp. 12–14.
5. Butler, Oldman and Wright, *Sheltered Housing for the elderly: A Critical
Review*.

6. Boldy, D., 'A study of the wardens of grouped dwellings for the elderly', *Social and Economic Administration*, 1976, 10, pp. 59-67.

7. Age Concern, *Role of the Warden in grouped housing*.

8. See, e.g., Boldy, 'A study of the wardens of grouped dwellings for the elderly'.

9. Boldy, D., Abel, P. and Carter, K., *The Elderly in grouped dwellings: A profile*. Institute of Biometry and Community Medicine, University of Exeter, Exeter, Devon, 1973, p. 36.

10. A landmark report was: Age Concern, *Role of the Warden in grouped housing*.

11. Ministry of Housing and Local Government, *Grouped flatlets for old people: A sociological study*. Design Bulletin 2, HMSO, London, 1962.

12. Age Concern, *Role of the Warden in grouped housing*.

13. Ibid.

14. This and the next section are derived from: Heumann, L.F., 'Sheltered Housing for the elderly: The role of the British warden'. *Gerontologist*, 1980, 20, pp. 318-29.

15. Chippindale, A., 'Society at work: A Warden's day'. *New Society*, 7 September 1978, pp. 508-9.

16. Boldy, 'A study of the wardens of grouped dwellings for the elderly'.

17. Heumann, 'Sheltered housing for the elderly: The role of the British warden'.

5 MANAGEMENT OF SHELTERED HOUSING

In this chapter we analyse sheltered housing management and recommend changes which we feel are necessary for the long-term success and vitality of assisted independent living. Our findings diverge from current practice and prevailing recommendations for change in sheltered housing management, both in Great Britain and the United States. Based on our analysis, we find that the concept of assisted independent living, as embodied in the older more established British sheltered housing programme, is being jeopardised by management practices at the local level. The success of sheltered housing is inevitably and unavoidably linked to other housing, health and social services that either complement, supplement or contribute to the sheltered housing service. Hence the management of all these interlocking elderly support services should be co-ordinated. Instead they are fragmented and disjointed; often working in ignorance of, or at cross purposes with, one another.

In Chapter 3 we found that the British sheltered housing system has evolved a variety of entry points by varying the degree of on-site support services, communal living and scheme size. However, individual local sheltered housing managers rarely, if ever, provide an adequate variety of entry points. Just as there is no planning mechanism to determine what type of sheltered housing is needed by the local elderly population, so too there is no mechanism to determine the total number of units within *each type* needed to retain an appropriate vacancy rate and reasonable waiting list. In Chapter 4 we saw that few managers have developed an adequate allocation and transfer process to keep a balance between active and inactive tenants in each scheme, and few managers have satisfactorily co-ordinated with health and social service providers to meet the needs of their expanding and ageing sheltered housing population.

Given this picture, we are perplexed by those recommended management reforms that only address prevailing management activities within existing fragmented administrations. Whilst we agree that many such reforms are necessary, we feel that the first priority should be attached to correcting the imbalance between the relatively small supply and large demand/need for sheltered housing units. Only after an adequate supply of units and alternative entry points are available can

160

management goals of retaining a balance of active and frail tenants and stability of warden (and other support) functions and workloads, be achieved. Without such an adequate and diverse supply, sheltered housing management will continue to be faced with incremental reactions to short-term emergencies related to long waiting lists and an ageing tenant population. We also conclude that this supply imbalance must be corrected across the entire spectrum of elderly assisting living, and that planning for the number and types of entry points must be co-ordinated by all relevant services.

Managers of the fledgling American elderly housing programme can learn a great deal from the British experience. British sheltered housing is a successful programme that is outgrowing its *ad hoc* and fragmented management system; in fact the continued success of sheltered housing may be jeopardised if the current management system does not become more consolidated and co-ordinated. In the United States, the 'programme' and 'on-site' manager are often the same person. Here, the concept of assisted independent living is threatened because too much management is being focused at the site. The apparent reasons for this centralised on-site management is the newness of the concept, combined with the urgent need for assisted independent living units. There are as yet no national associations to provide management guidance to local nonprofit developments, and even the largest public housing authorities are only now building their first assisted independent living schemes. Therefore, the person designated as the on-site manager is often the one most knowledgeable about planning for the entire programme.

As we reported in Chapters 3 and 4, the typical American scheme is quite large and service-rich (e.g. 100 units or more with meals, housekeeping and other services provided by on-site staff). As a result, on-site management is usually given to a professional career manager. The role of this manager includes long-range planning of 'the programme', advising a board of directors, and supervision of the staff and business operations of the scheme.[1] Where the British warden is typically a non-professional resident housewife with no central management role, a recent study of American on-site managers found that 72 per cent were male, they averaged 51 years of age, 66 per cent were college graduates, 23 per cent held graduate degrees, and 12 per cent were currently pursuing higher degrees in business administration and gerontology.[2]

Where the British management system requires greater consolidation and co-ordination, the American system needs to diversify and decentralise authority. This is likely to happen as the American programme evolves and expands. Now is not too soon for planners in America and elsewhere to take heed of the many management problems found in the older, yet growing, British programmes.

In the first two sections of this chapter we deal with the programme management problems of size and diversity that predispose all problems of site management — providing an adequate number and types of sheltered housing units. The third and fourth sections discuss management reforms of the two most important site management tasks, allocation of candidates to unit vacancies and management of the on-site support staff — in particular the resident warden. The fifth section addresses the central issue of co-operation and co-ordination of sheltered housing management with contributing service management, and ultimately the co-ordination of long-range analysis and planning by all services involved in assisting the elderly. The concluding section compares our proposals for management reform with alternatives discussed by other analysts.

The Need to Provide an Adequate Number of Units

Almost every manager interviewed in the Devon and West Midlands sample was at least aware of the importance of keeping a balance between active and inactive tenants in each scheme (see Chapter 3), and of the threat of a 'drift' towards dependent living for all tenants if a balance is not maintained. There was also a clear understanding that the greater number of inactive tenants the greater the chance of overloading the resident warden and undermining the very goal of assisted *independent* living. Nevertheless, most of the managers in our sample stated they have difficulty maintaining a balance of active and inactive tenants in their schemes.

Our study did not specifically probe the reasons why managers had difficulty maintaining a balance in their schemes, but this aspect was explained in a national study of the allocation of sheltered housing units.[3] The study, conducted in 1977, surveyed 72 housing departments and 35 social service departments in England and Wales. As with our sample, Bytheway and James found that most of the managers surveyed were aware of the importance of maintaining a proper balance of frail and active tenants in each scheme, but they had considerable difficulty doing so.[4] The reasons given were that despite allocation procedures which sought a balance, 'a majority of new tenants [being assigned vacancies] have health problems'.[5] The apparent reason so many persons with health problems are allocated a unit is because the normal allocation process is frequently bypassed, with almost half the vacancies being filled with 'persons in emergency situations'.[6] So many of the vacancies have to be filled by people with emergency health problems because so few vacancies occur relative to the large waiting lists. In short, demand/need far exceeds supply.

The average British municipality accommodates about 5 per cent of its elderly in sheltered housing with, according to Bytheway and James, an average waiting time for sheltered housing of three years.[7] This is far too long for any elderly to wait, let alone elderly with emergency health problems. The only municipality with reasonable waiting time in the West Midlands sample provided sheltered housing to about 16 per cent of its elderly population (including private sector wardens who visit elderly living in privately owned or rented housing). The waiting time in this case was six months on average. Enough units to house 16 per cent of the elderly is probably close to the supply generally required to provide an adequate vacancy rate and meet elderly sheltered housing need. In Chapter 1, using conservative assumptions, we estimate that close to 15 per cent of the elderly could benefit from sheltered housing (see Table 1.6 and accompanying text).

While management feels they are more or less compelled to allocate many of the limited number of vacancies to people with health emergencies, wardens are feeling overloaded. In Chapters 3 and 4 we document this drift toward increased tenant dependency and increased warden workload. The longitudinal data on Devon schemes covering 1973 and 1977, show a rise in the extent of support service receipt (Table 3.10), and in particular in the workload of wardens, especially outside of 'normal' working hours (Table 4.5).

In a study of 608 tenants of 51 sheltered housing schemes in England and Wales, Butler[8] found that only 41 per cent of the elderly moved to sheltered housing for health related reasons eight years previously, while two years previously 69 per cent moved for health reasons. He also found a correlation between the scarcity of sheltered housing and the age of tenants, i.e. places with a low supply of sheltered housing tend to admit older tenants.

Thus it appears that the quality of management of sheltered housing depends fundamentally on a considerable increase in the number of units in the sheltered housing stock. Current management problems in areas such as tenancy allocation and warden support are inseparable from, and predisposed by, the relatively low supply of sheltered housing.

The Need to Provide an Adequate Number of Entry Points

The second problem of programme management that predisposes all
site related management problems is providing adequate *diversity* in
sheltered housing entry points. In Chapter 3 we showed that the typical
housing authority or association provides only limited choice of
sheltered housing types. Often entire market areas, especially rural
areas, provide only one type of sheltered housing. Figure 3.1 illustrates
how sheltered housing types can vary by the amount of on-site services
provided, the amount of communal living and scheme size. While many
varieties of sheltered housing are possible, each local market would only
have to provide a few choices to meet the needs and tastes of local
elderly. All the entry point types could be designed to provide a similar
range of support and all could require termination at similar levels of
resident functional dependence. On the other hand, and perhaps more
likely, minimal and typical support levels could vary by scheme type.
Thus by providing an appropriate number of units and entry point
choices, sheltered housing could attract and acommodate different
personalities, life-style tastes and support needs. This would give both
the elderly and those in charge of allocation the flexibility needed to
keep a balance of active and frail tenants in each scheme.

For the elderly, a choice of entry points means they retain an
important element of control over their lives at a point when they are
making a very difficult and stress-related move. Having a choice means
they can visit and perhaps even sleep at alternative scheme types and
pick the one that suits them best. Feeling secure about their choice may
mean that fewer elderly will postpone their move until a crisis situation
arises. It may also result in quicker, less traumatic adaptation to
communal living arrangements. All of this could lessen the workload
of the wardens and strengthen the tenant support network within
schemes.

A choice of entry points also brings greater flexibility and meaning
to the allocation process. Greater flexibility, in that not all the medical
emergencies need to be concentrated in the same scheme type. Greater
flexibility, in that medical emergencies need not be the main reason
for moving to sheltered housing – a particular scheme can be
chosen for a different social, medical or environmental support
regime. Greater meaning, in that the allocation process could truly
serve to counsel elderly candidates and help them match their social,
health and environmental needs and tastes with the appropriate
sheltered housing environment. With a combination of an adequate

number of sheltered housing units and entry points, the allocation staff may even be able to become actively involved in outreach programmes such as explaining sheltered housing choices to the elderly community.

The logic and importance of providing an adequate array of sheltered housing entry points has not escaped most managers. However, the typical manager lacks the resources, staff skills and planning capabilities to address the issue comprehensively. In the West Midlands we observed several managers who were diversifying their sheltered housing entry points in incremental phases based on their own agency's perception of need and ability to respond. While this is better than doing nothing, these managers can have an erroneous perception of need priorities for the service area as a whole and duplicate each other's efforts. The result can be a surplus of entry points in some sub-areas and among some housing choices and shortages in other areas and among other choices.

To develop an appropriate number of entry points and units requires a comprehensive market area plan and co-ordinated implementation of that plan by all the agencies that develop, manage and service sheltered housing. Multi-agency cooperation in analysis and planning is central to many aspects of sheltered housing management and is discussed in detail later in this chapter.

Analysis of the Existing Allocation Process

In many ways the allocation process in use by British sheltered housing managers today is the immediate cause of the 'drift' toward more frail and inactive tenants. The allocation process in sheltered housing is meant to serve two different client groups which have conflicting needs. There is the group awaiting assignment to a sheltered housing vacancy, the most needy of whom have real health 'emergencies' which require an assisted housing environment. There is also the group residing in a sheltered housing scheme; their most urgent need may be a new tenant who is active and can help organise and run informal social and support activities (at the very least, someone who imposes no additional burdens on the warden). It appears, from our observation of allocation procedures and those of other recent studies,[9] that the allocation process generally pays little attention to the needs of sheltered housing schemes and tends to favour the selection of that person on the waiting list judged to be in greatest need.

The concept of assisted independent living, as embodied in sheltered housing, requires a community of elderly tenants who can exert some control over the organisation of the scheme, its social life and life-style. This requires a certain number of active and engaged tenants. Without them, the organisational control of the scheme will pass to the support service staff, creating a dependent, not an independent, environment. By considering only the needs of candidates on the waiting list, and choosing those in greatest need of assisted independent living, the allocation process can easily destroy that independent living environment for both the candidate and those already residing in the scheme. It does not matter if the allocation criteria used considers housing needs, social needs or health needs, if it considers only the needs of the waiting list population and not the needs of the sheltered housing scheme, there is a very good chance it will eventually defeat the purpose of sheltered housing.

Figure 5.1[10] illustrates the interdependence of the various support and other aspects of sheltered housing and how, in theory at least, they should affect the selection process for new tenants. It shows that there are several interactive factors that should influence who is allocated a given sheltered housing vacancy. First and foremost are the current tenants and their changing pattern of tenancy. The ageing process within the scheme is going to affect self-support or independence maintenance by individual tenants. The more tenants who are frail and disabled the fewer who can care for themselves. It is also going to affect tenant care activities for one another. This does not just mean domiciliary support in episodic or emergency cases, it means daily spontaneous and organised support with social activity as well. The more inactive tenants, the less chance for spontaneous social activity within the scheme. The ageing process will also affect the composition of the scheme: the number of couples, the ratio of men-to-women, the number of elderly friends visiting the scheme, the rate of turnover, etc. A group made up of all women, few visitors and low turnover can lead to group despondency and disengagement. In theory, the allocation system should take all these factors into account in replacing a vacancy.

Second, the allocation process must consider the resources for care and support within each scheme. A steady decline in independent living will affect the type of support resources provided by other tenants, will affect the volume and character of the workload falling on the warden, and will have implications on the volume and character of visiting health and social services. The allocation system employed

Figure 5.1: The Grouped Dwelling (Sheltered Housing) Scheme as a System of Care for the Elderly

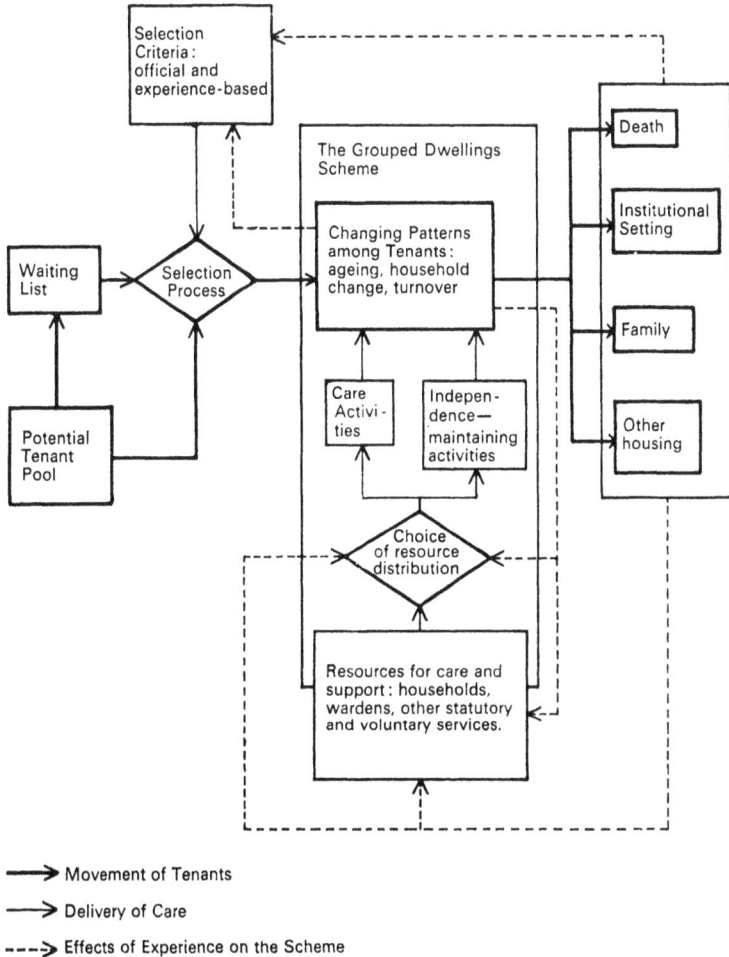

Source: Boldy, D., Abel, P. and Carter, K., *The Elderly in Grouped Dwellings: A Profile*. Institute of Biometry and Community Medicine, University of Exeter, 1973.

should bear in mind these various effects of changing tenancy. For example, it is possible for the warden workload and visiting services to increase and replace a declining tenant support network without creating undue stress on the providers. However, the presence of too many well-meaning providers could still unintentionally replace tenant control of scheme activities.

Finally, the allocation process must take into account the potential tenant pool and its interrelationship with the changing tenancy of the scheme. Those in charge of allocations must be aware of the changes in age and housing tastes in the general population, and how these changes are likely to affect demand for a vacancy in a given scheme. Each scheme, and eventually the entire programme, presents an image to prospective tenants. If a scheme loses its independent identity and tenant control, or even appears inactive and sedentary, it may lose its attractiveness as assisted *independent* living.

Taking all these chacteristics of a scheme and the supply sources for new tenants and support services into consideration is difficult. It becomes even more difficult when the allocation system must consider multiple sheltered housing entry points. Not represented in Figure 5.1 are variations in sheltered housing type which can vary the amount of tenant social and domiciliary support, the ease or difficulty in organising and maintaining activities, the type and amount of persons who desire each type of housing, and the amount and type of support personnel present. The allocation process under these circumstances requires a staff willing to assemble and match fairly detailed information about the prospective client and the prospective scheme. This cannot be handled satisfactorily by a single officer of a single management agency or even by a panel of professionals working within a single agency. The allocation process, like the development of the right number and types of schemes, is a market area function requiring the co-operation of all agencies involved in the provision of sheltered housing services. What is required are allocation panels made up of housing management, social work and medical professionals along with representatives of residential/nursing homes and warden's services, using the input of a prospective tenant's personal doctor where necessary. Such panels provide the best chance of finding an allocation solution that satisfies both the macro needs of the sheltered housing and support service programmes in the region, and the micro needs of a given scheme and its prospective tenant pool.

In the light of what we believe is needed, let us analyse the allocation methods currently in use.

Housing Priorities: Stock Utilisation and Tenant Need

Probably the most common method of allocating sheltered housing in Great Britain today is that employed by most housing departments. These housing departments define sheltered housing as part of their overall housing stock and their primary goal is its maximum utilisation. This includes the removal or improvement of substandard stock and placing persons in the most suitable and decent housing environment possible. Their allocation of households is based, first and foremost, on housing needs and housing priorities as opposed to medical or social considerations.

(a) They typically use just one waiting list for all prospective tenants, both elderly and nonelderly.

(b) They often employ a common 'points system' to prioritise households on the waiting list. The typical points system is based on need related to physical housing (e.g. living in overcrowded or undercrowded conditions, being the subject of slum clearance and loss of a dwelling, living in a unit that requires sharing a kitchen or bathroom, living in a unit without complete plumbing or heating, and other measures of substandard accommodation). The elderly with the highest points are then identified. Some authorities rely only on the ranking of elderly based on these 'housing need' points. Other authorities treat all elderly above a certain points total based on 'housing need' as their sheltered housing pool. They are then likely to employ two other variables: (i) the length of time on the waiting list and (ii) an assessment by a community physician or area medical officer. Those elderly with the greatest medical need and/or longest waiting time for sheltered housing are then the first to be allocated a dwelling.

(c) The entire allocation process is handled by a single officer of the housing authority.

(d) That officer usually recognises the need for balanced sheltered housing schemes and feels there is a problem of schemes becoming dominated by older more frail and inactive tenants. However, in almost all cases no effort has been made to modify the current points system which typically allocates according to housing need, medical emergency and time on the waiting list.

(e) When pressed to define a balanced scheme the officer in charge of allocations defines it in terms of a mix of tenants by age not functional ability or social independence.

(f) Many of the elderly on the waiting list originate from social service referrals or nominations, but the social services are not involved in the actual allocation process.

Social Priorities: Voluntary Associations

The second most common allocation procedure is that employed by many voluntary (nonprofit) housing associations. Their primary allocation criteria are related to 'loneliness' or 'isolation' as opposed to housing or medical need. For this reason they tend to house more single persons than couples, more women than men, and more low- to moderate-income than middle-income elderly. Medical condition does come under consideration in allocations in that these associations like to limit their units to 'well' and 'active' elderly upon entry. They frequently start with a very active population in new schemes as opposed to a balance of persons by age, functional and social activity levels. Although the local public housing authorities usually have 50 per cent nomination rights of elderly from their own waiting lists, further screening by the association and/or an 'understanding' with the housing authority tends to limit their acceptance to the more active elderly. Typical housing associations with this allocation philosophy would employ the following procedure:

(a) Because some of these associations are active nationwide or at least in multiple regions, they can allocate persons wishing to move from a distant city. Often the national or multiregional headquarters of the associations keep a waiting list from which they can refer applicants when a vacancy occurs in a desired locality. The area or local manager (often a local committee of citizens assembled to manage a single scheme) also keep a local waiting list, and have the final say as to who is chosen.

(b) Allocation criteria are decided by a central committee (if appropriate, at the association's national headquarters). The selection process usually does not involve a points system, a more flexible and personal scrutiny of each candidate being employed. A centralised formula and handbook are devised which outline the allocation criteria. Then the local manager or committee put together a list from local authority nominees as well as contacts with private physicians, clergymen and friends of current residents. The allocation process often includes visits and interviews with prospective tenants. If there are doubts about health status, a reference from the candidate's doctor can be required.

(c) After a list of eligible candidates is assembled, final choices are frequently made subjectively by the local manager or committee of the person(s) who would be most compatible with others in the scheme.

(d) In associations that house less than 15 persons per scheme, compatibility of new tenants is likely to include a subjective selection of the candidate whose personality is deemed most compatible with existing tenants. However, compatibility is usually interpreted in terms of maintaining a balanced scheme based on the tenants' age, activity and dependency on the warden. In some cases it is clearly not a balance that is being sought but maintenance of the most active population possible.

(e) The allocation process is typically handled by a local committee. Since that committee also oversees maintenance, finances and other administrative matters, its composition is likely to include a variety of skills not necessarily important for allocating vacancies. However, persons with medical and social service training are often included.

Special Eligibility: Voluntary Associations

There is a small group of housing associations that caters for various special subsets of the elderly population; and eligibility is limited to membership of these various sub-groups. The largest, and only *nationwide* association of this type, is the Royal British Legion Housing Association Limited.

The primary criteria for eligibility in Royal British Legion sheltered housing is that the candidate be 'active', retired, of pensionable age, a British subject or naturalised British subject, and has served for at least seven pay days in the armed services (active or reserve), the Mercantile Marine during hostilities, a Red Cross organisation that served with the armed forces, served with an allied nations armed forces, or be the widow or dependent of any of these. Given the major wars of the twentieth century, the Royal British Legion serves, and will continue to serve, a sizeable group of eligible elderly.

Other specialised voluntary associations cater for particular religious or occupational groups (e.g. Methodists or retired teachers).

Position on the waiting list seems to be the only other allocation criteria used by these agencies. Maintaining a balance, even by age, was not mentioned by those we interviewed. Allocations are sometimes handled by a single officer at a central office reviewing applications, or by a local committee in charge of one scheme. They frequently employ personal interviews with candidates.

Socio-medical Priorities

The final type of allocation process uses a professional allocation panel, either advisory to an agency officer in charge of allocations or directly. The panel can be made up of a variety of practitioners and providers, e.g. doctors, nurses, social service representatives (particularly social workers) and representatives of housing management. While these panels consider all facets of need (housing, medical and social) their primary concern is with socio-medical need, considering factors such as social isolation, loneliness and difficulties in undertaking various activities of daily living when allocating vacancies. Stated more simply, they look for persons who can benefit the most from a sheltered housing design and the presence of a resident warden. While the fewest number of sheltered housing management agencies currently employ professional allocation panels and socio-medical criteria, this appears to be the fastest growing allocation alternative. Many different types of management agency have adopted this allocation procedure, usually developing their allocation criteria independently. We have observed a public housing department, a social service department and a voluntary housing association in the West Midlands each of which has adopted this procedure. The housing department joined with a local health district and social service department to develop such a panel. The social service department which employs an allocation panel, has the responsibility of hiring and monitoring wardens and allocating places in sheltered housing but does not build or maintain the schemes. Its eight-person panel includes a warden, the warden supervisor, five other representatives from social services and only one representative from the letting office of the housing department. The voluntary housing association referred to was only currently developing such an allocation panel process at the time of the study.

We found no consistent effort to balance schemes among agencies which use this allocation panel approach. Panels which consider only elderly applicants, screen those they feel cannot benefit from sheltered housing. The candidates with the greatest and most urgent needs are given the highest ranking. As a result no balancing of schemes results.

We have observed in the West Midlands and elsewhere that allocation panels that are dominated by social service practitioners and administered by social service departments can redirect sheltered housing so that it becomes an alternative to Part III (i.e. a residential or nursing home). Optimal placement of social service clientele can become the predominant allocation variable, much like the housing authority criteria described above can lead to allocations dominated by goals of the optimal use of the housing stock. Both approaches can undermine the long-term viability of sheltered housing when they tip the balance towards less active and dependent residents. There is a difference however. There appears to be less overloading of the warden when social service departments tip the balance to more frail residents because they can assign home help staff to assist the warden. The similarity with Part III accommodation is, nevertheless, realised as soon as the tenants lose control of daily social interactions to such home help staff.

In conclusion, it appears that the vast majority of voluntary associations and municipal departments managing sheltered housing are not employing allocation criteria designed to meet the long-term needs of either the sheltered housing concept or its tenants. Most of the allocation processes in use tend to have short-term objectives which often serve either bureaucratic expediency or management goals that defeat the purpose of sheltered housing. We maintain that the best way to improve the allocation process is to remove the pressure to allocate vacancies to persons who have been on the waiting list the longest or who have the most immediate health-related need. The best way to do this is to increase the number of sheltered housing units and entry points. Any solution short of this requires denying a place in sheltered housing at times to elderly with the most pressing need and longest wait, in order to preserve the independent nature of those schemes which have too many frail and inactive tenants. In order to make the best use of available vacancies that occur in the existing stock, a single waiting list and allocation panel may be needed for an entire market area. The panel would have to be designed to represent all of the support service interests evenly and would have to consider both the needs of prospective tenants, and schemes, and have access to alternative solutions to sheltered accommodation in allocating units.

Management of a Network of Wardens and Peripatetic Support Staff

Chapter 4 described the warden's role, indicating that it is more varied and complex than the national government recognises or most local managers apparently realise. This variety and complexity will only increase as new varieties of sheltered housing are developed and more elderly survive to very old age with increasing support service needs. Hence management officers in charge of hiring, monitoring and supporting the warden will also have to adapt to the increasing number, complexity and variety of warden-related problems. This section describes the most important dimensions of these management changes. As background, it will be useful if we first review the findings from our analyses of the role of the warden in Chapter 4, as they pertain to management.

National policy still sees the warden's role as static and uniform, requiring no special skills other than the commonsense of a friendly neighbour who provides no direct assistance with independent living. There is no uniform definition or hiring policy among local managers. Some still adamantly cling to the lay warden model. Others, in increasing numbers, are hiring wardens with nursing and social work skills to meet the observed needs of their tenants; but they have not altered their official definition of the lay warden.

We found that different sheltered housing types alter the character and volume of warden services. We also found that as the proportion of frail-to-active tenants changes over time within a scheme, the complexity and volume of warden services increases. Our analysis indicated that wardens in all sheltered housing types provide important ongoing support with independent living, not just emergency services. The variable workload of the wardens is not reflected in the logic or consistency of pay scales, time off, or back-up support provided by management. Contrary to the beliefs of some management, we know of no evidence that professionally trained wardens will be underutilised or overcare for tenants. If management is truly committed to providing a balance of frail and active tenants in each scheme from the outset, professional warden skills will be needed; it is more logical to assume that the unskilled warden will be the one to overcare for tenants, not the skilled warden. In short, we found that a thorough evaluation and updating of management policy regarding warden duties, compensation and support was often overdue.

From our interviews with management, we see a growing recognition of the complex problems that are emerging with regard to hiring, monitoring and supporting wardens, but few fundamental management responses or 're-thinks' were observed. One reason for this may be the bureaucratic time lag between recognition of needed management changes and actual response. The typical sheltered housing programme and its related problems have grown most rapidly over the past eight to ten years. Even now, the typical authority has only 10 to 20 schemes and, thus, only that many wardens to oversee. Most of their sheltered housing employs only one warden type, most of the schemes are relatively new, and most are occupied with young and active elderly instead of a balance of active and frail tenants. Thus most wardens are currently still able to cope with limited management support. There has been no policy, or observed need for a policy, to monitor activities within a scheme until very recently. In fact, the management of warden activities seems to have been designed with the assumption that the wardens are self sufficient. Any need for management help was, and still is, supposed to be identified and initiated by the warden. Managements' response to problems within a scheme is more reactive than preventative.

Even though management is becoming aware of warden-related problems, we do not feel that the range and dynamics of the problems expressed by the wardens we interviewed are fully comprehended by their management. This may be a result of the longstanding belief by management that the warden can function independently with regard to day-to-day problems. Wardens have become accustomed to not bringing their problems to management, partly because they have been able to handle them on their own in the past, and partly because they have found no administrative staff available and/or equipped to handle their problems any better than they can themselves. With perhaps just one exception, we did not find any consistent management effort to monitor social activity and the warden's workload within individual schemes in order to identify and prevent impending problems.

Some examples are warranted of warden problems management recognises in part but not in full. Chapter 4 showed that many managers provide no help securing relief wardens for yearly holidays or time off. Some of their wardens cannot find an adequate replacement on their own and thus are not taking the time off away from the scheme to which they are entitled. Many managers are now aware that they need to provide relief wardens for time off, but they are less often aware that wardens also have a need for relief cover at other times. Such situations range from episodic work overloads due to a flu epidemic, to someone to stay with the housebound when a social outing is planned. Most management is not prepared to provide a system of relief wardens which could prevent work overloads to resident wardens and make it possible for them to provide special social services to keep their tenants active and engaged. Management, and particularly housing authority management, does not fully comprehend that assisted independent living fulfils complex social and functional needs and not just shelter needs. Furthermore, they fail to recognise that wardens, as the prime organisers of the social environment within the scheme (and often the prime provider of functional support as well) themselves have complex support needs. A warden who does not receive management help with a relief warden for statutory time off is hardly going to request a relief warden for on-the-job assistance.

Another example, and one that is likely to become even more important in the future, is calling upon a social service to provide visiting support to a tenant, and calling upon a residential home (nursing home) to find a place for a tenant. Most of the wardens we interviewed felt it was their responsibility to observe this need and initiate a request for such services or transfer. If the service or transfer was not forthcoming then the warden would attempt a number of strategies such as turn to the family, if any, for help and/or the tenant's physician, and/or social worker, and/or superiors in the agency administration from which service or transfer is sought. The last place to look for help would be their housing management supervisor. There are two reasons for this. First, wardens are often told this is the order in which to seek a solution. Second, and more important, because approaching management isn't likely to make any difference anyway. If management responds at all, they are likely to approach these other agencies on the same case-by-case emergency basis as the warden and with no more chance of success. Management is unlikely to have established an interagency understanding or policy about ongoing suport or transfer needs.

One of the major surveys of sheltered housing residents recently reported that sheltered housing tenants are more than five times more likely to use meals-on-wheels and more than six times more likely to use home help than the national average.[11] Given these enormous service demands, coupled with the continued increase in new sheltered housing schemes of recent years, no wonder social service departments are demanding closer ties to the planning and administration of sheltered housing, especially warden selection and management.[12] The wardens themselves are beginning to unionise in many areas in response to growing inequities in support and compensation, coupled with increasing workloads and responsibilities.

The Required Changes in Warden Management Practices

Initiative/Leadership. Underwood and Carver recently stated 'that all wardens should be given regular support and contact even if they never ask for it'.[13] Taking this type of initiative and leadership is perhaps the single most urgent change needed in sheltered housing management. Some of the following points illustrate the types of initiative required.

Monitoring Schemes. A description of a model sheltered housing management operation states, 'regular interval surveys are carried out on each scheme to identify circumstances such as: design faults that should not be repeated in the future, age of tenants, information on their fitness, mobility, aids they require, involvement with social service department, social activity, etc.'[14] Without this type of monitoring of scheme activities, management cannot present a clear picture of the overall service and transfer demands being made by their sheltered housing on other agencies, or develop an equitable system of tenant allocation, warden compensation or warden relief. The importance of data collection and analysis, regarding both existing and potential or incoming tenants, is so crucial that an entire section on analysis and planning is presented later on in this chapter. Suffice it to say here, that such data collection and analysis is costly and involved.

Specific and Realistic Statement of Warden Skills and Duties. The warden's role must be clearly defined so that the right candidates are sought and attracted to the job. This becomes more important as management introduces different entry points into sheltered housing, each with variations in warden duties. A full and precise definition may require the collective wisdom of a national policy review board. However, the following training and service requirements, while a radical departure from the current situation, are we believe applicable to many wardens in service today:

(a) Professional training in nursing and/or social work is increasingly needed.
(b) Wardens are expected to monitor at least basic health and functional ability changes in tenants and maintain the individual resident's functional independence without overcaring or undercaring for as long as the resident can function independently with visiting support.
(c) Wardens should have the ability to co-ordinate needed visiting services and personnel attending each resident and make sure they do not interfere with the independent nature of the scheme, or overcare for the resident(s) they are attending.
(d) Wardens provide episodic nursing, counselling and other support services, at times when visiting services are not available and/or in case of emergencies.
(e) Wardens must be able to identify and provide appropriate social and physical activity to match the needs of residents with different

functional and social limitations.

(f) Wardens must be prepared to provide the above services in the role of a family proxy. They are expected to make close personal and social ties with the residents.

(g) Wardens are expected to retain their objectivity and initiate transfers of more dependent residents for the good of the entire scheme.

Obviously this list is not exhaustive. The point we wish to make should, however, be clear. This type of statement will attract different candidates with different skills than current definitions of the warden service. Additional points pertinent to the type of warden being sought are made below under recruiting and training/retraining of wardens.

Warden Recruitment and Outreach. The varied skills needed by wardens are such that management can no longer be sure they are getting the best candidates without some increased attention to outreach and recruitment policies. Because the job requires both a caring support service attitude and professional skills, advertising for the right people at the beginning of career development may be warranted. The targets may be young to middle aged housewives who have interrupted schooling or professional practice as a nurse or social worker to begin a family and now want to return to a related job; alternatively, similar persons who are willing to receive appropriate training for the first time. Work with community colleges in developing a warden specialisation for nursing or social work students is suggested as an appropriate outreach activity. Many persons could begin as a relief or assistant warden, while completing their studies on a part-time basis.

Pay for Warden Service. This subject has been discussed in some depth in Chapter 4 where it was shown that there is presently no consistency, logic or fairness in payment for warden services. The combination of low pay and inconsistency in reward for services is a source of growing frustration for existing wardens and a deterrent to attracting the best warden candidates.

There is no reason why the basic means of compensating for warden services shouldn't remain free rent and utilities in the warden's dwelling connected to a sheltered housing scheme. This is, after all, an important symbol of the unique type of service expected from the warden. There should also be a consistent salary schedule based on length of service, workload and varying skills and expertise required. Progressive pay scales should include incentives for maintaining and improving skills, and they should be consistent throughout a market area. This will require co-operation between the various public and voluntary (nonprofit) managers of sheltered housing within such an area.

Warden Support/Relief Systems. As was stated in Chapter 4, there are two basic ways to compensate for increasing warden workloads and responsibilities. One is through increased salary, the other is thorough proper management back-up support. These are clearly complementary, not supplementary, management options. Three areas of management support are important to wardens. First, the basic recognition of an increased workload and/or responsibility. Schemes not only need to be monitored for changes in workload, management should meet with each warden and discuss such changes and possible responses. The management officer in charge of monitoring warden/scheme activity should be able to evaluate warden actions and suggest time and energy saving ways to organise or change duty patterns. It is also appropriate to organise warden get-togethers to discuss more efficient means of organising their work day. Some wardens just don't know when they are overcaring, and/or not encouraging tenant self-help fully, and/or inefficiently organising their daily routine. They not only need tactful administrative advice, they need to be assured that what they are experiencing is not atypical. They need to know that when workload and responsibility grow beyond the point where they can be remedied by resources within the scheme, management is prepared to help find temporary or permanent assistance and, if need be, help relocate tenants if warranted, or reassign the warden.

Second, sheltered housing management which is not already administered through a social service department, should support wardens where necessary by helping to secure visiting services and transfers for tenants. Transfers can be temporary, e.g. to day care facilities, or permanently to a more dependent care environment, depending on tenant needs. Preparation for such warden assistance amounts to establishing permanent interagency ties with these support services sources and transfer points in advance of need by the tenants. These support and transfer agencies should have a clear understanding of the likely future demand so that they can prepare for it. They should help define the circumstances under which their services will be sought, by whom, and also help define priorities for transfer or service provision. Perhaps the allocation panel discussed above or a similar panel structure could be developed to review long-range needs and transfers. The main point we come back to over and over again in this chapter, is that sheltered housing management can no longer function as an independent activity. There are just too many points of interdependency with management policies of other housing, health and social service providers.

The third area of support is direct warden back-up support within the housing management operation, as opposed to that from outside agencies. There are four possible variations for this support, but all centre on the idea of relief wardens.

First, as was clearly demonstrated in Chapter 4, there must be a pool of relief wardens to assure that wardens not only can, but do, take full advantage of weekly allotted time off and yearly allotted holidays. This time off with relief should be mandatory not voluntary. Even if the wardens stay home they need this time totally free from their jobs.

Second, there should be enough relief wardens to not only handle statutory time off and holidays but episodic needs for warden assistance as well. Examples of social activities that require a relief warden are where the number of elderly is increased by events that bring neighbours to the scheme for a day, and when trips away from the scheme are planned and a relief warden is needed at the scheme for those too frail to participate and/or as an additional 'supervisor' on the trip. Many social events will not even be attempted without such temporary relief. Medical examples include periods where there are temporary overloads in the warden duties due to events such as a flu epidemic. Professional examples are where the warden, with management approval, wants to attend a special course or conference or visit another scheme.

Third, there may be situations where an evaluation of a scheme may turn up a long-term overload for a single warden. Despite all efforts to keep schemes balanced between active and frail tenants, there may be schemes where vacancies are so infrequent for a time that the majority of residents become frail and require daily warden supervision and support. In such cases, there may be upwards of several years where one or more assistant warden(s) must be permanently assigned to a scheme, until turnover allows for a renewed balance between active and frail tenants.

There is strong support in some quarters that schemes in which the majority become very frail be allowed to 'retire' from a sheltered housing role and be remodelled as institutional homes.[15] We see the need for such a permanent change as a rare occurrence and one that should be avoided whenever possible. Most cateory 1 schemes simply cannot be physically remodelled to provide a secure and efficient institutional environment, and many category 2 schemes could only be altered at great expense and would require temporary relocation of the residents. A change from independent to dependent housing may require the actual transfer of management to a different agency, one that is capable of handling an institutional setting. Most important, such a permanent change may require moving the remaining active tenants to conventional sheltered housing. If such a situation occurs, permanent conversion should be seriously questioned. Because of all these reasons, we stress that the retirement of sheltered housing be very much the *exception* rather than the rule.

The fourth and final warden relief would be with actual support services, normally provided by social service departments, that either do not exist locally, cannot be provided for an extended period, or cannot be provided at 'off hours' of the day and week. Obviously a first step would be to negotiate for such services with the existing social services in the community. However, where this is unsuccessful the developer/manager may have to provide the support services through in house staff, purchase them from the private sector or from a public or voluntary service that doesn't normally provide such service (e.g. adapt a visiting meal service using a local hospital kitchen or college kitchen as the source of meals). It is unlikely that the relief wardens can or would provide such services, but the same monitoring and management mechanism used to assign relief wardens could be used to administer this support service programme.

In-service Warden Training and Retraining. Because there are a large number of wardens now in service who are facing social and quasi-medical problems amongst tenants which they are not trained to handle, there is an increasing demand for in-service training. Also, because of the growing variety of scheme types, there are potential situations where wardens will want to be retained to take on a new type of warden position or move into an administrative role. In-service training courses of many types can be invisaged but the most popular would include the following aspects: site management, programme administration, first aid, nursing, individual counselling and group counselling. We have touched on all of these various topics, with the exception of counselling, in the previous chapter.

Because of the close personal ties that evolve between warden and residents, wardens are frequently called upon to counsel residents about financial, social, health and personal problems. While a close tie

between warden and residents is a primary management goal of
sheltered housing, management has done very little to help untrained
wardens with the difficult counselling problems that result. Many of the
managers we interviewed were not even aware of the numerous
counselling problems indicated to us by wardens. Management
apparently feels that sound commonsense will handle most immediate
counselling crises, and for more chronic problems the warden can call in
professional help of an appropriate kind. However, the number of
occasions when the warden is faced with very immediate and emotional
counselling problems that cannot be deferred to someone else appears
to be increasing as schemes age; it is also often more difficult to secure
adequate counselling services for the elderly than it is to secure more
specific support such as meals-on-wheels or medical treatment. Wardens
need to understand the psychopathology of ageing. Lawton, in his book
on managing housing for the elderly,[16] discusses very immediate
problems that can arise due to depression, suicidal ideas, delusions,
hallucinations, ideas of persecution, alcoholism and other behavioural
problems with unique characteristics among the elderly. Counselling
with regard to all of these behavioural problems can be complicated
by loss of memory, wandering and disorientation, deterioration of
personal care, and various functional problems such as loss of hearing
and sight. Under such circumstances, it is hardly surprising that wardens
don't always know exactly who to refer a counselling problem to, or
what problem they are referring.

There are also immediate situations where the warden must either
listen, offer advice or give reassurance.[17] One cannot always rely on
common sense in choosing which to do. Advice and/or reassurance
can often be the wrong action. Listening, while often the best initial
action, is not always enough, and knowing how to listen is itself a
skill. For example, some counselling problems that can be solved simply
by listening involve interpersonality conflicts among the tenants. It is
not always clear if these should be heard one party at a time in private,
in small group sessions of key parties, or heard openly in a meeting of
the entire scheme. Knowing which way to handle the matter can be
critical to its resolution. Learning how to spot counselling needs and
when and how to use basic counselling techniques in dealing with both
individual and group problems is just one example of in-service training
that management should be developing for wardens.

Tenant Organisations. These are probably the most satisfactory vehicles
by which residents can become involved in the control of their own

environment, through which residents can retain some engagement with the larger community, and through which complaints can be constructively aired and resolved. Nevertheless, many managers don't even recommend that wardens organise their tenants, and none in our sample provided advice on how to start up such an organisation, how to structure it, what type of activities it can successfully engage in, and how both warden and management should relate to it once it is established. A well organised tenant council can make the warden's job easier. Typically, one of the first things organised is a 'buddy system' including ways to signal each other by knocking on walls if someone falls and cannot reach an alarm cord. Tenants often organise services to temporarily sick or disabled neighbours helping with shopping, cooking and laundry. They often elect a complaints committee or set up regular meetings of all the tenants and the warden to discuss problems and make suggestions. Lawton has found that other tenants are 'very effective in rebutting inappropriate complaints made by their peers'[18] and can thereby save the warden a great deal of time, energy and aggravation. Some tenant organisations require nominal dues or have fund raising activities which help to underwrite the costs of parties or trips away from the scheme. Some have organised groups to do volunteer work outside the scheme and many have an outreach programme to invite lonely elderly in the surrounding community to join their organisation and partake of social activities.

On the other hand, there is no doubt that tenant organisations can also be the source of additional work and aggravation for the warden. It is difficult to know just how much of a scheme's activities should be relinquished to a tenant organisation, especially when such groups are frequently run by a small but active and vocal minority. Cliques can form which isolate and ostracise certain individuals unfairly. The majority of activities can be oriented to the most active tenants, ostensibly preventing less active tenants from needed physical activity and social contact. Involving outsiders may be opposed by some tenants and/or cause physical and sensual overload of common spaces for other tenants. Perhaps the biggest problem for the warden is whether to remain an integral part of such an organisation or indicate a willingness to attend events only when invited.

Many wardens would like management help in relating to a tenant organisation. Schemes need to be monitored and wardens told when they are taking over too much or too little of the administrative responsibility. Perhaps the easiest mistake for a warden to make is to do everything herself, asking and expecting too little of the tenants and effectively depriving them of their independence. Wardens who see only the potential workload and aggravation in the concept of tenant organisation are likely to avoid or oppose it.

Management has a responsibility to develop a set of basic rules appropriate to each scheme and presented to each new tenant in writing upon admission. All other rules needed to administer the scheme should be left to the warden and tenants. However, some wardens need to be reminded that the fewer additional rules the better, that rules that serve the warden and not the tenants effectively stifle independent living and that *tenant established* rules and norms are generally the most effective and efficient way to manage a scheme.

Warden Organisation. Many of the problems wardens confront in relation to tenants, sustaining organisational activity and guiding the social management of their scheme can be most effectively resolved where the programme managers organise the wardens and facilitiate regular meetings between them. Management can also organise special seminars and workshops given by experts in sheltered housing management and sponsor visits to sheltered housing schemes to observe experimental management techniques and model tenant organisations. Wardens should also contribute to the overall management of the programme and tenant allocation policy through either elected representatives or by participation on a rotating basis.

Wardens of voluntary housing associations often report to a lay board composed of community leaders. The warden are often expected to be professional advisors to the board because they are seen to possess expertise and knowledge about management which the board lacks. Too often, professional managers of large housing authorities forget that wardens are confronting management problems daily and have a different and valuable view of the overall programme administration. A warden's organisation might be encouraged to develop its own outreach programme to the community, encouraging individual wardens to speak to religious and civic groups on the aims of sheltered housing and particular activities in their schemes. Much of the experience wardens have gained is useful to other organisations working with the elderly. This type of exposure and recognition is also important to wardens who are often too isolated.

It is not usually easy for management to sponsor unionisation of its employees, but in the case of the warden there should be many benefits. Wardens' unions are already forming in several places. The increased support and compensation being called for by these unions will probably increase the cost of providing sheltered housing. However, there are also needed changes which will make sheltered housing a stronger programme in the long run. It would be both admirable and prudent if management led the way in this area.

Warden Reassignment or Dismissal. The managers in the West Midlands sample were asked a series of three questions designed to shed light on an area that is seldom discussed: How do you determine if a warden is incompetent in the job, and how do you either dismiss or reassign her? The answers reflect little if any management policy. In effect the unanimous response was that there are no grounds for dismissal short of committing a criminal offence. The first question presented the managers with a statement and question about monitoring warden activity:

> Some housing managers try to minimise warden rules preferring to leave the running of sheltered housing up to the warden's initiative. On the other hand some wardens welcome a clear briefing on their role and a follow-up check on their work. Which method do you most agree with and why?

All four of the public agency managers and one of the housing association managers said they try to minimise rules and leave the site management to the warden. Two stated that minimal rules applied (e.g. the warden should visit each unit once every 24 hours and be on call), another said 'we offer guidance if asked but do not lay down rules', and the remaining one said, 'we are very anti rules'. The first of the two voluntary associations which provide strong control guidance described how the warden was initially briefed and how a local housing committee and regional officer actually oversee warden management of the scheme on a weekly basis. The second has developed a 'Management Handbook' of rules and duties and assigned a local representative to regularly visit each scheme. The second question asked was:

> Do you have signs you look for that tell you all is not going well in a sheltered housing scheme (e.g. the warden is overworked and near exhaustion or incompetent)?

No agency had specific signs they looked for, and none monitored schemes specifically looking for problems with the warden service. Three public agencies said they could tell by 'tone of voice in telephone conversations [with the warden]' and/or said they met quarterly with all wardens in a general meeting to discuss problems. The three voluntary associations felt it was something that would be picked up as a rule by weekly or 'frequent' visits to the scheme by a local housing committee, local representative or regional officer. The most unique response was that of a housing authority which had assigned a warden and relief warden for each scheme. Both the warden and relief warden are supposed to monitor each other's performance for stress and get feedback from residents. In addition a district welfare officer visited each scheme regularly to observe. The final two-part question asked:

> What constitutes ground for warden dismissal? Have you ever dismissed a warden? If yes, explain the circumstances?

Two respondents answered they had no official grounds, a third answered that 'we try to prevent a need for dismissals through good initial screening of all candidates'. Three said in effect it is difficult or impossible to dismiss on anything but criminal offences. One voluntary association respondent said they dismiss wardens for 'unsociable and/or immoral habits and failure to carry out their duties'. Two agencies had never dismissed a warden. Three had dismissed wardens on grounds of stealing from tenants, shoplifting and absconding with money collected for rents. The remaining two agencies tried to dismiss people for other acts. One agency 'suspended a warden who used a pass key indiscriminantly and frightened tenants. She appealed, and is now working elsewhere in the department'. The other manager said they were successful in several cases of 'counselling and persuading' wardens to leave who had 'family problems' and 'personal money management problems' that began to interfere with the quality of their work.

Co-ordination of Sheltered Housing Management

The recent retrenchment by government will cause many readers to find our proposed increases in total sheltered housing units, sheltered housing entry points and warden support and renumeration unrealistic if not impossible. Any such retrenchment with regard to sheltered housing will, we feel, prove to be a false economy in the long run. Sheltered housing, when developed to its needed capacity and managed properly, is a most efficient and humane form of long-term assisted independent living. Part of our overall recommendation strongly supports government economies which combine lower management cost with greater management efficiency. As part of our proposed expanded sheltered housing service we would call for an end to competing and overlapping bureaucracy in the management of all aspects of assisted independent living for the elderly. If no other management change occurs in this time of tight money, government should demand co-ordination of all local services with an interest in independent living for the elderly — namely housing, health and social services. The public will only come to see retrenchment as a sham and hypocrisy if it is aimed singularly at sheltered housing starts and elderly services delivery and not at the disjointed and inefficient administrative bureaucracies.

Not surprisingly, this point has widespread support. However, because it will result in the elimination of some management control and political power within some agencies, there is very little concrete action on the part of government. For example, a joint statement by the British Department of the Environment and Department of Health and Social Security (DHSS) extolled 'The importance of collaboration between health, social services and housing authorities in the development of overall services for old people',[19] without any indication of how this can be accomplished or what initiatives central government will take. Similar statements can be found in sections of the 1974 and subsequent US Housing Acts dealing with deployment of housing and related services for elderly in need of assistance with independent living. (A more recent DHSS consultative document has, however, made a number of suggestions regarding collaboration and the means whereby increased resources might be devoted to community care.)[20]

By combining recent research findings and pragmatic observations from housing, health and social service researchers and practitioners, the planning and management interdependence of all assisted living services for the elderly becomes obvious. A Department of the Environment Study re-established the importance of sheltered housing as fulfilling a 'housing need' for most elderly at the time they move to sheltered housing. It found that 59 per cent of tenants moved to sheltered housing because their previous dwelling was too big or too expensive, or unsuitable because it contained barriers, provided insufficient heat, or lacked a kitchen or bathroom, while an additional 29 per cent had to relocate because their previous house was demolished or sold.[21] These housing problems are critical in determining the overall need for sheltered housing.

Once the elderly are resident in sheltered housing and become more frail and housebound there is strong evidence that sheltered housing fulfills an important 'social need'. A recent study of a sample of elderly aged 75 and over, selected from four socially different urban areas, asked respondents what they thought were the advantages of sheltered housing. The most common replies were that 'help was available when needed' (34 per cent), that it 'protected against loneliness' (20 per cent), and that it 'provides a sense of security' (5 per cent).[22] These social factors are equally important in determining the number of units to build and the type of support services to provide. Sheltered housing clearly serves both housing and social needs, and considering one without the other can result in a distorted planning perspective.

Once elderly become frail, health service needs become a part of the sheltered housing support system. One recent case study concluded that area health authorities should contribute to the construction costs of sheltered housing facilities in proportion to the degree of benefit derived by the health authority because sheltered housing schemes postpone or even prevent the need for elderly residents to transfer to the institutional settings provided by the health authority.[23] Another study of a sheltered housing scheme designed to give an enhanced degree of medical care, concluded that the collaboration between health and housing authorities on this one scheme is encouraging. However, more formal and concise operational policy and cut-off points need to be defined between long-stay hospital care, residential homes (run by social services), and sheltered housing in order to identify the housing resource needs of all three throughout the elderly population now and in the future.[24]

The two most important points of management collaboration in sheltered housing are the initial allocation and the transfer of residents. Housing authorities must be aware of the growing need for visiting health and social service support to sheltered housing tenants. The increasing, and in some areas heavy, demands made by sheltered housing residents on health and social services entitles these authorities to have a voice in the allocation processes and to be fully informed of future change in demand for their services due to expansion of sheltered housing schemes and/or increasing age and dependency of sheltered housing tenants. This is true regardless of any cost savings to these other authorities resulting from delivery of services to grouped schemes or possible postponement of entry into their service. Sheltered housing *requires* the expert input into allocation and planning of these other authorities because sheltered housing addresses social and health needs as well as sheltering needs. We agree with Butler, Oldman and Wright,[25] that if any one of the three authorities is in charge of allocation and planning then there will be a tendency to fit the elderly candidate into a pre-defined set of services related to the professional perceptions and goals of that authority and its staff. Limiting allocation criteria to any one authority will miss out on some needed resources, and will consequently force misuse of the available support services. The allocation of different types of sheltered housing and visiting support resources requires a total assessment of an individual sheltered housing candidate's social environment, life style and support needs. This can best be done by establishing a forum through which potential elderly clients in need of some kind of assistance meet with a panel of professionals representing all the services, a panel with access to vacancies in a full spectrum of sheltered housing and other support service alternatives.

The reasons for a co-ordinated transfer policy have been stressed throughout this chapter.[26] We have shown that there is still a great deal of confusion about the low transfer rate from sheltered housing to residential or nursing homes. Some argue that this statistic merely points to the great success of sheltered housing – the lack of *needed* transfers. While this may be true in part, more convincing reasons, given the increase in frail and dependent sheltered housing tenants and overworked wardens, are: (1) few vacancies in residential homes and, in turn, long stay hospitals, offered to sheltered housing tenants, and (2) the lack of co-ordination and planning across the entire housing continuum. Earlier we argued that the drift toward sheltered housing schemes with more frail and inactive tenants is due to the high need for, and small supply of, housing which produces too few vacancies, which are allocated to those judged most needy and/or who have been on the waiting list the longest. The drift is also due in part to problems of transferring tenants who require constant personal or nursing care. The lack of an adequate 'vacancy rate' and the resulting tendency to allocate these dwellings to the most needy and those longest on the waiting list, is endemic to the entire housing continuum. Without comprehensive and co-operative planning and appropriate additional housing development, many of the programmes will be altered and compromised.

Because all aspects of assisted independent living are interrelated and to some degree complimentary or supplementary, comprehensive and co-ordinated *planning* by all support services is necessary. The following subsection discusses such co-ordinated planning efforts.

Co-ordinated Regional Planning and Analysis

In order to plan sheltered housing accurately, management requires an accurate means of determining the number of elderly who will need and desire such housing as opposed to a complimentary service provided by another agency (e.g. visiting services to conventional housing). Demand for sheltered housing will, however, be in part determined by the availability of alternative support solutions. Furthermore, adequate sheltered housing management requires knowledge of current and future resident demand on the warden as well as visiting support services. The data collection, storage, retrieval and analytical skills required to complete such comprehensive analyses are daunting. In almost all cases, the costs of completing such analyses are beyond the capabilities of most housing managers acting alone. However, more or less identical information is needed by all the managers providing complementary or supplementary housing and/or service combinations in the same market area. Co-operation is the obvious solution.

A 'needs assessment' is a major analytical tool that can be used for such detailed planning. The typical needs assessment of the elderly would estimate the number and characteristics of the elderly in a local service area who require assistance with various aspects of daily living and lack adequate and affordable private support. Detailed cross-tabulations are required which describe the elderly by housing and household characteristics along with other indicators of need, describing specific support and which can be met by specific support services. A detailed matrix describing elderly with single and multiple needs and their household size, income, etc., can be created by variable cross-tabulation. This needs matrix can then be matched with elderly desires for alternative services and the supply of those services. The results yield a comprehensive picture that can be used to set spending and development priorities, identify services that are over- or under-provided and new services that need to be created.

A recent government study in the United States has shown that a local needs assessment model using a random sample survey of the elderly proved to be very accurate and useful.[27] In large urban areas equally accurate results are possible using secondary data and detailed estimating models.[28] Both methods demonstrate that a needs assessment approach can be used to help determine imminent needs of the elderly and the costs and benefits to them of alternative support service approaches. Unfortunately both studies conclude that detailed and accurate assessments are extremely costly and beyond the funding and staff capabilities of most local service agencies.

This conclusion was reinforced by a nationwide analysis of needs assessments conducted by a random sample of 263 local planning agencies serving the elderly in the United States.[29] This study found that almost 90 per cent of the needs analyses completed by agencies were below the quality required for accurate planning. In fact, the typical needs assessment was counterproductive, often resulting in incorrect or misleading findings.

The reasons for these inaccurate and misleading analyses were varied and highly localised (e.g. variations in availability of secondary data, variations in collecting primary data, identifying the appropriate needs indicators to fit local market conditions, etc.). This prohibits rectifying the problems with national government guide-books for conducting a proper needs assessment, yet the individual local agency cannot be expected to assemble the in-house expertise required to carry out the necessary specialised data collection and analyses. However, the study found that there are often a number of housing, health and social services agencies providing overlapping planning services to the elderly within the same market. If they co-operate and pool their planning resources along with increased state and federal advice and aid, detailed and accurate needs analyses would become economically feasible.

The situation is similar in Great Britain, although one particular approach to joint planning, referred to as 'balance of care', is starting to have some success.[30] This approach brings together survey data concerning the characteristics of the elderly and their *current* forms of care, and value judgements of an advisory panel (consisting of health, social services and housing representatives) regarding *acceptable* and/or *desirable* forms of care. The resulting balance of care model allows the resource implications of different assumptions regarding forms of care, numbers of different types of elderly to be provided care, and available finance, to be explored. The approach has influenced and assisted joint planning in both Devon and Cornwall and is now being taken up in other areas of Great Britain.

Both co-ordinated planning and management arrangements are warranted at the local level in both the United States and Great Britain, including all the service agencies, public and voluntary (nonprofit), serving the elderly. It is intolerable to allow retrenchment in direct services before economising by eliminating administrative/management duplication and inefficiency. A single, accurate and detailed needs assessment of a local elderly population will reduce the duplicity in analytical activity, and the double counting of need, while identifying the

highest priority elderly needs and needy elderly. In this way, local
service agencies can maximise whatever support service resources are
available, be the economic climate one of prosperity or austerity.

Differing Management Conclusions

There is no doubt that ameliorating the 'drift' in sheltered housing
environments towards a dependent majority of residents in individual
schemes is the recommended focus of management activity. All the
major analyses in recent years have recognised this problem and
proposed solutions. We have concluded that this 'drift' is caused by an
imbalance between the small supply and large elderly demand/need for
sheltered housing. It is our conclusion that once an adequate supply of
units and alternative entry points are available, the management goals
of retaining a balance of active and frail tenants and uniformity and
stability to the warden functions and workload, becomes possible.
We also conclude that the supply imbalance must be corrected along
the entire spectrum of supportive housing for the elderly; an adequate
vacancy rate is required at all assisted living entry points. Planning for
the number of types of assisted living entry points must be co-ordinated
by all services involved in assisting the elderly.

   Not everyone agrees with this scenario, or, if they agree, feel it is a
realistic solution given the current economic recession and government
austerity. However, it is our feeling that the alternative solutions are
interim and do not fully recognise the primary cause of the sheltered
housing management dilemma. Let us analyse three of the more
popular counter scenarios and solutions.

Scenario 1: Excess Sheltered Housing Demand is a Result of Service
Inequities Which Favour Sheltered Housing
Implied solution: Rectify the inequities and supply will equal demand/
need

This scenario agrees that demand/need excesses for sheltered housing
are a root cause of the drift in tenant dependency, but it concludes that
the causes of the excess demand are service inequities which favour
sheltered housing over other means of assistance with independent
living. Another way of looking at it is to maintain that sheltered
housing is a victim of its own success. The scenario proceeds as follows:

1. Living in sheltered housing produces three advantages to tenants

over elderly persons living on their own in conventional private housing. First it provides an entrance into the service network; residents become more visible to all other support professionals.

2. Second, sheltered housing residents are grouped together allowing economies of scale in all support service delivery when compared to conventional private housing. This does not escape visiting services which want to show they are reaching more elderly for less cost.

3. Third, grouped living produces camaraderie and support among tenants. This, plus the organisational assistance of the warden, means that sheltered housing residents are a relatively more informed, aggressive and visible group. They see to it that they and their neighbours get all the available support services for which they are eligible.

4. All this results in inequities in service distribution when comparing sheltered housing residents to conventional elderly residents. This has been argued in the study we quoted earlier which showed only 2.6 per cent of the elderly at home nationally receive meals-on-wheels while 16 per cent of the sheltered housing residents receive meals-on-wheels, and only 4.4 per cent receive some home help service nationally compared to 30 per cent in sheltered housing. The degree of handicapped in sheltered and ordinary housing is similar but the support is most definitely *not*.[31]

5. This increase in support service combined with independent living does not escape the elderly 'grapevine', and waiting lists swell out of proportion. The more elderly living in conventional housing who see happy, independent, secure, sheltered housing peers with easier accessibility to a wide range of support, the more elderly who seek sheltered housing.

Solution: Deliberately limit the service supply to sheltered housing and/ or cut back sheltered housing construction and eventually the excess demand for sheltered housing will dissipate in favour of other assisted living alternatives.

The first statistic that flies in the face of this scenario relates to the many wardens in our survey, as well as other surveys, who have complained that their needy tenants are neglected by visiting domiciliary services because of the presence of warden support. Still, Butler and Oldman's statistics[32] seem hard to refute; sheltered housing tenants get much more domiciliary aid than conventionally housed elderly with similar disabilities. It may be possible, however, to reconcile these apparent contradictions. While Butler and Oldman

found that the degree of handicap of persons in conventional and
sheltered housing is similar, there are other differences between
sheltered and conventional housing residents in their national survey
that could account for the differences in service receipt. Only 30 per
cent of the elderly at home live alone compared to 70 per cent of the
sheltered housing elderly. Thus we could conclude that more persons
moving to sheltered housing have no private support network and must
rely on public domiciliary services. Only 24 per cent of sheltered
housing tenants were home owners before entering sheltered housing,
compared to 50 per cent of comparable conventionally housed elderly.
Home ownership correlates with financial resources. Thus we could
conclude that more conventional than sheltered housing residents can
afford private domiciliary support. There are also other factors
additional to demographic statistics. We have seen that, due to the
backlog for sheltered housing, many who are allocated units have
emergency needs for housing and domiciliary service. Hence even if
functional ability (handicap) level is similar between sheltered and
conventional housing residents, those entering sheltered housing are
likely to represent that proportion of the conventionally housed
handicap at the margin where they can no longer cope with their
handicap on their own, while those who remain in conventional housing
are likely to represent those who can still cope. We quoted studies in
Chapter 1 indicating that elderly often wait until a crisis situation
before moving from conventional housing. Coping on their own for as
long as possible is a way many elderly postpone the recognition of
growing support dependencies. Entrance to sheltered housing,
everything else being equal, could mark the point of personal admission
for many elderly that they can no longer go it alone and must seek a
wide array of help for the first time.

Based on these findings we might now ask whether Butler and
Oldman didn't uncover a degree of *undersupport* by visiting domiciliary
services to conventionally housed elderly, rather than a degree of *oversupport* to sheltered housing residents. Part of the variance in support
service use uncovered, may indicate a real need for better outreach to
hard-to-reach conventionally housed residents, not a signal that
sheltered housing residents are overserved. It may also indicate that
there are many rugged individuals out there who actually thrive on
shunning public support even though they know all about it and, in
most people's opinion, need it. This must remain their choice; each day
to them without support may be a personal victory and reason for
living. There is of course another personality type which needs support

and does not shun it but seeks it out. Surely the former group is not more noble or praiseworthy, just different; and surely the latter group shouldn't be ignored simply because they are more likely to seek sheltered housing and support services.

In conclusion, we do not feel this scenario is proven or necessarily logical. Given the many warden comments about the lack of needed visiting domiciliary support in sheltered housing we feel this scenario and its implied solution is dangerously misdirected.

Scenario 2: The 'Drift' Toward Dependent Care is Inevitable Because the Fastest Growing Demand for Sheltered Housing is From the Oldest and Most Frail Elderly
Implied solution: Accommodate the 'drift' by converting existing schemes and building new schemes to fit a 'very sheltered housing' or linked schemes design

We have already recognised 'very sheltered housing', beyond the on-site care provision of category 2, as providing legitimate alternative entry points to the sheltered housing continuum. What we called 'service-rich' sheltered housing in Figure 1.4 covers four 'very sheltered housing' types. We included two of these types in our Devon and West Midlands samples, category 2½ (alternative eight in Figure 1.4), and linked schemes (alternative nine in Figure 1.4). However, where we propose very sheltered housing as an important life-style choice and alternative entry point into sheltered housing, some analysts have proposed this single alternative as the long-range solution to the sheltered housing 'drift' toward institutional housing.[33] Others fear this is becoming the unplanned and incremental response to the increasing number of frail tenants in sheltered housing.[34] The scenario presented by proponents of this solution to sheltered housing 'management' problems unfolds as follows:

1. The number of very frail elderly, over the age of 75, is by far the fastest growing subgroup of elderly living both in sheltered housing and in the community.
2. The goal of sheltered housing is that it should be the 'final home' of the elderly. Any move after entering sheltered housing will be traumatic and tantamount to adopting the 'conveyor belt' principle of care for the aged.
3. Yet most conventional sheltered housing (category 1 or 2) is unable to meet the needs of the very frail, given current staffing.
4. The very frail elderly are the primary cause of an increasing warden

workload, her inability to adequately provide for the more active tenants, the collapse of tenant control of a scheme, and the drift toward an institutional setting.

5. The austerity movement has placed very real and severe restriction on the expansion of expensive visiting domiciliary support as well as expansion of nursing or residential homes and geriatric hospital beds.

6. Current sheltered housing can be developed to contain the problem of frailer tenants within the existing structure with less expense and disruption than any other support alternative. In many schemes it can mean no alteration to the physical structure, no changes in the basic tenant/warden relationship, and no change in the social organisation of the scheme. The existing organisation can minimise the number of assistant wardens and home helps needed. Additional staff can be added as the margin of total need within each scheme expands.

Solution: Convert all sheltered housing to accommodate the most frail.

All signs indicate that this is the path of least resistance and will be how sheltered housing evolves without planning and additional commitment of resources. It may well constitute the best solution given a society committed to incremental action and a marginal commitment of new resources. However, as proposed it tends to be a 'laissez-faire' reaction to past practices and current trends and largely overlooks the costs and consequences.

The greatest potential risk has to be that of losing assisted independent living environments and the sheltered housing concept. For once you *allow* sheltered housing schemes to become dominated by frail and inactive tenants who cannot maintain and control the organisation of the scheme, support staff will step in to fill the void with no way to ever re-establish assisted independent living. It doesn't matter how incrementally you add additional staff, the point will come when the scheme will convert to institutional living. Not only will there be no organisational mechanism to revert to 'true' sheltered housing, but there will be little hope that such a scheme could ever attract active elderly tenants again.

This scenario makes what we believe are three false assumptions: first, an explicit assumption that the frail elderly will become so dominant that they will become the norm, not the exception in society; second, another explicit assumption, that current sheltered housing is incapable of adequately accommodating even a few frail elderly with the help of visiting support services; third, an implicit assumption that the chairfast, bedfast or confused elderly integrate well with active elderly.

While it is true that the group over 75 years of age is the fastest growing subgroup of the elderly, the evidence quoted in Chapter 1 indicates that only about 10–15 per cent will ever need public assistance with independent living and only 4 per cent will ever need *long-term* (more than six months) institutional care (see Table 1.6). The fact that so many frail elderly congregate in sheltered housing is, as we have argued, because there are too few units and too few entry points. This is forcing the allocation process to increasingly assign vacancies to the most needy. In effect, this scenario would have us risk the conversion of a successful assisted independent housing programme to an institutional housing programme simply because the successful programme needs to be expanded and society apparently lacks the will.

The second false assumption in this scenario is that sheltered housing could not even accommodate a 'fair share percentage' of frail elderly. If there were enough sheltered housing schemes, each scheme would only have to accommodate 10 per cent or less of the very frail tenants (at most 3 to 4 persons for the average scheme) at any one point in time. All the evidence we and others have observed[35] is that the typical category 1 or 2 scheme can, without much difficulty, accommodate a small number of very frail elderly, sharing care between the warden, active neighbours and visiting support services. We know of schemes which have provided hospice care for dying residents so long as the constant surveillance and nursing care only lasts a few months. The only reason pressure is currently growing for transfer of sheltered housing tenants to institutional care is because the proportion of frail elderly in sheltered housing shows signs of growing intolerable for the system, and because the accompanying low number of vacancies in institutions is preventing even elderly who would like to move from doing so. Based on our conversations with wardens, even long-term bedfast and incontinent tenants are tolerable so long as there are only one or two per scheme. The only 'conveyor belt' application appears to be for very confused and mentally unstable persons and short-term institutionalisation near the end of life.

Third, we have recognised that a subgroup of the elderly want the security and/or need the support of a category 2½ or linked scheme sheltered housing option. It has been theorised that such arrangements produce economies in shared services and amenities and a better standard of service.[36] However, there is also evidence that this often only works for persons who *choose* it. It appears that to convert all sheltered housing to such close communal living would be a less tolerable categorical entry point to assisted independent living than if we retained category 1 and 2 as the exclusive entry points. While linked schemes present theoretical economic advantages, they do not appear to work in practice. Three points stressed by Derek Fox[37] are worth repeating. First, active elderly and frail elderly don't mix well. In fact they tend to separate into two non-interrelating groups. A move to more residential care is seen as a downgrading of status by active elderly. Second, the continued search for service economies at the expense of independent living can lead to larger and larger colonies of old people 'segregated and inward looking'.[38] Third, and most important, the types of support service required by semi-independent and dependent elderly are quite different. The inevitable predominance of the dependent services can inhibit and stifle the more assisted-independent services, and accelerate the trend toward dependency for all the residents. Thus we feel adoption of this scenario can only exacerbate the 'drift' toward institutional care and signal the death of a successful sheltered housing programme.

Scenario 3: The Dependency Drift Can be Accommodated if Sheltered Housing is Divided into Two Separate Management Programmes of Assisted Independent Living
Solution: Retain category 1 as a housing programme with housing objectives. Turn category 2 and more sheltered category types over to local social service departments

This scenario is proposed by the researchers of one of the most extensive studies of the allocation process in sheltered housing management.[39] Their scenario proceeds as follows:

1. The drift in sheltered housing management and the growing importance of social service input at all levels of administration is becoming increasingly recognised. Consideration is being given not just to co-ordination of housing and social services but to a major revision in local government responsibility and the merging of the two units into one department.
2. Bytheway and James[40] set out to see if closer working ties between the two departments are possible. Based on their interviews with respondents from both departments they find irreconcilable differences.
3. They find that housing respondents believe independent living can

best be retained through the minimisation of support services to tenants, and social service respondents see support services as an integral part of retaining independence. They conclude that local government must retain a clear division of responsibility in administering sheltered housing.

Solution: In order to solve the growing drift toward elderly who require more supportive environments with domiciliary services, separate management of sheltered housing is recommended. The housing authority would be in charge of all category 1 schemes and the social service authority would administer category 2 schemes and residential homes. Category 2 would serve as an alternative placement location to Part III accommodation but not be an equivalent housing provision, so that two separate waiting lists would be maintained. Category 1 would serve only active elderly. With the separation of sheltered housing management, the housing authority could assume its goals are housing in nature and balanced but predominantly active schemes. Category 2 allocations could be based more on emergency need.

There are four reasons why we feel this is a poor scenario. First, it assumes what the authors call a 'socio-architectural' difference between category 1 and 2 housing which is not warranted. As was shown in Chapter 3, housing authorities currently do not differentiate between these two categories in allocating tenancies and tend not to transfer between them. Therefore, both categories have been assigned more active and less active tenants, and both suffer from the drift caused by low vacancies and emergency allocation policies. Separating the management by category type will not solve the current problems. Furthermore, we have shown there is no architectural correlation between the needs of the tenants and the two categories. Indeed, housing authorities prefer to place more frail persons in category 1 bungalows rather than upstairs in a category 2 scheme with no lift (elevator).

Second, the authors are placing category 2 and Part III accommodation under the same department and recommending that category 2 be regarded as an alternative to Part III in the placement of social service clients. They then recommend that category 2 and Part III remain separate forms of housing provision. Given the fact that Part III, like sheltered housing, has long waiting lists, how long is it going to be before category 2 and Part III 'emergency' allocations are identical? In fact, if category 2 is truly treated as a 'placement' alternative to Part III, we perceive a rapid merger of the two housing types in fact, if not in name, for the very reasons we have stressed throughout this chapter. The less active category 2 tenants will not be able to 'compete' with the support service staff for control of the scheme and the scheme will become institutionalised. Once this happens, all the elderly that want true assisted independent living will be left with the housing authority category 1 schemes, and we are back where we are today, except with roughly half as many sheltered housing schemes to allocate.

Third, if housing authorities take this proposal seriously and only cater for active tenants, this scenario represents a far clearer 'conveyor belt' approach to elderly housing than currently exists. What is more likely to happen, of course, is very little movement between category 1 and 2 leaving the housing authority with the same problems they have now, just less flexibility.

Finally, this scenario can only reinforce the ideological differences between housing and social service professionals. It actually justifies all their suspicions of each other. What we need is a programme that diminishes and reconciles their differences. We feel this can only come about if sheltered housing is retained by the housing authority with their skills related to developing and maintaining the physical 'plant', and encourage a real partnership between all concerned housing, health and social service parties in the planning for, and management of, sheltered housing. This would include joint representation on allocation and transfer panels; co-ordinated representation in the planning of admission and discharge policy to and from sheltered housing, residential homes and hospitals; co-ordinated planning of the amount and types of housing, support service staff and forms of care generally needed throughout the elderly support system.

Notes

1. Lawton, M.P., 'Planning and managing housing for the elderly'. John Wiley, New York, 1975, 136 pp; Thompson, M.M. and Donahue, W.T., *Planning and Implementing Congregate Housing for older adults*. Monograph, International Center for Social Gerontology, Washington, D.C., 1980.

2. American Association of Homes for the Aging, *A Profile*. The Association, Washington, D.C., 1978.

3. Bytheway, B. and James, L., *The Allocation of sheltered housing: A study of theory, practice and liaison*. Medical Sociology Research Centre, University College of Swansea, 1978.

4. Ibid., pp. 69 and 81.

5. Ibid., p. 104.

6. Ibid., pp. 80 and 104.

7. Ibid., pp. 43 and 102.

8. Butler, A., 'A profile of the sheltered housing tenant'. *Housing*, 1980, 16, pp. 6–8.

9. Bytheway and James, *The Allocation of Sheltered housing: A study of theory, practice and liaison*; Butler, A., Oldman, C. and Wright, R., *Sheltered Housing for the elderly: A Critical review*. Research Monograph, Department of Social Policy and Administration, University of Leeds, 1979; Temple, C.M.M., *Allocation: Its relevance to the role of sheltered housing and in meeting the needs of the elderly*. Masters in Social Science Dissertation, Centre for Urban and Regional Studies, University of Birmingham, 1980.

10. Boldy, D., Abel, P. and Carter, K., *The Elderly in grouped dwellings: A profile*. Institute of Biometry and Community Medicine, University of Exeter, 1973.

11. Butler, 'A profile of the sheltered housing tenant'.

12. Bytheway and James, *The Allocation of sheltered housing: A study of theory, practice and liaison*.

13. Underwood, J. and Carver, R., 'Sheltered housing: How have things gone wrong – what's coming next?' *Housing*, April, 1979, pp. 8–9.

14. Ibid.

15. Lawton, 'Planning and Managing housing for the elderly', pp. 263, 264.

16. Ibid.

17. Ibid.

18. Ibid., p. 259.

19. Department of the Environment and of Health and Social Security, *Housing for Old people: a consultant paper*. HMSO, London, 1976.

20. Department of Health and Social Security, *Care in the Community: A consultant document on moving resources for care in England*. HMSO, London, July 1981.

21. Department of the Environment, *Housing for the elderly: the size of grouped schemes*. HMSO, London, 1975.

22. Abrams, M., *Beyond three-score and ten: A first report on a survey of the elderly*. Age Concern, London, 1978.

23. Underwood and Carver, 'Sheltered housing: How have things gone wrong – what's coming next?'

24. Godber, C., 'Collaboration in sheltered housing'. *Housing*, April, 1978, pp. 10–11.

25. Butler, Oldman and Wright, *Sheltered Housing for the elderly: A Critical review*.

26. See also Chapter 3 and Butler, Oldman and Wright, *Sheltered Housing for the elderly: A Critical review*, p. 88.

27. United States Comptroller General, *Conditions of older people: National information system needed*. General Accounting Office, Comptroller General, Report to the Congress, Washington, D.C., 1979.

28. Heumann, L.F., *Identifying the housing and support service needs of the semi-independent elderly: Toward a descriptive planning model for Area Agencies on Aging in Illinois*. Housing Research and Development Program, University of Illinois at Urbana-Champaign, 1977.

29. Heumann, L.F. and Lareau, L.S., *Developing a nationwide planning tool for state and local agencies providing housing and support services to the elderly*. Housing Research and Development Program, University of Illinois at Urbana-Champaign, 1980.

30. Boldy, D., Canvin, C., Russell, J., and Royston, G., 'Planning the Balance of Care'. In Boldy, D. (ed.), *Operational Research Applied to Health Services*. Croom Helm, London, 1981.

31. Butler, A. and Oldman, C., 'The objectives of sheltered housing: Implications for future provision'. *Housing Review*, March–April, 1980, pp. 48–50.

32. Ibid.

33. Harbridge, E., 'Very sheltered housing: A better option?' *Community Care*, July 1980, pp. 23–4; Lawton, 'Planning and managing housing for the elderly'.

34. Boldy, D., 'Sheltered Housing for the Elderly – The Alternative Refuge?' Community Care (in press); Tunney, J., 'Sheltered housing: Homes sweet homes?' *Roof*, September 1979, pp. 149–50; Butler, Oldman and Wright, *Sheltered Housing for the elderly: A Critical review*.

35. Tunney, 'Sheltered housing: Homes sweet homes?'

36. Fox, D., 'Housing needs of the elderly'. In, Canvin, R.W. and Pearson, N.G. (eds.), *Needs of the elderly for health and welfare services*. Institute of Biometry and Community Medicine, University of Exeter, Publication No. 2, 1973.

37. Ibid.

38. Ibid., p. 88.

39. Bytheway and James, *The Allocation of Sheltered housing: A study of theory, practice and liaison*.

40. Ibid.

6 THE FUTURE OF SHELTERED HOUSING

In this book we have been analysing the British model for sheltered housing. The model consists of four unique components: a variety of housing categories to allow the elderly a choice in communal living, relatively small scheme size, location of schemes in residential neighbourhoods, and reliance on a single live-in staff person, the resident warden, who co-ordinates support and social activity at the margin of individual need. In our opinion this is the most humane and successful formula for long-term assisted independent living in use today in Western society. The model allows the elderly participants maximum choice and control over their life-style, and lets them retain close access to lifelong community ties. The model is also the most successful we have seen at minimising the institutional atmosphere that can develop in long-term assisted living environments. Above all, British sheltered housing is the best tested model in use today; and it appears from our observations to be equally popular with residents, staff and management.

Despite all its positive aspects, the future of British sheltered housing is uncertain, and its transferability to other Western countries seems doubtful. In one sense British sheltered housing appears to be jeopardised by its own success. No matter how fast new schemes have been built in recent years, demand continues to outstrip supply; most impaired elderly cope so successfully, turnover is low and vacancies are rare. But the real threat is not success. If sheltered housing was both successful and cost efficient there would be little opposition to stepping up construction and expanding the variety of category types. However, British sheltered housing *is* being challenged on the grounds of cost inefficiency, not only by British housing managers and economists but also by other societies looking at the programme. Some critics feel the British programme contains some expensive 'luxury' components when compared with other forms of assisted independent grouped living. Perhaps the most costly component is small scheme size, especially when it occurs in older schemes where many tenants require extensive support to remain in an independent environment. We recognise that small scheme size can be a key to the success and popularity of sheltered housing, especially for elderly whose ability to engage in community activities is severely limited by advancing disabilities. In this chapter we examine the successful components of the British programme and explore how they can be retained and still accommodate the realities of rising building construction, building management and support service costs in a climate of economic recession. All public social programmes are currently coming under government cost scrutiny. We feel it would be better for this scrutiny to include programme proponents seeking to retain and maximise programme benefits, rather than be completed only by those purely seeking cost reductions.

The Emerging Problem

There are four potentially costly elements in the current sheltered housing programme. All four relate to the goals of small scheme size and low key background support with daily living at the margin of individual need.

Construction and Maintenance Costs

When the sheltered housing programme was first conceived, land and building costs were half what they are today in most Western countries,[1] and overhead and operating costs over the life of a building were not major considerations. As land costs have risen it has become cost efficient to make maximum use of each site; as construction costs have risen it has become cost efficient to develop one large scheme in place of three smaller ones. The most dramatic savings appear when comparing a lifetime of heating and maintenance on one large building versus several smaller ones. The larger scheme makes more efficient use of maintenance staff, equipment and energy consumption. For example, average annual energy consumption measured in BTU/square foot of a highrise apartment compared to bungalows or townhouses (terraced housing) is 50.6 BTU compared to between 68.9 and 82.6 BTU, respectively.[2] Based on such figures alone, most American developers will not consider building a scheme of below 80 to 100 units in a tower block design.

Support Service Costs

As people age and become more frail and dependent they require more support. A sheltered housing programme that relies on visiting support services can become quite expensive, especially where schemes are small and visiting support staff must spend a large percentage of their time arranging appointments and travelling from one location to another. If a scheme of 30 units can claim more efficient use of peripatetic staff than individuals scattered throughout a community, then schemes of 80 or 100 units might claim even greater efficiency by using such staff for some services and on-site staff for others. Some would also argue that the warden in her role as support service co-ordinator gains increased flexibility and efficiency in a larger scheme where she can combine her special skills and interests with one or more other warden(s), and where she can make better use of resident communal support and family and voluntary services in place of public services.

Warden Support

No one is more important to the British sheltered housing concept than the resident warden. Yet the potential of overworking the warden can be higher in smaller schemes where adequate relief and support is not available at nights and at weekends. A large scheme makes it more economical to have on-site staff 24 hours a day and provide warden relief and support with great flexibility and cost efficiency.

Warden Services

We have seen that as more elderly residents become frail and disabled the warden's job becomes more important and more demanding in terms of both time and skills. More professionally trained wardens requiring higher salaries are already a reality. The warden role is evolving as uniquely different from either nursing or social work. Few wardens are equally skilled at all the varied tasks, such as counsellor, support co-ordinator, family proxy or facilitator of social enagement. Larger schemes may allow two or more wardens to pool their skills and make more efficient use of their time thus justifying higher salaries.

The Emerging Solution

As reported in Chapter 3, several West Midlands managers are increasing the size of their purpose-built sheltered housing schemes, as well as converting existing tower blocks to sheltered housing use. In the rest of Europe and North America the equivalent to sheltered housing almost always consists of 80 to 100 units or more. These countries have uniformly concluded that small scheme size is uneconomical. There have been a number of reasons why local managers in Great Britain have been able to postpone an increase in scheme size until recently.

These reasons all relate to the presence of the resident warden.

With the resident warden, British sheltered housing has a central facilitator and organiser of support services to individual elderly service recipients. No other country has developed an on-site manager who consistently serves as an advocate and organiser for tenant support needs. In other countries there is no one to co-ordinate service delivery at the point of service reception. In the United States in particular, each service agency is a separate entity which contracts independently with the individuals receiving services. The agencies are frequently unaware of what other services are being provided or needed. Not only are there frequent duplications of support effort and monitoring costs, but there is no guarantee that some persons are not being oversupported at the cost of their long-term functional independence, while others are not missing key services needed to retain functional independence. Furthermore, there is no one person making maximum use of voluntary support from neighbours, family, voluntary agencies or the warden herself. We have observed that a well-trained warden can build on and co-ordinate free support resources in the community far better than any equivalent on-site manager in the United States or Europe. As we reported in Chapter 5, wardens may be such skilled advocates that their tenants can come almost to monopolise the time of visiting support services in the community.[3] Hence the overall success of the warden in securing a range of visiting support has helped to make small sheltered housing schemes viable support environments for the functionally disabled, and has postponed any cost evaluation to determine if larger schemes with more on-site support might not represent a more economical means of service delivery.

Another factor that has helped to minimise the cost of small British sheltered housing schemes is the relatively small salary paid the resident warden. It is very doubtful that persons of equal skill could be attracted to such a position in the United States, for a similar salary plus rent and utility reductions. In addition to higher salaries, wardens outside of Great Britain would also probably demand shorter working weeks with guaranteed relief for time off. These are all demands that would, of course, increase the cost of sheltered housing, but they are only just now being felt in Great Britain. Such costs are, no doubt, beginning to contribute to the pressure for larger schemes.

In many American cities there isn't an adequate visiting support network available in the community. This has also made small schemes with only a resident warden on-site a difficult, if not impossible, model to copy. America's response to the lack of proper public support networks to assist with independent living has been to develop service-rich facilities with all the needed support services provided on-site. This is, of course, only economical in very large schemes of 100 units or more.

Even in American cities where visting services are abundant, the lack of support at nights and at weekends has been enough of a reason to build large service-rich schemes from the outset. Once again the presence of the warden has helped postpone the conversion to larger service-rich schemes in Great Britain. Despite the generally accepted view that wardens should not provide direct services, we have seen in Chapter 4 that wardens *do*, filling in particularly at night and weekends for visiting support services, thus postponing the need for other support solutions. Only as the number of persons requiring support has grown and overburdened wardens has pressure begun to mount for other solutions.

Finally, the lack of viable neighbourhood support networks has diluted the importance of small neighbourhood-based schemes in some countries, especially the United States. The price of metropolitan sprawl in America has often been the inability to provide adequate municipal, commercial and residential infrastructure which can help support disabled persons whose mobility is limited to a small area. Where there is extensive inner-city decay and abandonment and suburban and rural absence of supportive neighbourhood environments, building small sheltered housing schemes that depend to some extent on neighbourhood support, just does not make good sense. Many British neighbourhoods may have also undergone a decline in neigh-bourhood support, be experiencing rising crime rates and the like. However, as before, the presence of the warden has helped lessen the negative impact. Wardens can and do accompany tenants on trips away from the scheme or run errands for tenants, and thus help compensate for the greater danger, increased barriers, greater distances, etc., the elderly face when venturing out alone into neighbourhoods which are becoming increasingly less accommodating. Only now, as wardens begin to express their concern regarding overwork, in part caused by unsupportive neighbourhoods, are British managers beginning to think more about large service-rich and self-contained facilities.

One emerging solution for urban areas to these rising cost trends, not only in Great Britain but throughout Western society, has been high rise/high density self-contained schemes. Several of the British managers interviewed in the urban West Midlands sample felt that they could successfully adapt the critical warden concept from small to large schemes. In fact they see the move to larger schemes as a means of improving and strengthening the warden service role. Where larger schemes have been attempted, the managers have retained something like the 30 to 1 tenant to warden ratio by assigning the appropriate number of wardens, with each generally provided with some separate communal spaces to use on given floors of the highrise and each with an assigned number of elderly to visit and monitor. In addition, it is also generally felt by management that the multiple wardens in larger schemes can pool their skills and time with regard to specialised social activities and act as back-up support for each other. For example, during an afternoon quiet time on a typical day when many less active elderly are in their own units resting, one warden could provide craft activities on-site for those active residents who are interested while another warden could take a small group on an outing, either touring or shopping, swimming, etc. In this way it is felt that large schemes can create new and better social programmes, staffing flexibility and financial savings.

Alternative Solutions

Moving to larger schemes can produce some cost savings through management, maintenance and support service efficiency, and has the potential to produce some new benefits from pooled warden resources. However, it can also produce some severe 'costs' for tenants, as described in Chapter 3. In particular, large schemes can mean greater segregation from the community and from familiar neighbourhoods, and increased complexity in tenant organisation and communal living. All of this can make adaptation to highrise living more stressful and confusing, especially for persons with failing mobility, eyesight, hearing, and the like. We feel there are more sympathetic ways to adapt and expand the British sheltered housing concept, keep the groups of elderly small and within supportive residential neighbourhoods, and retain the warden concept of support organisation, all without building new schemes of 30 or fewer tenants. This can be done by expanding the warden concept into the private sector and/or conventional housing. Sheltered housing wardens have been so successful that some municipalities have begun to introduce warden-like roles into the community. 'Private sector wardens', as they are called, are typically housewives assigned to visit and check on the elderly within a residential neighbourhood and make sure they receive emergency aid when needed, are made aware of support services, and help them form their own support and social networks with neighbourhood peers. We feel this concept can be greatly expanded by combining it with untapped resources in existing vacant housing and commercial buildings available in many urban areas and various recent technological advances in communications between a peripatetic warden and dispersed residents. We see three variations in which the private sector warden concept can be adapted and expanded to existing building stock.

Air Space and Vacancies in District Shopping and Office Centres

This solution was recently suggested in part by Edgar Rose[4] and really contains two ideas for acquiring either cheaper land or existing non-residential vacancies. First, most Western countries now have regional (often suburban) shopping centres which contain many of the commercial facilities the elderly need and use all located in a compact area, often under one roof. Some of these centres include office space on the second floor accessible by elevators (lifts). Often these centres have not attracted and retained all the commercial and office rentals expected and now have large vacant spaces. Other shopping centres possess 'air space' (or legally developable air rights) which they can sell or lease for far less than it would cost to buy and develop new land. The lower land costs and/or vacant existing office space may make it economical to continue to provide smaller sheltered housing schemes with a conventional warden. An alternative would be to build onto, or convert, this space to accommodate small groups of four or five bedrooms or bedsitters (efficiencies) around communal space where elderly can look after each other with a private sector warden assigned to (say) every eight or ten such groups.

The availability of vacant second and third floors above commercial and office space is also common in many centre city areas and in the first and oldest commercial rings travelling out from the city centre. It is equally possible that these existing upper storey spaces could be converted to sheltered housing using a peripatetic warden support concept.

Criticism of this idea is levelled mostly at its limited usefulness. The savings from leasing air space as opposed to purchasing and developing land may not be enough to warrant smaller sheltered housing schemes. Since the scheme must still be built, construction costs might also mandate larger schemes. Converting existing office and commercial space represents a larger potential cost saving, but it is questionable just how much of such space is readily usable by functionally disabled elderly. We know of no careful inventory of such vacancies for this use, although we believe that a large number exist. Nevertheless, it is likely that where they occur in smaller cities they will often include steep stairs and no elevator (lift), making them costly to convert, while in larger cities they will often occur in less than desireable locations. So, while this seems like a useful idea in urban areas where it can be applied, it will not by itself provide the answer to the large unmet demand for sheltered housing.

Expansion of the Abbeyfield Concept

The Abbeyfield Society is a nationally active voluntary housing association in Great Britain. Instead of building new schemes, the association purchases and converts existing old and large residential and commercial dwellings to serve as sheltered housing for five to ten elderly residents. The schemes are managed, and much of the conversion work is completed, by a voluntary committee in the community where the scheme is located. These converted schemes fit the category 2½ description, with all rooms and living functions shared communally except for a private bed/dressing room. A recent evaluation of Abbeyfield schemes and residents nationally showed the concept to be economical and popular.[5]

As currently conceived and operated, Abbeyfield is a small programme. In the West Midlands, for example, there are only a few Abbeyfield conversions, in each of only a few municipalities. The concept might be more readily expandable if several existing structures could be converted in a single area or on a single residential street by a municipal authority. Economies in social service delivery, meal planning, food purchase and other services could then be realised. There might even be enough economies for both a live-in cook/housekeeper in each scheme and a peripatetic warden assigned to (say) every 5 to 10 schemes.

The major problem related to expanding the Abbeyfield concept is similar to that of the previous solution. There are unlikely to be many situations where a number of buildings in a common locality are all vacant, large enough to adapt, and reasonably inexpensive to convert to sheltered accommodation. In fact, finding a single house in a suitable environment that is economical to convert seems to be a major contributing factor keeping the existing Abbeyfield programme so small. Where the idea can be applied, it appears to be a constructive addition to the range of ways that sheltered housing can be retained and expanded despite increasing government austerity.

The Shared Housing Concept

This final variation holds perhaps the greatest potential as a future means of continuing and expanding the British sheltered housing concept. It uses an abundant existing housing inventory, with little or no conversion costs, and has the potential of providing a great deal of support and security with cost economy. It employs three concepts already in existence but never brought together in one programme: shared housing, private sector warden and recent technological advances in security/communications.

Over the past half century Western societies have held detached or semi-detached housing as the ideal. The United States in particular has built thousands of such residential neighbourhoods. The oldest of these exist on the boundary between the inner city and the first modern suburban ring. The houses, physical infrastructure and commercial services in these neighbourhoods are, in most cases, still in very good condition. These neighbourhoods are usually very safe and secure and in many ways come closest to an ideal residential neighbourhood for the elderly. As it turns out, many of the residents of these neighbourhoods are already young elderly or near elderly whose children have recently grown up and left home. The housing has been characterised as 'empty nests' because they are occupied by single elderly or near elderly couples. They are also seen as the greatest untapped housing resources of most Western countries,[6] because the housing stock is so underutilised.

There are recent estimates that as many as a million and a half such homes in the United States have already been converted (some illegally due to local zoning restrictions) to create 'accessory apartments'.[7] Accessory apartments are created when elderly owner occupants convert the empty space in their single family homes into two or more units. When totally separate units are created with private entries, bathrooms and kitchens, conversion can run as high as $10,000 per unit.[8] However, when an elderly owner occupant takes in one or more elderly tenants and they all share the house communally, there are often no conversion costs. It is this second concept of *sharing* a home with renters rather than *converting* a house into separate accessary apartments which we wish to explore here.

Shared living among the elderly is not new. It is most likely to occur spontaneously in warmer resort or 'sun belt' areas of the United States and European countries where there is a predominance of both elderly home owners and renters. 'Share-A-Home' of Central Florida is one of several formal programmes designed to bring elderly homeowners and

elderly renters together.[9] Sharing allows elderly homeowners to stay
in their homes with companionship, security and additional income
to pay for rising property taxes and maintenance costs. It provides
elderly renters with companionship, security and often cheaper rent in
more pleasant surroundings than they could otherwise afford. A recent
evaluation of 243 Share-A-Home participants revealed that over two-
thirds indicated overall satisfaction with the programme. Participants
perceive companionship and assistance with household tasks as the
major advantages; loss of privacy and problems with interpersonal
relationships as the major disadvantages.[10]

Since most of the Share-A-Home participants are widows in their
early 70s, additional health and health-related social problems are not
found in the Streib[11] study may possibly arise as the participants age.
Typically, the voluntary (nonprofit) sponsors of these programmes
serve only as brokers, bringing prospective elderly owners and renters
together. The programmes are not funded to provide ongoing service
to help with support and counselling problems, likely to arise if, and
when, shared living becomes shared dependency. It is here that we
would recommend the introduction of the private sector warden
concept.

The problems likely to arise in a shared home can also occur within
conventional elderly households, and a private sector warden could
provide help in either case. However, because the shared housing
participants do not also share longstanding friendships or family ties,
their newly formed household may require special or more frequent
counselling and support from a neutral but trusted third party. Elderly
housemates who were initially matched because their needs and
resources were complementary, can undergo rapid health and
personality changes which threaten functional independence. Such a
situation can become awkward, stressful and burdensome if the housemates do not know each other well, have lease commitments, and have
no one else to turn to for relief. The private sector warden can visit
and monitor daily living, provide shopping, transportation and
domiciliary support on an episodic basis, call in long-term support
from professional visiting services, and serve as a third party consultant.
A lay warden as friendly neighbour could have a major role in such a
setting and could, we feel, monitor 50 or more shared homes or conventional elderly households within several city blocks.

Perhaps the greatest challenge to this idea is in regard to the private
sector warden. The major problems experienced with the past use of
private sector wardens concern the breach of security, breach in

emergency support, and the loss of continuity of social service that can occur when the warden is making rounds visiting residents or running errands. Because so much of the warden's time on duty is likely to be spent visiting residents spread around a neighbourhood or running errands for them, it is felt she (he) is out of contact for too much of the time. This is especially true as residents age and are more likely to need the warden in an emergency situation. It is also difficult for residents who don't live in the same facility as a warden to understand exactly when she (he) is on or off duty.

There are several recent technological developments in portable and stand-in communication devices which may answer the breach in security that can occur between a private sector warden and her dispersed residents. The first is a stand-in call service.[12] With this device, the homes of the elderly being served by the private sector warden are wired by emergency call system to the warden's home via the telephone network. When on duty and at home, the warden speaks directly to residents who pull an intercom cord in their bathroom or bedroom. When she is on duty and away from home, visiting residents or running errands, one of two call forwarding devices can be employed. If the warden wishes to remain in contact with all residents while visiting in the neighbourhood it is now possible to switch any calls coming to her home to a battery-operated short wave radio device she can carry with her. This will allow her to hear and speak with the resident calling. When she is off duty or when she is away from home and outside the signal range of her radio device, the warden can simply switch the intercom call system through her telephone to a nearby warden or a central switchboard shared by a large number of private sector wardens and outlying elderly without a warden's service. There is still no dialling; and with this call forwarding service residents pull a cord and talk directly to someone who advises, reassures or calls out help.

In cases where the elderly have a severe episodic illness or chronic condition that makes even reaching an intercom cord difficult or risky, there is another new electronic device called a Companion Service,[13] which is designed to trigger an alarm and signal the warden whenever an individual's normal movement patterns are interrupted for an abnormal length of time. The cost savings combined with constant contact and the personal care of a warden using these electronic devices make the entire package of shared homes and private sector wardens a very economical and realistic solution. (For an account of alarm systems available in Great Britain see Butler and Oldman.)[14]

We began by looking for new housing alternatives, where small grouped living could be combined with the warden concept of support for functionally disabled elderly. We have concluded with a description of a new private sector warden who could become the primary support co-ordinator for *all* elderly living in the community who require assistance with independent living. The term *primary* support as used here is analogous to the primary approach to nursing services used in hospitals and as juxtaposed to the *team* approach to hospital nursing services. The team approach has proven inefficient and untrustworthy at times, even in the restricted confines of hospitals, because each specialised provider in the team is only concerned with his or her special function. Some services, and a great deal of information, must be duplicated by each different provider, yet no one person is responsible for the comprehensive needs of the recipient. The cost of duplicating information services, and the chance of totally failing to provide a particular support service, increase when one leaves the confines of a building. In fact, each peripatetic community service in most United States cities is a definite separate entity — there is little or no attempt at a co-ordinated team approach. For this reason, the private sector warden concept as *primary* service co-ordinator and family proxy to elderly recipients of peripatetic services becomes so important and is potentially so useful. A private sector warden can provide real economic savings as well. One saving is as a result of providing many episodic service needs herself and by harnessing the support of a network of elderly neighbours under her 'charge'. Because she takes a comprehensive approach to individual support needs, the warden can produce additional savings by informing and co-ordinating visiting providers, and preventing costly duplication of services, and oversupport of residents. Finally, if she/he can prevent unnecessary support dependencies by helping to extend the independence of elderly recipients, she/he will help prevent the premature need for additional support services. Most of all, this system is humane. It provides the elderly person with a dedicated friend and neighbour for daily support contact and an advocate to counsel and arrange visiting support providers when needed. There is far less chance for a visiting home help, social worker or public nurse to make close and lasting ties with the elderly they serve. Their heavy monthly caseloads and specialised service role prevent them from taking on the role of the warden.

If economic recession and government austerity are long-term realities, both in the United States and Western Europe, and we fear they are, then the expansion of the private sector warden concept in combination with the concept of sheltered housing is, we feel, an excellent way to retain and expand the overall British sheltered housing concept. This need not become the *primary* focus of a government's assisted independent living programme. In fact, in order to provide elderly with variety and choice in sheltered housing, this should be just one alternative offered, in combination with as many of the other emerging and existing alternatives proposed throughout this book, as makes sense in each local economy. This includes larger and higher density purpose built sheltered housing schemes, Abbeyfield type housing conversions, and the various types of space leasing and infill construction described in this chapter. Finally, but certainly not least, it should also include the various categories of traditional purpose-built small sheltered housing schemes of the British variety, wherever affordable.

Notes

1. Stokes, B., *Global housing prospects: The resource constraints*. World watch paper No. 46, Worldwatch Institute, Washington, D.C., 1981.
2. Hannon, B., *et al.*, 'Energy and labor in the construction sector'. *Science*, 1978, 202, pp. 837–47; Keyes, D.L., 'The Influence of energy on future patterns of urban development'. In Solomon, A.P., *The Prospective City*, MIT Press, Cambridge, Mass., 1980, pp. 309–25.
3. Butler, A. and Oldman, C., 'The objectives of sheltered housing: Implications for future provision'. *Housing Review*, March–April 1980, pp. 48–50.
4. Rose, E.A., *Housing for the Aged*. Saxon House, Teakfield, Westmead Farnborough, 1978.
5. Morton-Williams, J., *Survey in Abbeyfield Houses: For the Abbeyfield Society's Commission on Growth*. Social and Community Planning Research, London, 1979; Abbeyfield Society, *The lights are green: The report of the Abbeyfield Society's Commission on Growth*. Abbeyfield Society, Potters Bar, Herts, 1979.
6. Hare, P.H., 'The nation's largest untapped housing resource'. *Christian Science Monitor*, August 19 1981; Baer, W.C., 'Empty housing space: An overlooked resource'. In Montgomery, R. and Marshall, D.R. (eds.), *Housing Policy for the 1980s*. Lexington Books, Lexington, Mass., 1980, pp. 29–36; Bradshaw, J. and Wright, K.G., 'Staying Put'. Revised proposal to the Joseph Rowntree Memorial Trust for an Evaluation study of 'Staying Put', University of York, Social Policy and Research Unit, Institute of Social and Economic Research, July 1981; Scholen, K., *Unlocking home equity for the elderly*. Ballinger, Cambridge, Mass., 1980.
7. Hare, P.H., 'Carving up the American dream', *Planning*, July 1981, pp. 14–17.
8. Hare, P.H., 'The empty nest as a golden egg: Using the unused space in single family neighbourhoods'. Draft of an article for *Perspectives on Aging*, 1981.
9. Streib, G.F., *Alternative living arrangements for the elderly: A research study*. Center for Gerontological studies and Department of Sociology, University

of Florida, Gainsville, Fla, 1980.

    10. Ibid.

    11. Ibid.

    12. Davis, M., 'Stand-in call service provides relief for the warden'. *Housing*, August 1979, pp. 16, 17; Day, J.B. and Epps, B., 'Rescue service for the elderly', *Housing*, August 1979, pp. 12–15.

    13. Gerontological Society and The Western Gerontological Society, *National Research Conference on Technology and the Aged: Project Narrative*. Gerontological Society, Washington, D.C., 1979.

    14. Butler, A. and Oldman, C., *Alarm Systems for the elderly: Report of a workshop*. Department of Social Policy and Administration, University of Leeds, March 1981.

APPENDIX: WARDEN ACTIVITIES BY ACTIVITY TYPE AND SERVICE FUNCTION FOR THE DEVON AND WEST MIDLANDS SURVEYS

Activity type and number	Service function[a]	Survey use	GENERAL SUPPORT TO TENANTS
G1	O	D	The reception of new and/or potential tenants and introducing them into the scheme.
G2	O	D	Giving advice on, and finding out about, what facilities are available for tenants including form filling, telephone calls, financial advice, etc.
G3	O	D/WM	Liaising with doctors, social workers, hospitals, etc., and the calling in, and arranging for the provision of, domiciliary services.
G4	O	D/WM	Regular visiting, either daily or weekly visits, often to all or the majority of tenants.
G5	O	WM	Contacts all residents regularly by intercom.
G6	O[c]	D/WM	Specific visiting, including making a cup of tea, reading letters, etc., possibly to more than one tenant at the same time.
G7	O	D/WM	Liaising with, and encouraging the continued involvement of relatives and friends.
G8	P	D	Collecting and delivering pensions plus general shopping at the same time.
G9	P	D	Collecting and delivering prescriptions, from surgery and/or chemists, plus general shopping at the same time.
G10	P	D/WM	General shopping.
G11	O[c]	D	Making and receiving telephone call(s), including the delivery of telephone message(s). Also sending telegram(s).
G12	P	D	Looking after tenants' pets such as dogs, cats and budgies (parakeets).
G13	P	D	Putting out and taking in dustbins, waste sacks (trash and trash cans).
G14	P	D	Regular administration of tablets, medicines, eye drops.
G15	P	D/WM	Housework activities such as cleaning windows; tidying cupboards; putting out and/or taking in washing; fetching coal and/or lighting fires; moving furniture; gardening for individual tenants; measuring and/or cleaning, fixing and/or hanging carpets and/or curtains; washing and/or ironing garments.
G16	P	D	Repairing, adjusting etc. tenants' 'appliances' e.g. adjusting TV set; fixing electric kettle, mending fuse, helping use washing machine, changing light bulb, mending cupboard, repairing door handle.

217

GENERAL SUPPORT TO TENANTS

G17	P	D	Personal tasks for tenants ('non-emergency') such as doing up shoes, washing and cutting hair, cutting nails.
G18	O^c	D	Preparing tenant for, and/or transporting to, hospital or residential home ('non-emergency'), clinic, dentist, election, holiday etc. Also visiting tenant in hospital.

'EMERGENCY' ACTIVITIES

E1	O	D	Answering the alarm bell (not false alarm) plus any attention at that time (i.e. can involve other 'emergency' activities).
E2	O	D	Answering the alarm bell (false alarm), i.e. rung in error.
E3	O	D	Contacting and discussing with relatives (or vice versa), in connection with an 'emergency'.
E4	P	D/WM	Cooking, preparing a meal for a tenant.
E5	O	D	Dealing with the breakdown of services such as central heating, gas, water, etc. Tenant losing key, arranging for new lock, etc.
E6	O	D	Dealing with emergency illness and death, ranging from emotional upsets and falls to attending a tenant's funeral, etc. Could involve a number of 'emergency' activities.
E7	P	D	Home nursing, i.e. bathing, washing feet, checking and dealing with catheter and/or colostomy bag, dressing ulcer, washing down after an attack of diarrhoea, giving tablets/ medicines in an 'emergency', giving insulin injections, etc. Attention involving rendering first aid.
E8	P	D	Putting tenant to bed (including giving tablets) or getting tenant out of bed, including dressing and/or washing.

COMMUNAL ACTIVITIES

C1	O	D/WM	Encouraging and/or organising communal activities, including preparing the room, and/or taking part in activities.
C2	O	D/WM	Making and maintaining contact with groups and individuals in the area and using their resources.
C3	O	WM	Originally start a tenants' committee.
C4	O	WM	Continue to head a tenants' committee.
C5	O	WM	Organise social outings.
C6	P	WM	Prepare/serve communal meals.

HOUSEKEEPING AND ADMINISTRATION

H1	S	D/WM	Cleaning and looking after communal areas.
H2	S	D/WM	Reporting on the fabric of the dwellings and carrying out minor repairs such as unblocking the toilets, putting light bulbs in the hall or centre. Responsibility for the heating system and other

HOUSEKEEPING AND ADMINISTRATION
equipment such as lifts (elevators), TV relay,
call-bell system, fire alarm system.

H3	S	D/WM	Rent collection and related activities such as passing on the rent to collector(s), delivering to district council offices. Record keeping (excluding diary records kept for the study).
H4	S	D/WM	Preparing, booking, etc., the guest room (or room being used as such).
H5	S	D/WM	Grasscutting and/or gardening for the scheme as a whole.
H6	S	D/WM	Liaison with other wardens, either relief(s) or in neighbouring schemes. Wardens' meeting(s).
H7	S	WM	Arrange for relief warden for weekly time off or yearly holiday.
H8	S	WM	Keep records of changes in the health, emotions, hygiene, etc., of residents.
H9	S	WM	Take special training courses to gain new organiser/provider skills.

Notes: a. Service functions are divided into 'Organiser' (O) and 'Provider' (P) services. Housekeeping and administrative duties are listed as 'support' (S) activities. b. Not all of the activities listed were employed by both surveys. The letter (D) means the activity was listed in the Devon survey; the letters (WM) mean the activity was listed in the West Midlands survey. c. The reader might interpret some activities listed as 'organiser' activities to be 'provider' services. We chose to be very conservative in our interpretation of provider services. We felt all extensions of the original 'friendly neighbour' role or duties of the warden should remain organiser activities; namely, visits to tenants' flats even if it includes making tea or reading to them, receiving and delivering phone calls, preparing tenants for trips away from the scheme, etc.

INDEX

Abbeyfield Society 86, 210, 215
accident 57, 117; prevention 12
Activities of Daily Living (ADL)
25, 29–31, 34, 101–2, 135, 172,
190
Age Concern 144
alarm system (calls) 11, 17, 65, 80–1,
84, 92, 96, 127, 140–4, 213;
see also intercom
almshouse 74, 78
Altenwohnhauser 65
Altenwohnheime 11, 65
Altenwohnstifte 65
Anchor Housing Association 86, 111
apartment 11, 16, 48, 55–6, 94,
103, 126, 211; see also flat

barrier free 11, 16, 32, 36, 56, 63,
68, 89, 105
bedsitter 209
behaviour problems 182; see also
mental disability
bungalow 16, 49, 56, 81, 89, 92,
95–6, 103, 106, 109, 116–17,
199, 204

caretaker 13
chiropody 100–1, 113
chronic diseases (conditions) 12, 28,
46, 49–51, 56, 66, 70, 73–5,
77, 109, 127, 150, 154
church 86
clergymen 170
cohort 19
community services see domiciliary
services
congregate housing (living) 11, 16,
23, 56, 65; see also sheltered
housing
Congregate Housing Service Program
63, 85
Council for Jewish Elderly 58
counselling 181, 182, 205
crime (rate) 56, 94–5, 157, 207

day care 42–3, 57, 101, 113, 126,
150, 179
demographic statistics 16, 18, 19,

35–6, 112, 156, 194
Department of Health and Human
Services 67
Department of Health and Social
Security 187
Department of Housing and Urban
Development 63, 67
Department of the Environment
65, 107, 187
disablement see functional dependence
district council see housing authority
doctor 68, 75, 80, 85, 98, 109,
153, 168–70, 172; see also
physician
domiciliary services (care) 12, 13, 41,
49, 68, 75, 82, 84–5, 102–3,
123, 127–9, 135, 139, 150, 166,
168, 193–6, 199, 212; and costs
24, 25; see also support services

efficiency see bedsitter
elevator 106, 109, 199, 209–10;
see also lift

family support 13, 16–17, 19–21,
33–5, 40, 42–3, 50–1, 55, 57,
67, 70, 72, 75, 121, 127, 176,
206–7
first aid 181
flat 49, 56, 94–6, 102, 146, 148;
see also apartment
flatlet 81, 83, 103
functional (in) dependence 12, 14,
16–20, 22, 25, 28, 31–2, 34–6,
38–46, 50, 55–7, 65, 66–71,
73–4, 84, 90, 96–7, 110–11,
118–20, 124, 127, 130, 141–2,
148, 156, 164, 169–70, 177,
194, 206, 212

granny flats 55, 58; see also Kangaroo housing
grouped housing 16, 78; see also
sheltered housing
Guttman scale 29–30, 32

Hanover Housing Association 86

220

For Product Safety Concerns and Information please contact our EU
representative GPSR@taylorandfrancis.com
Taylor & Francis Verlag GmbH, Kaufingerstraße 24, 80331 München, Germany

www.ingramcontent.com/pod-product-compliance
Lightning Source LLC
Chambersburg PA
CBHW050433280326
41932CB00013BA/2095